DON'T LEAN ON YOUR EXCUSES

A WORLD CHAMPION'S COURAGEOUS STORY THAT INSPIRES LIVING WITH NO REGRETS

Marcelo

Always be the
best you can be Steve

STEVE JUDGE

Printed in the United Kingdom
First Printing, 2019

ISBN 978-1-9160846-0-5 (Paperback)
ISBN 978-1-9160846-1-2 (eBook)

Librotas
Portsmouth, Hampshire
PO2 9NT

www.librotas.com

Contents

Dedicated to Mum and Dad

'You made me who I am today'

Steve's Tunes for the Journey

	Chapter Title	Song Title	Artist
	Prologue	We Close Our Eyes	Go West
1	One Leg or Two?	I Believe	Stephen Gately
2	Chin Up and Look to the Future	Action	Def Leppard
		Adiemus	Karl Jenkins
3	The Great Escape	Don't Give Up	Chicane & Bryan Adams
4	Growing Bone and Independence	Get Up	Mike and the Mechanics
5	Living with Consequences and Regrets	The One And Only	Chesney Hawkes
6	Don't Lean On Your Excuses	Go For It	Heart And Fire
7	The Torture of Progress	It's Gonna Be Tough	Chesney Hawkes
8	Uncaged	Danger Zone	Kenny Loggins

	Chapter Title	Song Title	Artist
9	Let's See What This Baby Can Do!	You Can't Take Me	Bryan Adams and Hans Zimmer
10	The Foundations of a New Life	You Get What You Give	New Radicals
11	The Challenger Within	Open Road	Gary Barlow
		Far and Away – Book of Days	Enya
12	Coincidences, Karma and Good Luck	Lose Yourself	Eminem
		The Garden	Take That
13	Achievement Through The Cultivation of Time	Run for Your Life	Bucks Fizz
14	Seizing Opportunities	Something Inside So strong	Labi Siffre
15	Change the Plan, Not the Goal	Night Swimming	R.E.M.
		Never	Footloose soundtrack. Michael Gore/Dean Pitchford
		St. Elmo's Fire (Man In Motion)	John Parr
16	True Elite, True Achievement	One Vision	Queen
		Explosion	Eli 'Paperboy' Reed
		Hannah's Theme	The Chemical Brothers
17	Achievements and Accolades	Thunderstruck	AC/DC
18	To Conquer a Dream	Only If	Enya
19	A Tough Year	Papercut	Linkin Park
		Titanium	David Guetta & Sia

	Chapter Title	Song Title	Artist
20	Turn Your Excuses into Challenges	Champions – Duracell 2012 Olympic Games Song	Duracell B.o.B. and O.A.R.
21	And the World Thought I Had It All	Hall of Fame	The Script
22	Pushing the Senses	Keep on Movin'	Five
23	Suffering in Silence	Hold On	Skepta
24	I'm Done and I'm Finished	The Phoenix	Fall Out Boy
	Prologue	It's A Beautiful Day	Michael Bublé

Family Thoughts, Feelings and Reflections

Another 'Judge' family fun run done. From left to right: Bruce, Dad, Sugar the dog, Mum, Dawn (race numbers for her and Sugar) and me.

Mum

Much of Steve's drive and determination as well as Dawn's and Bruce's stems from our family life. All five of us were always wanting to go forward in all that we did, individually and as a family. As a mother it gives me an immense glow inside to witness my children making progress in their lives and fulfilling their potential.

We are always there for each other and supporting with our own strengths. At Steve's major events Bruce would have a stopwatch and Dawn would have a very LOUD voice and I would always be in the right place at the right time.

I am very proud of Steve's 'journey' as I am with all of my children and what they have each achieved within their life.

Dad (written by Steve)
1939–1998

Dad was always about the family. He always had some sort of 'action plan' that encouraged and supported fun and creativity.

Through our recent family discussions, as we are now, we agree that Dad would be so proud of us all and our families. We reckon that he would probably give us a score of 9 out of 10 for what we have achieved in our lives, maybe even a 10 out of 10. However he did also used to say that there was always room for improvement.

Dawn

Since Dad passed away Mum has always been there for all of us, full of energy and drive, ensuring we all had the desire of independence and self-reliance throughout our lives and choices. There's nothing like family at the end of the day. If my brothers hurt, I hurt. If they're sad, I feel sad and concerned and want to make it better. When they're happy and achieve, I'm ecstatic! There is always a strong link and tie.

Mum and Dad were quite a powerhouse of advice, guidance and fun for everything anyone could ever need in their life. Steve, Bruce and myself were extremely lucky they got together and we are gifted with their genes – but better than that is their legacy as this comes out in everything we now do. I see everything Steve talks about and felt during his journey in all of us in varying degrees!

Bruce

It's funny being Steve's brother. Funny in lots of different ways. Although we don't talk all the time we always just click as soon as we meet up, which can be months apart. I love being so similar and often so different. We have done an incredible number of things together, like getting cold on mountains or competing our heart out. Team Judge is invincible and always good fun, laughing at the same things and the same jokes. I am so proud to have been able to support Steve through some of his international competitions and incredibly proud when he beats all the competition not just for Great Britain but for the Judge family.

Reviews

"Steve Judge exudes such positivity, determination and inspiration that, once you've read this book, you'll have squared up to any fears and self-doubts. Where you go from there is entirely up to you but, warning you, just reading his book makes you want to run up a mountain! If you are looking for a book that will heal, stretch, inspire, and challenge you to persevere and overcome, this is your book."

Alex Peace-Gadsby OBE, Chief Commissioner
of Scouts for England and entrepreneur

"The first time I met Steve over a cup of tea I had no idea of his backstory or his injury and so the first time I heard him speak I was shocked. His story of fighting back from adversity is an inspiration to anyone who needs help to understand how to fight back from some of life's biggest obstacles."

Lee Jackson, international speaker and past president of the
Professional Speaking Association in the UK & Ireland

"What happened to Steve Judge could happen to anyone – a car crash, with serious consequences. But how he dealt with it is extraordinary and this story serves as a masterclass in finding resilience and raw ambition to overcome whatever life throws at you. As you might expect, the story speeds along – his physical recovery is utterly fascinating – and his dry humour helps to mop up the emotion of it all. Happily, at no point does Steve lurch into preaching 'at you' in the way that some motivational authors might. The lessons you learn from Steve's experience and impressive achievements are yours to find. The Steve Judge story will stay with you – you simply take what you need from it."

Penny Haslam, award-winning speaker and former *BBC Business* presenter

"This book gives an open and real account of what can be achieved when you set the right goal. The tools that Steve shares are easily transferable in all of our lives, both personal and in business. Poignant, persuasive and powerful."

Brad Sugars, global entrepreneur, international business speaker and author

"Captivating, motivating and emotional! Easy take-away which will help anyone focus on their business goals. I highly recommend this book to anyone who has a vision for what they want to succeed in."

Claire Young, *Apprentice* finalist 2008, entrepreneur and business owner of School Speakers

"The book mirrors how Steve performs on the stage with a combination of fun, laughter and joy with the intense and serious undertones. The chapters are broken up into easily digestible chunks with the use of diary entries and the notes on his thoughts and feelings from when he was there in the moment. You can feel how much Steve has opened himself up with inserts like 'My White Tiger' which connects with me as once again he brings in the personal touch. Steve Judge is a person that you just don't forget. His story is inspirational."

Martin Johnson, author of *I Am Human: 30 Mistakes To Success*

"Only looking back to learn, only looking forward to dream, this book inspires, entertains and educates all in equal measure. Steve shares with the reader why pressing play on today is so very important."

Brad Burton, founder of 4Networking, business author and motivational speaker

Don't Lean on Your Excuses | Steve Judge

Prologue

"GO GB!!!"

"COME ON GREAT BRITAIN."

The crowds were screaming.

Hearing their cheers lifted me up as I sprinted towards the finish line.

It was October 2011. I was at the Ming Tombs Reservoir in the Changping District of northern Beijing, China. These were the closing moments of the Paratriathlon World Championship Final (swim, bike and run). My heart was pounding, my body aching. The thin, humid air hugged me, making me feel a little uncomfortable, as I'm used to the invigorating freshness of the British weather.

The race had started an hour earlier, with fifty elite athletes from around the world competing against each other for one of the highest accolades of the year, the ultimate prize: the amazing achievement of becoming champion of the world. I was experiencing a mixture of nervousness and excitement, as the enormity of finally being there, representing my country at this huge event, weighed down on my shoulders.

The swim had started off in the reservoir packed with athletes, and I had avoided being punched or kicked at the mass start. Everybody fights for position and this is mixed with competitive testosterone, a touch of nerves and everyone heading for one focal point ahead. Each elite athlete focused on their goal and on staying strong, keeping in their rhythm, and remaining in their line, despite others who may dare to encroach. Gliding through the water, I grabbed mouthfuls of air with each turn of my head. I used every muscle in my body to pull myself through the water of the 750 metre course.

The thousands of lengths of the pool that I had done in the early mornings, conditioning my body in strength and efficiency, gave me the muscle memory to concentrate on the job in hand. I watched my sighting around the buoys so as not to deviate too much and keep the distance to an efficient minimum. The long endurance-based lake swims that I had subjected myself to in all conditions gave me the stamina and strength I needed to pursue the title.

On the return journey I made every stroke count. I pulled fiercely with my arms, knowing that they could rest a little on the bike. I powered myself out of the water and straight into transition one (T1) on automatic pilot. I slickly took off my wetsuit as I had done in training many times before – sometimes at the local lake but most times running around my garden with just my swimming trunks on and the neighbours wondering what the hell I was doing…but I'll cover that later.

My bike shoes went on and I twisted my race number belt round to my back and grabbed my helmet, fastening it underneath my chin before wrenching my bike out of its holding and pushing it to the end of T1. Taking a running jump onto it, I propelled myself around the 20km bike course which circulated the reservoir we had just swum in.

I pushed myself to extreme limits on the gradients and hung on tight on the downhills, going fast on the corners. From the tough cycle rides through the unforgiving environment of the Derbyshire Dales I'd learnt only to dab the brakes when essentially necessary because 'momentum is key'.

The course was as the video had shown – the video I had meticulously watched over and over again before even arriving in the country. I wanted to power through the urge of taking on fluids. "I'm good, I don't need them!" I said to myself, but luckily my brain knew better. Not on the uphills or downhills but just as we had planned on the recce the days before, on the flat stretches I released my hand from the bike and squirted the homemade salty energy drink into my wide open mouth.

I gasped for air afterwards, like a deranged rabid dog, as froth and foam seeped out of the corner of my mouth. Sweat, snot and dribble ran down my face; I couldn't wipe it off as my hands had more important things to do…I was holding on for dear life while my legs pumped hard. I dug in deep. The burning pain in my legs was excruciating and the fatigue was grinding me down… I chanted "e-KILL…e-KILL…e-KILL". Not a death chant, just an abbreviation of 'Eckington Hill', the charming yet steeply undulated village where I live and had spent many a painful, exhausting and even tearful hour training on my bike in all conditions and weathers. I was a long way from there now but the memories spurred me on. My exhaustion and lack of breath prevented me from saying the full name, but it felt like a very apt chant.

The scenery was a blur. I was thinking about me, my body, my bike, my actions on this course, my decisions, and was pushing my body so hard that I could feel my legs burning and my lungs screaming for oxygen. 'Gears! Don't forget to use your gears…for crying out loud,' I screamed internally, 'don't trash your legs. You're going to need them for the run.'

My competitiveness made me push myself hard on the bike, using so much energy, but I had to control myself and keep some reserve in the tanks for the final part of the event.

I was quickly through the second transition (T2) and onto the run section of 5K. Now I was relying solely on my numerous hours of training, going from a fast 22mph on the bike to a running speed of 6mph, which felt like a snail's pace. I struggled to feel my legs after what I put them through on the bike and had to trust myself that they were still down there doing 'their thing'.

From the early mornings when only streetlights shone my way, to the lunch times when my work colleagues rested and chatted while I pounded the streets squeezing in those extra miles of training, all for this: everything had led to this moment. My subconscious was on autopilot. I was like a triathlon machine...Go, go, go!

Pushing the pain and exhaustion away, I got on with the job in hand, getting as much air in my lungs as possible to survive the course. Running was my life and always had been from the early age of ten when I started doing 10K runs with my family. Running through the local woods as a teenager behind my family home had brought me so much inner strength and elation. I thought of the more recent distances that I'd covered in training around my village and around the streets where I worked, and the numerous laps around the two lakes of Rother Valley Country Park. It was a special place for me where I had cried in pain and disappointment but also in exhilaration and achievement. All of these memories pushed me forward on this lapped circuit, and I could see my competitors hunting me down. USA and France were hot on my trail. I stayed focused and looking straight ahead.

I recalled the speed sessions that I had done on the track with Bob Pringle and the Sheffield Tri Club. I remembered to lift my knees up, keep my chin up and look ahead... Focus... Push hard... Keep going. I felt the wind through my hair as I glided on. In my peripheral vision, I saw a blurry mass of Union Jack flags being waved and the cheering crowd gave me a continuous drip feed of energy.

I was focused, I wanted this. NO! I needed this. I had been feeding this need for over nine months, although in reality it had been more like nine years. Some called it 'obsession' but I labelled it 'dedication'. To work towards something that was vitally important to me, my health, my wellbeing, my purpose. Feeding the need gave me focus, structure, a goal. In the months leading up to this event, I had visualised every minute detail and it was all coming to fruition. As an elite athlete I was prepared and conditioned for every situation and eventuality. I was flying…I was 'in the moment'…I 'had this' – or so I thought.

The final corner led down to a 200 metre sprint finish section ending at the finish line, which was positioned right in front of the grandstand. As I came around this corner, the noise and the cheering hit me. Hearing my name shouted out, at high volume, was empowering.

"Come on JUDGE!" shouted those who could read my name printed on the front of my tri suit.

"Come on Steeeve" shouted the people who knew me and had helped and supported me on my journey…And then it happened. I couldn't have primed myself for this or even visualised this. As I gasped for air to fill my lungs, the noise of the crowds and the sight of the finish line in front of me put the biggest smile on my face. "Always smiling" – people branded me with this statement and it was true. To be honest I used and controlled this to raise my spirits and stature. But this time I was not in control. I needed oxygen and I couldn't get it because of this ridiculously huge beaming smile plastered over my face.

'Focus…Focus…Keep going…Serious. Just keep going, push hard, go for the finish line and I can smile later'…But it wasn't working…I couldn't help but smile with such utter euphoria.

I kept running, smiling and gasping for air. I glanced behind me as I approached the finish line and then eyes front.

'I've done it…I've DONE it' and I felt a wave of elation, amazement as well as a passionate anger.

It was a feeling which transformed from "I've done it" to an "I told you I could do it…and here I am".

I had smashed through the barriers of non-believers and non-supporters. I had proved statistics and assessments wrong because there is no such thing as normal, so don't judge me!

I punched the air in triumph and conviction. I raised both hands as I crossed the finish line in celebration. I turned to the crowd in the grandstand and acknowledged their support and encouragement.... "Come ON!" I shouted to myself. YES! I did it. I had finished and YES, I had achieved.

Shaking hands with my fellow athletes, I finally absorbed my surroundings, noticing the flash of the bulbs from photographers that made me blink and hearing the noise of the crowd around me.

The finisher's medal round my neck that along with the smile says everything about what I had just achieved. Beijing, China, World Championships 2011.

An official came up to me, gave me a bottle of water, a towel and put a medal round my neck with words of congratulations. "Wow... is that it...did I win? What medal have I got...what colour is it?" I looked down at this medal round my neck. It was very shiny and silver and I started trying to read what it said. A bit dehydrated, exhausted and lightheaded, I tried to focus on this medal and soon realised that it was in Chinese...and...I don't speak Chinese. I turned it over and read some writing in English: 'Finisher's medal'. Baffled for a moment, I looked around at the other athletes and realised that everybody was wearing the same medal. 'Just a finisher's medal.' But then I looked down and I saw that my hand was grasping it really tightly.

Don't Lean on Your Excuses | Steve Judge

I looked at this medal, a beautiful shiny silver medal, and I said to myself, "Yes…I did it!"…It was like I was in a film and everything around me had gone into hyper speed but it was silent. The race officials and flags circulated around me. The euphoric atmosphere and rapture of the grand final of the Paratriathlon World Championships.

I looked down at my tri suit in the colours of my country. I felt so proud and honoured to be representing Great Britain. I glanced over to the reservoir where the event had started and smiled in amazement at what I had achieved. "I finished," I said with a smile. All the training, dedication and commitment, and I did it.

This had been my vision, not giving in, knowing how far to push myself and not letting time pass me by, in the words of the Go West song 'We Close Our Eyes'.

I looked back down at my medal and beyond to my legs, and felt my heart beating faster. I went from beaming from ear to ear to then feeling overwhelmed with emotions. I found myself clenching my teeth to stop my eyes from welling up. I squeezed the medal even tighter, so grateful and proud of what I had achieved, to not only be here right now but also because of the fact that I'd just completed a triathlon. This was amazing in itself but it was more than that. I felt the accomplishment on an emotional level within myself but also physically, as I stared at my two legs that had propelled me round the course because nine years ago I'd been told that I might never walk again.

CHAPTER 1

One Leg or Two?

BEEEEEEEEEEEEEEEEEEEEP!

The sound of the car horn woke me from my unconsciousness. Dazed, I opened my eyes to see the car wreckage surrounding me. Remembering what had happened, I looked down to my legs. They were out of sight, hidden due to the twisted metal, dashboard and console. They wouldn't move and I attempted to reach down to see if I could free them, but was restricted. In hindsight, not being able to assess the severity of the situation probably saved my life. If I had been able to reach further down, I would have realised that my left leg had been wrenched apart at the knee and was now twisted at a 90 degree angle. If I had felt my right leg, I would have noticed that it disappeared about 6 inches below the knee, and I would have brought my hand up covered in blood. As a trained first aider, I know that having information like that could have well put my body into a state of shock and without proper treatment it could have quickly spiralled out of control. Instead, my assessment brought me to the conclusion that I was stuck. Well and truly stuck and in an enormous amount of pain.

The year was 2002. It was two o'clock on a rainy Sunday afternoon in April. I was driving home from Sheffield on my own when I suddenly remembered we needed some milk. Ahead of me lay a fork in the road. Instead of going right for home, I took the left road for the shop. Little did I know that this decision would change my life immeasurably. The minor road took a gentle curve to the left. It had been raining earlier so the surface had a light sprinkling of water. Skirting around a large housing estate, the road was empty in both directions. I wasn't speeding or driving in a reckless manner. It was a Sunday and I was just going to get some milk.

Suddenly the car lost traction as it skidded. I lost control and the car started turning sideways whilst still moving forward. I tried desperately to do something. I turned the steering wheel but nothing! It had no effect. I dabbed the brakes, trying to keep my composure, but there was no reaction. I desperately slammed my foot down on them in complete terror.

In a state of panic I looked out of my car door window and saw my fate approaching. The car was heading directly towards a huge tall metal pole at the side of the road. My eyes widened at the realisation of the imminent impact. I had no control. There was absolutely nothing I could do... just a surreal emptiness of solitude and helplessness. Seeing the pole getting ever closer, I knew it was going to crash into the driver's door. I squeezed tightly on the steering wheel and screwed my face up, bracing for the impact. The car bumped up the kerb sideways and smashed into the pole... then there was blackness.

BEEEEEEEEEEEEEEEEEEEEEP!

The noise from the horn was loud and annoying. I felt sick. I just wanted it to stop. I felt stranded and embarrassed. I just wanted to get out of the car, disown it, walk away, go home and hide. My legs were numb with pain and I felt shaky…I felt really shaky. Uugh…that damn noise!

I looked at the door to open it, but there was no chance. It was crushed and twisted and stuck fast. In that moment I realised the extent of the situation. I was stuck good and proper. There was no walking away from this. I wasn't going to be able to sort this out myself. I needed help. My car was trashed and I couldn't get out. But what about me? How badly was I injured? I felt faint. Oh shit! This was not good.

The window was smashed clear. Initially I tried to free myself because I always like to be independent first. Still to this day I'm prepared to struggle to great depths before I show incompetence and need. I don't like asking for directions; I like to be able to say "I've got this". I started screaming for help as loudly as I could, my voice croaking with desperation. I shouted over the noise of the horn, both of us screaming in competition. After a couple of long agonising minutes, a passer-by ran up to the car and asked if I was okay. "Can you call 999 please," I desperately asked him. "I'm stuck, I can't get out." "They're on their way," he said. "It won't be long." I also pleaded with him to turn the horn off. To my immense relief, he went to the front of the car and somehow managed to disconnect the horn so that the terrible sound finally stopped.

Silence. It felt so much better without the noise. I rested back in my seat and breathed. But without the noise, my brain started to think and assess the situation. I felt the pain in my legs. Now I started feeling cold.

There was a small gathering of people around the car now, some from the housing estate, others from cars that had stopped. "Won't be long now mate, hang on in there." I was told that the emergency services were on their way which kept me optimistic, but I was feeling weaker and weaker as every minute and second passed by. I was breathing in deeply and out slowly. Keeping myself calm but flinching with pain. I was unsure how much longer I could cling onto my optimism… and my life.

At last a paramedic arrived. She talked confidently to me as she assessed the situation. She told me that everything was going to be OK. Suddenly I felt safer, stronger, and my hope grew. It was like the cavalry had arrived. The superhero had landed. Help was here. Alongside her presence and words of reassurance came the administration of drugs through an intravenous drip. I'm in no doubt that this also added to my overall feeling of calm!

One by one the emergency services arrived: the police, ambulance and fire brigade. I even heard a helicopter overhead. I was aware of them discussing the situation and how to address it. I kept breathing, long breaths in through my nose and as slowly as I could out through my mouth. "It's going to be fine," I said to myself. "They've got this."

Eventually, a fire officer came to me and explained that they were going to cut the car apart to release me. Over the next hour and a half they worked on the wreckage, careful not to make my injuries more severe. He explained every step of the process, so I knew what was happening.

"OK Mr. Judge, we're going to cut the rear wing so there will be a bit of a noise and it will vibrate so you may experience a shudder; just hang on in there."

There was a howling noise with each incision as the hydraulic cutters did their work and the car shook a little. After that they moved around and did the same again to another part of the car. At this stage I was feeling content with the numerous professionals looking after me and with the highly efficient way they were dealing with the situation. I sat there with the drugs being pumped into me, breathing slowly, in and out.

Eventually they were able to release me. With great speed they removed me from the wreckage along with what was left of my legs and promptly secured the bleeding. Due to my legs being crushed, the main artery in my leg was squashed, so blood was unable to flood out of the open wound. Considering how long I had been trapped in the car, it was fortunate that the blood flow had been limited. Losing blood would have sent my body into shock, and eventually I would have lost consciousness and very possibly died at the scene.

The ambulance doors closed with a solid thud behind me. With me strapped tightly to the stretcher, the two guys in the ambulance introduced themselves as Steve and Steve. I felt an instant connection, safe in the hands of the two Steves, and we all smiled when I told them I was also called Steve.

Steve said to me, "OK Steve, we're going to take you to the nearest hospital, is that ok Steve?"

"Yes Steve," I said. Then the other Steve said, "We're going to drive very fast Steve, is that okay Steve?"

"Yes Steve," I responded.

"And very safely, is that ok, Steve?"

"Yes Steve," I replied.

The blue lights flashed and the siren wailed as I travelled along, feeling the sway of the ambulance as it sped along the roads of Sheffield. My journey of recovery had started. With the help of the two Steves I was now physically moving. In fact, moving very fast towards help, expertise, safe hands, reassurance and my recovery. My optimism was high and my positivity renewed. I liked Steves!

I was unaware how much medication was being pumped into me, keeping me alive, but it was clouding my judgement and thoughts and keeping me ignorant to the true reality of the situation. As soon as I was freed from the wreckage I had started to lose more and more blood, so it was also critical to keep pumping blood back into me.

The car hitting the post at 40mph with a side impact on the driver's door had literally bent the car in half. The impact was about a foot away from my head, and with this distance as well as the air bags being deployed, the only injuries I suffered on my upper body were a few cuts and bruises. The accident could have been worse and even though this information was not a great help at the time, I clung on to this later in my recovery.

Both of my legs had been crushed from the knee down. My left leg had been knocked sideways, causing my knee joint to be wrenched apart. All four of the ligaments that held my knee together had been ripped out and my joint was dislocated. My right leg bore the brunt of the hit and the lower leg had been crushed. My fibula and tibia bones were shattered and knocked out, and there was also severe skin and muscle damage. The leg was partially amputated as it was only held together by skin and a bit of muscle.

I also learnt later on that due to the severity of my injury, the paramedic at the scene had concluded that the appropriate action was to amputate my right leg below the knee at the crash site. An amputee team had been sent there, but on arrival they couldn't get sufficient access to the wound to administer the procedure. As the rescue unfolded they reassessed and thought that there was a slim possibility of saving my leg and so they did not follow through with the initial plan.

My initial memories of hospital are vague. The medical staff were fighting for my life. My body had been through so much trauma and I had lost a dangerous amount of blood. Life-saving decisions had to be made.

The police knocked on the door of my mum's house in Bawtry near Doncaster. She had been living on her own since my dad had passed away four years previously.

My mum's a strong, fit and able woman and along with my older brother and sister we used to look forward to the 'Mothers' Race' on school sports day. Mum was always the hot favourite and never let us down as she sprinted up the track crossing the line in modest victory. Possibly a 'tad' embarrassing, but I would be full of pride and excitement as my beaming smile always showed my mum how much I loved and admired her. And despite my mum's strength of character I will always be grateful that after breaking the news to her that one of her sons had been involved in a serious car accident the police then insisted on driving her to the hospital. They knew that no mother who has just been given such shocking news would be in a good state to drive herself. It affirms for me the skill, care and compassion that our servicemen have for the public which so often gets overlooked.

My fiancée was also contacted by the police and rushed over to the hospital along with her dad. It was amazing to see my gorgeous fiancée amongst all of what was going on around me. Despite all of the practitioners giving their full attention to saving my life I felt very much alone. To see familiar faces in a sea of busyness brought me a wave of warmth and comfort. I also felt embarrassed and guilty for being the reason they were dragged out on a Sunday evening and at the realisation that I would not make it to work the next day. It was bound to be another manic Monday in the laboratory where I worked as a Quality Manager.

I really don't like inconveniencing people, never have and never will. I felt this guilt and I was angry that there was nothing I could do about it.

They told me that my mum was on her way before I was taken down to the operating theatre around seven o'clock on the Sunday evening. I met my surgeon and we briefly discussed what was going to happen. Sheffield Northern General Hospital specialises in orthopaedics. If I had been taken to any other hospital it would have almost been guaranteed that my right leg would have been immediately amputated. The surgeon explained the severity of my injuries. My left leg would be set in a plaster cast to deal with later. This first operation was to concentrate on the right leg. "Mr Judge, you have extreme trauma to your right leg and we are going to do our absolute best to save your lower leg and foot. However, you have to consider the fact that we may have to amputate if there are complications," he said.

This was the first time that I heard this word 'amputation'. I was shocked and confused due to complete ignorance that I had been wrapped in for the last couple of hours. I understood that they were making life-saving decisions but amputate? When I had woken up that morning I certainly didn't think that by the end of the day someone would be looking down at me and telling me that they might have to remove my leg!

I'm the good looking one on the left, that's my brother on the right. Retford Lions 10K, 1983.

I was just 28, with no kids, and being legless was associated with a Friday or Saturday night out. Now this phrase had a whole new horrific meaning! But I needed my leg. I was a runner. That was my thing and always has been. From fun runs with the whole family in the early eighties up to now as a member of my local running club, Killamarsh Kestrels. But it was more than that. If anyone asked me why I ran it was to be in control of my own body as I pushed it physically. It brought me wellness and liberation. It released the endorphins that brought me happiness as a result.

I need to run. It was part of my 'Friday night routine' before I would go out with my friends. I run when I'm happy, I run when I am sad. It's not just fitness or 10K races; it's more than that. It helps my mindset, it's who I am. It's part of me. I have to run... I can't not run! Amputation was simply unacceptable.

Looking into the surgeon's eyes, I explained to him what kind of person I was. That I was fit, healthy, sporty and I would be committed to anything like physio or rehabilitation, should any be required of me (looking back, I was so ignorant of what that would entail). I stressed how passionate I was to keep my leg. Finishing my plea, I looked him in the eyes and remember saying to him "Please do the best that you can... I have faith in you." There, I had said my piece and there was nothing more to do but relate my situation to the lyrics from the Stephen Gately song 'I Believe'. I too had put my faith and my belief in the hands of others and I believed.

I was wheeled into the operating theatre. Anaesthetic was pumped into my body as I started counting backwards. 10, 9, 8, 7... The countdown of handing my body over to the surgeons and operating team. For them to do their best and make decisions that would affect my life forever. In reality this was a life-saving operation and this is what was explained to my mum and fiancée. The operation wasn't just about saving my legs, it was more about saving my life.

Apparently there were extensive and heated discussions during the operation about what actions to take. To save my ankle and foot they initially had to remove four inches of shattered tibia bone. They cleaned up the remaining ends of my bone and then joined them together which dramatically shortened my leg. They saved as much skin tissue and muscle as they could and wrapped it round the wound. This was then held together with an external fixator (Ilizarov apparatus). The best way to describe this piece of equipment is that it consists of four metal rings that go around the leg like four small bicycle wheels. The metal spokes of these wheels (rings) went into my leg, through the bone and out the other side. Each of these rings was then connected down the length of the leg by metal rods, so although the leg was held together there was flexibility within the spokes. Additional skin was then taken from my right thigh at the top of my leg and this was placed on my reformatted lower leg. The tool used to do this can be described as a sharp clinical potato peeler which literally peels off the skin which was then laid on my open wound.

I've made my operation sound quite simplistic and matter of fact, but it was a very complicated and technical event lasting around 8 hours. From what I have been told, amputation is a lot easier to conduct with more guaranteed results. What that team of highly trained practitioners did in that time was clearly incredible and brave. I thank them wholeheartedly for making those difficult decisions and following through on the actions they took.

My mum, fiancée and her dad were put up in an overnight room and were given continuous updates throughout the night by the surgeons. By 3am the next morning, the operation was complete and the lead surgeon explained what they had done. I was in intensive care, and although all had gone well, the fact that my body had been through so much trauma along with the invasive operation meant there was still a high risk that I might not survive.

My mum called my sister and brother, Dawn and Bruce, to explain the severity of the situation, and both burst into tears upon hearing the news. It was hard for my mum to listen to the sobbing of her offspring. It's one of those phone calls that you never want to receive. They dropped everything to be with me, and it breaks my heart to know that my accident inflicted that kind of trauma and upset on them. There it is again: another pang of guilt and sadness. Logically I know I did nothing wrong but the torment and regret is there and I hate it. Fearing it might be the last time they would see their younger brother alive, my brother and sister travelled three hours from Hertfordshire to Sheffield as soon as they could.

CHAPTER 2

Chin Up and Look to the Future

I slowly opened my eyes and the bright light hit the back of my skull. I moved my limp head sideways, checking out my surroundings. My shoulders felt like they were pinned to the bed in discomfort. A wave of pain swept up through me, forcing me to close my eyes tightly and grit my teeth. My body was rejecting the unnatural concoction of the anaesthetic which was making me feel sick. My mouth was dry and it hurt when I swallowed. My body had been chemically and physically tampered with.

I lay there and as I looked around the room I was again piecing together parts from my memory. It was like waking up with the worst hangover of my life, but instead of the laughter, the fun, and embarrassment came flashbacks of the skidding, the screeching and the screaming. I was drained and exhausted and I ached all over my body. My legs were throbbing. I couldn't move them; it felt as if they were held down by lead weights. I tried lifting my head up to see them, but the pain in my neck and shoulders made it difficult. Then the realisation hit me: How many legs have I got?

With all my effort I gritted my teeth, and by slowly lifting my head up, I could see thin bedsheets covering parts of my legs. I grabbed at the covers to reveal the results of the operation.

There at the end of the bed I could see my right foot – phew! They hadn't amputated! Internally I smiled. I knew it would be ok… I knew it. My left leg was in some sort of plaster cast and my right leg had a big black metal cage thing surrounding it. Staring at my feet, I tried to move them. First the right foot… hmm, nothing. Then I looked at the left foot. I tried to move it…nothing! My legs both felt so heavy and I couldn't move either of them. My head dropped back on the hospital pillow and I stared at the ceiling. I breathed in and out to recover from my efforts. Maybe the anaesthetic hasn't worn off yet, I thought. They're going to be in a mess, but at least I've got something to work with.

A solid spasm of pain shot through my whole body. I was so weak, fragile and completely exhausted. I needed energy. I needed water; my mouth was so dry.

I was in the HDU (High Dependency Unit) where there was one nurse to every two patients on a 24-hour basis. My situation was still critical: I needed close attention, monitoring and numerous blood transfusions.

I lay there focusing on their familiar faces as my situation was explained. Then I did a double take… Dawn and Bruce? I was amazed and so happy that they had travelled all the way from Hertfordshire to come and see me. We're a strange family when you look at us, as we don't all live near each other and don't call each other much, but when we get together it's always awesome. We are so connected; we laugh and joke and have such a fun time. I would describe us as close.

One such memory I have is in 1998 when we all met up at Mum and Dad's house. We ate and drank round the BBQ. By now Dad was bedridden with cancer so we took it in turns to pop in to see him. He was so weak that he could hardly hold the little bottle of French beer in his hand. He was battle-worn after receiving over 120 blood transfusions and numerous doses of chemotherapy over the past seven years. I don't remember much about our conversation because for me with my optimistic outlook this wasn't going to be the last time that we would speak, but I sense now that Dad knew otherwise. I remember him telling me that he was proud of me. He told me to keep doing what I was doing and then he looked at me and said, "Steve, always, in whatever you do, be the best that you can be."

I remember it clearly because he mentioned it like a statement. I nonchalantly confirmed that I would by saying "Of course, Dad" but little did I know that those would be the final words that he would say to me and I to him. Now I wish I'd said more and I wish that my last three little words to my dad were "I love you" but they weren't and the moment was gone as my dad passed away a couple of days later.

I was not always one for words but I have always been one for action. I was going to be the best that I could be in everything I chose to do, for me and for my dad.

As I gazed at Dawn and Bruce stood there at the side of my bed in the hospital I remember crying, partly in happiness but also for the inconvenience I was putting them through. I tried to display strength and optimism but in reality, I didn't know what was going on. The next day, after assessment by the senior surgeon Simon Royston, I was wheeled into the operating theatre again. Another ring needed to be added to the cage, which made a total of five rings. I felt like a limp puppet without a voice or opinion and completely in the hands of the professionals around me. 'Just fix me. Just make me better and let me know when you need me to do something.' I was OK with that thought.

Simon conducted his rounds later that day and gave me a rundown of the situation and the severity of my injuries. Although my right leg was four inches shorter than before, they were going to follow a procedure that would have the potential to lengthen my leg. In eight weeks when the bone had married up and sealed, they would carry out another operation to break the good bone in my leg. Then, using the external fixator, the leg could be lengthened by twisting bolts by just one millimetre every day. This would in theory gradually extend the leg back to its original length over a three-month period.

"Mr. Judge, with all that your legs have been through there is a great risk that your body won't take to the work that we have done. You have a long way to go with both legs and your overall recovery. It's because of this that I have to tell you that due to the extent of your injuries, you may never walk again."

I remember lying there, trying to take in all of the information he was telling me. A lot was hazy but when he said that last line it was like a spark went off inside me. I heard that ever so clearly. It was like someone had just turned the volume down on all of the background noise.

"You may never walk again"!

I felt a hollowness in my stomach and felt like I was sinking into the mattress. He said some other stuff after that, but I can't remember any of it. I think when I'm given information like that I can look at it in two ways – fight or flight. Where flight would have been turning over in bed and giving in. And where fight was…well, the opposite. I was thinking 'No way, no way…NO WAY! That's rubbish, that's ridiculous, I have TWO legs, I've just got to get them working.'

I remember looking back at the surgeon and thinking, 'Who are you? You don't even know me! Who are you to tell me that I may never walk again?' I felt an anger inside me, in my gut, deep inside my stomach, and my heart started beating faster and the adrenaline started building up. This is a familiar feeling; I have often referred to it as my inner white tiger which is my inner resource to channel anger, frustration and excitement. The tiger is controlled, elegant and slick as it prowls; it thinks and reflects before acting on its impulses. I really wanted my tiger to pounce and growl 'this situation is a load of rubbish', but in reality I was shattered so my tiger knew the priority was to contain its compulsions, to plan and most importantly sleep, as cats generally do.

Perhaps I was in denial of my potential fate, but I said to myself: 'I'll show you; I'll prove you wrong'. I clasped onto the word 'may'. You MAY never walk again...which in my head also meant that on the flip side I may walk again...always the optimist.

I'd learnt through my years of the power of words and how I used them could really support my optimism. The more I did it the easier it got. Looking on the bright side, turning a negative into a positive. It came down to choice and how I decided to look at things. I'd learnt not to overanalyse situations. I'd found that a little bit of ignorance is good but you do have to mix that in with a little bit of experience, some knowledge, risk and some common sense. If I mixed it correctly, then I had the recipe for success and happiness. The more I did it the better I got. In this situation we were dealing with the human body, my body. I wasn't prepared to be compared to a statistic or the average person. Everybody is different and the human body is an amazing thing.

It would be this knowledge and wisdom along with the strength of my inner white tiger that would get me through the tough times. When asked by a friend about the white tiger, I wrote this poem to describe its attributes, as my white tiger is something like an inner spirit within me. It has immense energy and power as well as passion and courage and it is there to support and resource me.

My White Tiger by Steve Judge

Wise in his experience and of that of others
Heart and soul full of passion, competitiveness and power
Ingenious as he prowls and plans before he pounces
Terrifyingly courageous from compulsions if not caged
Energy resourceful as sleep is to recharge

Tenaciously driven towards goals
Intelligent as he absorbs and adapts from others
Generous as his kind heart helps and supports
Eloquent in his pure colours of magnificence
Resourceful in the dedication of time and energy

I'm no Superman; I did hear the negative side to the comments. I did cry myself to sleep numerous times as I mulled the words over in my head. 'I may never walk again.' Every morning I would wake up and see the day as a new beginning. It was a choice. To think positively about what I could achieve in that day that would literally take me one step closer to my goal.

As you can tell, music has always been important in my life and it could be because of my mum. She ran a local 'keep fit' class through the eighties and nineties and so was constantly playing music throughout the house as she perfected her routines and choreography. We had every single 'Now That's What I Call Music' compilation album and so I was brought up on a selection of popular music. I'll never forget how my mum came home shocked from a class once, as she had been teaching the ladies of the village to express themselves to the lyrics of Prince & The New Power Generation – 'Sexy M. F.' (you may have to look up the lyrics yourself on this one).

Lying in my bed, I listened to music on my cassette tape walkman that my fiancée brought in for me with a selection of my compilation tapes that I had put together when I was motivating myself before a run. Now these tunes were helping me not give in to the darkness of the night.

Def Leppard's song 'Action' pumped my blood and riled me to the point of not being prepared to be pushed around by anyone or by anything. I'm in control of my own destiny and I'll be calling the shots. The music played on.

In the HDU, there was lots of noise and hustle and bustle surrounding me as I just lay there, feeling terrible. I was uncomfortable and unable to move. Pipes were going into me, supplying me with blood. I had oxygen pipes from my nose and other cables monitoring my progress. My neck and shoulders ached and it hurt to turn my head or look around. It felt like I was caught in a spider's web. I knew that these pipes and instruments were keeping me alive and that was important, but it bothered me that I couldn't work out what was going on around me. I asked my fiancée to draw a picture of me and label up all of the pipes and leads so I could work out what was going on. I'm a visual person and looking at the picture helped me a lot.

I spent five days in the HDU before being moved into an orthopaedic ward with eight beds all occupied by older men, except mine. I was the 'new boy' in town and learnt quickly that there was a pecking order of seniority, which mainly revolved around the possession of, and thus responsibility for, the TV remote control. My greenness and juvenility in this environment doomed me to the frustration of being subjected to endless hours of the Chelsea Flower Show, which blasted out of the one television at the end of the room. It was a nightmare. I just lay on my back staring at the ceiling. I felt old before my time.

I had to get better and I had to get out of this place. My main mission was trying to eat food to get some energy inside me. I needed this vitality from eating so I could fight and recover, but even this was incredibly difficult. Chewing the food took so much out of me; it was exhausting and swallowing was painful. This period of time at hospital was heartbreaking. I felt so low; I was spending all my time and energy just on survival, breathing, drinking, eating. The change was slow. I was stuck in bed, I couldn't get out and I was exhausted and frustrated. As the days passed and I realised the reality of my injuries, my optimism faded.

Patients would come into the ward, be dealt with and leave a couple of days later. One guy had completely rolled his car and trashed it. He was in for less than 24 hours and then deemed to be OK and fit for release. My mum travelled the one-hour trip from Doncaster every day to see me and every time she sat at my bedside I held onto her and cried. The words 'Why me?' spun around in my head. I was drained.

Diary Entry: 30th May 2002

Mum

I love you so much it's hard to explain.
I look so forward to your 2 o'clock visit.
It gives me so much to head towards.
To be up in bed and waiting.
You enter the room so happy it takes all the pain away from me.
You look after me as only a mother could,
You speak to me as only a mother can,
You love me as only you can.

Thank you for your prayers
Thank you for everything
I need you

Steve

I asked my mum to start a hospital diary as I didn't have a clue what was going on, and I've included some of these extracts in the book. I wanted to know the details of my injuries, what medication I was on, what operations I had had and other such information. The only other time I've had a diary was when I was travelling around the world for nine months after I was made redundant from my first role as a maintenance fitter working down the coal pits in Yorkshire. I'd put the £600 of redundancy towards a round-the-world ticket. The pocket diary size ensured that my entries were short and specific. I got the idea from my dad who kept a similar diary when he travelled around the world on an overland trip from 1964 to 1967. It was a brief record of his escapades with his travelling companions including his marriage to my mum in Australia in December 1965. Every day there was an entry of the temperature which my mum rolled her eyes at, saying in a dismissive tone, "Typical engineer"…I didn't get the negativity; I thought it was a great idea.

After a couple of days I finally had enough strength to pick up the pencil myself. I continued the report of what was going on but also how I felt. I wrote down how many hours of sleep I got and how many mouthfuls of food I consumed. After a couple of days, I realised I could turn back a few pages and see the difference. In a small way I was measuring my progress and I had benchmarks. This gave me something to work with and improve on. Any slight feeling of normality was progress for me and letting out a burp or fart felt great and was duly logged.

Diary Entry: 1st May 2002

> Shoulders are aching, feel stiff – Did physio and exercises.
> Need to keep eating and drinking peppermint water.
> Stomach digestion pains, injection given at 7.30pm to stop clotting.
> End of the day, fart score equals 9.

Even at this early stage the diary entry included physio and exercises. My initial physio was very much to help me breathe and encourage more movement and blood flow. As my recovery progressed so did the exercises. My body was compensating for the pain that it was in and protecting it through swelling or muscle tightness and the physio exercises were to counteract this. Throughout my rehabilitation I found the physio painful, boring and monotonous. But at no point did that ever stop me from doing them. I was being given the route to my recovery. If I wanted to get better then this is what I had to do. It wasn't a choice or a question, it was what had to be done. This was my body and I more than anybody was prepared to take action.

Using the pillows I would wedge myself to sit upright in the hospital bed, chin up and looking straight ahead. I carried out some of the breathing exercises that I had learnt in the past. Building up the oxygen and energy from within, I needed all the help I could get. Whatever it took, no regrets.

Through my years as a runner I had experienced my fair share of physio and my compulsion and commitment was always strong as I wanted to get back to running; I needed to get back to running. During a particularly long injury recovery where I was unable to run, I thought about what I could do rather than what I couldn't do. I started going to the gym and I got into cycling, eventually completing a 100 mile audax cycle ride. I even did a stint in amateur dramatics at the local theatre. This required commitment to learning how to act as well as all the lines; there was some pressure, and responsibility. Not to mention the adrenaline and endorphin rush that I got from being on stage.

My impatience to get better drove me to research deeper and I learnt about the seven chakras within your body and even taught myself yoga and breathing exercises to focus and master channelling energy and spiritual power. As I carried out my routine, I always played the same piece of music. The tune was 'Adiemus' which was written by Welsh composer Karl Jenkins. Please do listen to it (I have it listed on my YouTube channel).

I experienced such wellness and purity from being in touch with my body and its spiritual essence. I felt taller, lighter and uplifted. I remember an almost out-of-body experience where it suddenly became really easy and I could hold my yoga position for longer than normal and I remember thinking 'Whoa...this is cool' and found myself smiling. This dedicated practice mixed with the physio aided the recovery of my groin injury and gave me a whole new insight into what could be achieved with the power from within.

Now, looking down at my trashed legs, I knew that through the rehabilitation my arms were going to be crucial for support and independence. Whether I was in a wheelchair or on crutches, my arms needed to be strong and in good working order. I had to start thinking about what I could do rather than what I couldn't do. I did some tricep presses by lifting my bottom off the bed and back again. Then I noticed that attached to my bed was a one-inch bar that stretched up and then over the bed. I presumed it was to hang intravenous drips on or other equipment for the patient. By stretching up with one hand I could just about reach it, so I grabbed hold of it firmly and then reached up to grab it with my other hand. I was now hanging there like a cheeky monkey looking up to the nurses' station and making sure that no one could see me, as I was pretty sure the bar was not designed for this kind of activity.

I slowly started pulling myself up, not quite reaching the bar with my chin but not far off. I lowered myself back down and then did a few more. It felt good and it felt naughty. I had adrenaline running through my body releasing some endorphins. It was like something out of a Rocky movie where nothing was going to hold me back. I kept going until I started feeling shaky and then in a controlled manner I slowly released the bar and sunk back into my bed. Wow, that felt great; my heart was pumping and my arms tingling. It wasn't much but it was something and that was exactly what I needed at this stage. I was doing something positive to work towards my goal and as well as that, it was good for my muscles and adrenaline to 'kick start' my body into action.

My healing process was complex, but as with all illnesses and injuries one of the main things I needed was rest and recovery and good quality sleep. I was hooked up to a morphine drip and if I required more pain relief then it was just a case of pushing a button. The drawback for me was that I could only press the button when it shone green as it was a measured and restricted supply. That's clearly a good thing but at the time I didn't see it that way! At times of extreme pain and discomfort I would stare at this light until it shone green and then immediately press the button.

The pain was like a shallow electric shock that was pulsing and pumping. There was a constant dull ache followed by a sharp piercing sensation before the whole thing would start again. I was constantly trying to ignore it and concentrate on my breathing. Breathe in…deeply…breathe out…slowly, but invariably the pain would overpower and interrupt me. I would grit my teeth and breathe…but there was always one eye on the button waiting for it to light up. At times my arm was outstretched and my thumb hovering over it. Waiting, waiting…it was like being sat at the traffic lights staring and waiting for the lights to change to go, go go.

'GREEN!'

Button pressed, I released my breath, eyes closed and time to relax for a moment before the cycle began again. I felt the effects of the morphine as it slowly dulled the pain and I would enter into a semi-relaxed state. When this happened, I began to think clearly and logically, and I would take this opportunity to take in my surroundings before the pain would start again. I've never been one for using medication like Paracetamol and Ibuprofen and will only use it when completely necessary, and the same applied here. Through the day I could do the exercise and physio until exhausted, resulting in the ability to have a nap or sleep more naturally without so many drugs. I used the medication mainly just before I went to sleep in the late evening so that I would get good night's sleep. I would then wake up from a good rest with the energy required for eating, exercises and to continue the healing process. This was my 'game plan' and this is what I did to the best of my ability.

I was always getting visits from numerous friends, family, work colleagues and even my local vicar, Reverend Norman Harvey. I was always so delighted to see them all and would sit up in bed and put on a brave face about the situation as I could see from their faces that they were truly shocked at what they saw.

On one occasion I had just been transferred from a morphine intravenous drip to pills. Due to the weight that I had lost there was a slight miscalculation on the dosage because I was as high as a kite. When my eyes opened I clenched my fists and focused very carefully on each visitor that had travelled all the way to see me. Breathing in and breathing out. Forcing my eyes open and telling myself 'Concentrate, concentrate...' but they lazily drifted towards the ceiling. I was hallucinating images and colours and the words I said were garbled as my head hit the pillow yet again and I was out. After this embarrassing episode I was driven more than ever before to stop using these drugs as soon as I could. I still needed them at the moment but as soon as I could I would deal with the pain through my own methods.

Twelve days after the accident I had an operation on my left knee. My cruciate ligaments were ruptured and dislocated. My posterior ligament had been pulled off the bone and the interior ligament was snapped. Basically the four big rubber bands that held my knee together were all broken or no good. My knee joint could have been bent in any which way it wanted to.

The operation took a total of 5½ hours and my mum described the surgeon to me as he emerged from the epic operation. Paul Sutton, always so smartly dressed and well turned out, was physically exhausted in his sweat-drenched gowns.

Hearing this filled my heart with pride. He did that for me: he pushed himself to the limit like when you're studying until your head hits the desk or an athlete who nearly passes out or is sick as they cross the line. I needed to know that everybody was doing their best which they absolutely were, and I would continue to do the same.

Mr Sutton had been the best that he could have been and that was good enough for me. He had rebuilt my tendons, reconstructing my kneecap and replacing my broken ligaments with transplant ligaments from a pig. A pig! I don't ask many questions, to be honest, as it seems to be working but I've always felt a little bit strange since whenever I eat bacon sandwiches. During this operation, the medical team investigated the lack of feeling and movement in my lower leg. Due to nerve damage, they concluded there was a high probability that my feeling would be permanently affected, and that I would have a 'drop foot'. This meant that I might be able to move my foot left, right and downwards, but I would not be able to lift it upwards. A 'drop foot' carries lots of movement implications and I may have to wear a splint for the rest of my life. The other possibility was the nerve might just be squashed and over time the feeling and movement might come back. My optimism and ignorance of the analysis meant the information I took on board was that it would get better through time.

As the anaesthetic wore off a sharp pain started to emerge from my left leg. It was immense and there was a long-lasting dull ache around my left knee area. Following the operation I was instructed to carry out bending physio to help the movement and flexibility within the joint. I was exhausted from the operation as well as putting up with the spasm and discomfort from my right leg. I knew and understood that it was an essential part of recovery from the operation and important to my overall recovery, so I bore the pain to enable the best possible outcome from the operation.

Sat on the bed with my legs out in front of me, my left leg was strapped into a mechanical machine that slid forward and back, bending my knee up to a certain set degree. The goal was to get it to 90 degrees, so over time the degree of angle would be increased. A couple of days after the operation the practitioners once again set the machine up, telling me to work on an angle of 75 degrees.

I knew from my own notes on the last couple of sessions that 75 degrees was unrealistic and therefore I set the initial angle at 60 degrees. As the machine worked, over the next hour I managed to increase the angle, pushing through my pain threshold bit by bit. It was agonising and I gritted my teeth as my knee joint was wrenched by the machine and the sweat ran down my face. I had to dig deep for the determination to turn the dial one more degree, each time slowly increasing the angle.

By the end of the hour I had reached a satisfying 70 degrees and I was very pleased with my efforts. The practitioners then came back and asked how I had got on but they were very disappointed with what I told them. They gave me a lecture about how important it was to do the physio exercises to the best of my ability and said they were concerned about my commitment to getting better.

It was a huge blow, and my heart sank. I didn't want them to think I didn't care. It was hard to be told to try harder when I'd actually been giving it my all. It almost made me feel like rebelling and doing the opposite. These people didn't know what kind of person I was. Inside I was furious with them and later I sobbed. How could they doubt my commitment?

As planned, I did the physio exercise again later in the day. Despite the pain and the lack of encouragement, I managed to get my leg to 81 degrees and had to wring out my towel because it was completely soaked from bucketloads of my sweat. I wanted them to understand me. I am competitive and I will push myself through pain; just tell me what to do but don't tell me I am not working hard enough. I needed them to know me and then work with me, and not to question my drive and commitment. My goal was to get better and get out of hospital; that was sufficient motivation for me. All I needed was people to show me how to achieve it. I would take it from there.

CHAPTER 3

The Great Escape

It had been two weeks since the accident, and when I tried to wiggle my toes, nothing was happening. My brain was sending the signals, but nothing would budge. But I had feeling in my foot, well sort of, because when I touched it with my hands it felt weird, like 'pins and needles'. Something very tingly and ticklish and almost a distant sensation but nothing like I was used to. The penny dropped as I recalled a joke.

> *Doctor: How can I help you?*
> *Patient: I hurt all over my body.*
> *Doctor: Oh dear, show me where exactly.*
> *Patient: I have pain here (prodding their arm), I have pain here (prodding their leg) and I even have pain here (prodding their head).*
> *Doctor: Hmm, I see what the problem is; you've broken your finger.*

Maybe the feeling was coming from my hand telling my brain that it was touching my foot and my brain creating some sort of reaction. I had an idea and asked the patient next to me to touch my foot very gently as I closed my eyes. "Have you done it yet?" "Yes," they said, sounding ashamed.

I opened my eyes and saw them looking guilty, as though they had done something wrong. My heart sank at the realisation of the situation. To me my foot was dead. No movement, no feeling and yet my physio consisted of massaging my foot with my hands and manipulating the toes to keep them mobile and avoid them stiffening up. I had a physio resistance band that I would put around my foot and pull towards me and let my foot just bounce back to its resting position. All the exercises seemed to be pathetic; they didn't do anything but I carried on with the exercises as I was told, three times a day. During my sessions I would stare at my foot and urge it to move. 'Left...Right...COME ON! Up...down... Aaaargh.' Nothing, absolutely nothing. I tried to scrunch my toes but it was useless, and it felt like a waste of time. But still, I persisted.

It was as boring as physio exercises always are but the way I saw it was that I was stuck here in this bed in this hospital and my sole purpose was to get better. If that was what I had to do as part of my recovery then that was what I would do, that was my job. Up to this point I was calling my left foot my 'good foot' although I think I was clutching at straws. I needed to make sure that I had no regrets. When I looked back I didn't want to find myself saying things like "Oh, I wish I'd tried harder" or "I wish I'd done more exercises". I didn't want that feeling that maybe I could have changed the result.

I held on to the hope that there was still a possibility that some feeling might come back to my foot and if it did then I wanted to ensure that my foot had not seized up due to lack of movement. I programmed my mindset so that I started querying if there was anything else that I could be doing to advance my progress. Instead of moaning about the exercises that I had to do, I asked the physios if there were any more. This was my foot, my body, my goal and my consequences. My motivation was to get better.

The nerve pain that I got from my left leg was excruciating. During the day I was able to distract myself so as not to focus on the pain so much but at night there was no escape. It felt like my lower leg and foot was being crushed and on top of that there were sharp electrical pulses that made my body flinch and jerk in an almost spasm-like state. There was also a constant 'hummm' of pain that wouldn't go away, a bit like a mosquito buzzing in the room when you're trying to sleep. It was annoying and the longer it went on, the more angry and tired I became.

I would reach down to my leg, massaging it, slapping it and even hitting it. It did nothing. It was hopeless. "GO AWAY," I would sob. I felt like I was going insane trying to think of what else I could do. I reached out to the physios for some kind of resolution to this hell and it was explained to me that the feelings that I received from my left leg went up the nerve system following my spine and registered as pain in my head. This is the same route that messages of pleasure follow and only one can be registered at a time. Pleasure or pain, you can't have both. Following this theory on a couple of occasions, my fiancée would tickle and scratch my back, giving me relaxing pleasure which then overpowered the nerve pain messages that I was getting from my leg. It worked and the mosquito was squashed, giving me a break from the constant pulses of pain. It allowed me to close my eyes, take a deep breath and drift off to sleep. That moment of pleasure didn't last for long but for that short moment in time I had peace, and was able to think clearly and revitalise my positive outlook to battle on through to the next day.

I lay there in the hospital bed staring at the ceiling and thinking of all of the things that I wanted to do. My impatience and frustration made me very anxious and caused my heart to beat fast in annoyance. It was like a spring inside me was being coiled tighter and tighter, squeezing my lungs and making my heart beat fast. My white tiger was inside, and now he was waiting to pounce and was scratching on the cage door.

I wanted to make every minute of every day count and appreciate all the things that I had but I was still thinking about the things I couldn't do. Simple things like going to the toilet when you want to go, watching the TV when you want to and eating what you want when you want.

I was really low and regretting the things that I had taken for granted, the simple things. The only way to move forward was not to give up. Going through my head were the lyrics of Chicane and Bryan Adams' 'Don't Give Up'. How there would be dark days but I've dealt with these before, I can do this, I believe and I won't give up.

Every day I would be brave and optimistic but every day I would ask the ultimate question "Why me?" Every day I was unable to hold back the tears and the demoralising feelings. Every day I would use this anger, frustration and impatience to push myself, to continue on this journey in front of me. I would do everything I could to get better and work towards my goals. Looking down at my legs I concluded that I would never run again. It wasn't worth me trying to kid myself and saying "Hey...never say never." I had to bury that thought and move on. It was easier that way. I desperately thought about what I could do rather than what I couldn't do.

10K Personal Best achieved with my race number to match my vision of beating 38 minutes.

I remembered the action I had taken when I wanted to get my 10K run time under the unattainable 38 minutes. I had stuck Post-it notes which said "38.00" around my home, where I worked and even in my wallet. By having these visual reminders the goal of 38 minutes was drilled into me. Then at the next event I received my race number: Number 380 and I thought 'Are you kidding me!'

It was taunting my inner tiger to rise and retaliate with unprecedented action. On that day I recorded my fastest ever 10K time of 36.51. As always, I recorded my performance notes scribbled on the back of my race number and on this occasion, there were two quotes:

Quote 1. *Don't Give Up*

Quote 2. *You've got to push it and push it and push it and when you feel that you can't push it anymore…then…you've got to push it.*

With this thought, I grabbed my pen and my notebook and I started sketching. I was sketching a picture of me, not in the state that I was in but rather a future state. I was standing, and both of my legs were fixed. At the side of me were my discarded crutches. I was stood there on top of a small mountain looking forward towards the future. As I stared at the drawing my eyes started to well up and my mouth began to quiver. I wanted it…I wanted it now. I had an urge to throw off the bed covers and drag myself out of the hospital. Seeing the thing that I really wanted sparked a flame inside me for me to conceive the idea. Staring at the image I believed that I could do it and inside I knew that I was going to achieve it. I also thought to myself that I'd never tried horseriding but I was rubbish at drawing horses so I never did one.

I know I said earlier that actions speak louder than words, but there is also a time when words are very important, and I chose words that would shape my mindset and help my progression. I consciously said to myself almost as a mantra that the accident hadn't ruined my life, it had just changed my life, which was true in many ways.

Keeping a diary allowed me to remind myself of these positive words and also measure progress.

Diary Entry: 1st June 2002

Slept only with medication
Exercises
Breakfast
BORED
Dinner, Exercises
BORED
Mum came over.
BORED
My fiancée came over and once again I just want to go
home with her.
SO BORED, I must go home soon.
Tea, Exercises
Sleep but very noisy. Can't wait until I can go home.

*Another mountain conquered all in the name of fun, challenge and
adventure. Life skills and opportunities. From left to right: me, David, Zoe
and Adrienne. The Lake District. Venture Scout camp, August 1991.*

I'd been stuck in a hospital bed for three weeks by now. I was bored
and frustrated and I just wanted to get out and explore. I'd always
loved the outdoors from my upbringing. We were very much an

outdoor kind of family with walks or gardening and family BBQs rather than being inside round a table. My main hobbies were running and Scouting. From the age of eight years old I had loved the fun, challenge and adventure that Scouting brought to me. As I progressed through the 'ranks' I loved getting the badges that were on offer. I was the Scout that took the badge book home and would look through it in my bed at night. I would decide which badge I wanted next and then I would ask my mum, dad or the Scout Leader to help me work towards it.

I carried on with Scouting through my young adult years and following in the footsteps of my sister and brother I too achieved the highest award possible, the Queen Scout Award. It had been a journey in itself achieving this badge with many barriers in the way. With the help of my mum and dad and Venture Scout Leader Pete Jarratt we worked through those challenges to eventually achieve the amazing accolade.

I guess thinking about it now, I guess I was already setting up a foundation of setting goals and working towards them without realising it, and I was also discovering life skills and seizing opportunities. Now my next goal was to get a wheelchair and to do that I had to prove my upper body strength. I had to be able to transfer myself from the bed.

Despite the fact that wheelchairs were in short supply, I was eventually rewarded with the prize of my very own one along with the chance to venture out. When the nurse entered the ward and pushed the wheelchair in my direction, it was like he was pushing a golden chariot symbolising trust, independence and freedom towards me. It was the same feeling as when I was seventeen and passed my driving test and was able to go out on my own for the first time...with the window down... and the music blasting out.

I took it very slowly at the beginning as I was very conscious of the big metal cage on my right leg that was stuck out in front of me and I certainly did not want to be using that as a bumper. I grabbed every opportunity to slide myself out of my bed into the wheelchair and explore the vastness of the hospital. Ignorant of the rules, I would mischievously go down the long corridors, navigating the lifts to the numerous floors, and investigating areas that fascinated me. The activity gave me a lease of life and it was good therapy and exercise. The public phones down on the ground floor next to reception meant that I could spend evenings phoning my friends and family. This was far better than the lack of intimacy I had when I used the trolley phone on the ward. I could surprise them for a short chat and update. I was as emotional as them when I replaced the receiver and cut off my line to the ones I loved.

On one exploration I found myself at the main entrance of the hospital. Seeing the doors to the outside world open and shut in front of me beckoned me to go closer. My frail, skinny body felt the chill of the air blowing intermittently through the doors. I kept a steady pace so as not to draw the attention of the reception staff as I slowly cruised past them, staring straight ahead and avoiding eye contact. Nearly there, just a few more metres, and the doors opened for me like the pearly gates of heaven. The light was bright and the fresh air blew in my face as I closed my eyes and breathed it in. It had been a long three weeks since I'd felt the wind on my face.

My freedom chariot rolled out of the door and I turned left onto the pavement but then suddenly my chair wobbled as it hit uneven ground, causing my front wheel to spin. I grabbed the rear wheels and quickly controlled the movement as a gush of nervous heat ran through my body. 'Oh my gosh! this is on another level.' I was scared but I continued round on the pavement as the surface got smoother and I gained in confidence. Dealing with slopes, cambers, pebbles and edges, I continued for another hundred metres before I stopped at an imaginary boundary. I wanted to keep going but I knew that I couldn't, not today. The air was cold. I turned my head and stared up at the sun that I'd not seen for weeks. As it beamed down on me brightly it symbolised energy, power and fulfilment.

The adrenaline pumped from the extra effort that my arm muscles had used. A frail strength built up the emotion inside me. I looked behind me, initially with a sense of achievement, but then my head dropped in sorrow. The hospital resembled pain and torture and unhappiness to me; I didn't want to be there anymore. I hated it. Turning my head back and looking out in front of me represented moving forward, freedom, my home and back to normality. I just wanted to go home; I just wished the accident had never happened. I wished everything could go back to the way it was. Why did it have to happen? WHY? For the first time there was no need to stifle my crying as nobody was near me. I wailed with such anger and sorrow. Tears ran down my face, my nose sniffled and my lips quivered with saliva. I didn't try to stop myself this time. I needed the release. Many minutes passed as my shoulders shook up and down and I sat hunched in my wheelchair, continuing to cry. I wanted to be independent. I wanted my legs to be better again, I wanted to be back to normal again. It was so unfair – why me? Why me? Why me?

I was exhausted and cold and my survival instinct kicked in. I needed to get back to hospital. In my weak and dizzy state I turned the wheelchair round. I slowly powered myself back to the place that I hated. Up in the lift, along the corridors and back to my firm sterilised bed. No tears left inside me but just sadness. I lay there with my head on my pillow, completely and utterly defeated. The sound of the Chelsea Flower Show highlights playing on the TV. Deep down I knew I was a long way off being released. I knew that there was still a lot of recovery and monitoring that I had to go through. For now there was no escape, and I knew it.

My time in hospital passed agonisingly slowly as I counted every hour of every day of every week. The commitment to my routine of physio and activities progressed me forward until eventually I was close to being discharged…with conditions! I needed to convince the hospital and reassure them that when I got home I would be ok. My friends and family leapt into action, setting up the downstairs of my house with a bed in the living room and a makeshift toilet in the enclosed front hallway. We had to remember not to use the front door from now on.

Equally important was a wooden ramp that was manufactured by my friend's dad Pete which enabled me to get in and out of the patio doors on my wheelchair. My fiancée would look after me when she was not at work and my mum would travel over and take me to the various appointments that I still needed to attend in the daytime. A district nurse was also arranged to be in attendance as required to change the dressings on my legs and any other duties. The plan was submitted and eventually on the 4th June 2002 I was given the 'all clear' and the necessary authorisation to grab a big bag of medicine, bandages and swabs from the internal pharmacy and say my farewells. I owed my life to this hospital and so much more on top of that but now I was so glad to say goodbye. I duly passed on the TV remote control to the next patient in line. As I handed it to him I smiled and said, "With great power comes great responsibility."

Leaving through the front doors and feeling the fresh air of freedom on my face was euphoric and I breathed it in. I didn't look back but instead just kept my head down and moved on forward to my fiancée's car. I felt like I was 'on the run' but I also felt lifted and excited. I had done it! It took some time but I'd got out of there…job done, goal achieved.

Manoeuvring my legs carefully into the passenger seat I closed the door, breathed and smiled. "Let's go home," I said, and we drove off. Little did I know that it wouldn't be long before I was back there in the same ward and in the exact same bed as last time.

CHAPTER 4

Growing Bone and Independence

My heart was beating fast as we pulled into our estate and then I smiled as I saw our house. Our three bedroom detached home looked smaller than I had remembered but it was a shining light in the gloom. Using the wooden ramp to enter, everything looked a little different as there was a bed in the dining room. The lounge was as I remembered and I transferred over to the sofa and breathed a sigh of relief. I'd made it. The downstairs toilet and bathroom set-up was ok but eventually I ended up dragging myself up the stairs to use the proper bathroom as it made me feel more human. As I was vastly underweight I had been given the green light to eat as much as I wanted and whenever I wanted. A dream to some but clearly a necessity for me. There was no real thought of nutrition taken into consideration as my diet mainly consisted of Coco Pops and fish finger sandwiches washed down with numerous cups of tea...with two sugars.

Thoughts, Feelings and Reflections
June 2002: Please

Please let me have one night's sleep
Go on – just one
Please

My nights alone downstairs were horrific. I lay there in the silent darkness with my pain and I tussling it out against each other. The constant pain exhausted me but consequently didn't let me sleep and didn't give in. I would lie there resigned to the ongoing pain like a ragdoll just hoping that at some point before morning I would pass out and sleep.

As the mornings came I held onto the words of Mike and the Mechanics: 'Get Up'. My frustration compelled me to do something about it and get on with my life. I made my day busy by looking after my cage and my leg, keeping the pins clean and applying cream. Daily ablutions took a long time and took a lot out of me. Getting washed and cleaning my teeth resulted in me having to rest afterwards and recover. I built up my independence around the house but even with a grabber stick there were some things that I frustratingly still could not reach. As a hunter gatherer I ventured into the kitchen and rummaged through the cupboards for certain 'pickings'. The height of the worktop still restricted me on various practicalities which included the washing up. That would have to wait a little longer.

The deal for me being let home was that I still had to attend various appointments at the hospital. My fiancée was back at work and so my mum assisted me with the appointments. The skin specialist, physio, pain clinic, pharmacy. My mum would drive an hour from her house to pick me up and then drive into Sheffield Hospital which took another hour. She would stay with me all the time and then make the return trip home. It was a long and exhausting day for both of us.

I didn't want to inconvenience anybody and I also wanted to be independent. How could I do this when I needed these people? I found a leaflet at the hospital one day which offered a community taxi where people volunteered to take patients into hospital or even on days out. All you had to do was book it in advance and pay a subsidised fee for the petrol. This was an amazing service and not only did I feel that I was being slightly independent, it also gave Mum a rest. It was also nice talking to the volunteers and having them help me in to get to the various appointments.

Open-plan waiting rooms mean that you can't help but compare your injuries to those around you. The more you look, you can nearly always find someone who is worse off than you. When I entered the arena with my five rings on my leg…not three…not four…but five, you could sense the intake of breath. The nudging and the turning of heads in acknowledged amazement. Whispers…"Look, he's got five!"

Never one to do anything by half measure, I was clearly in the elite class of orthopaedic injuries and was very much considered 'top dog' when it came to waiting room conquests. I myself would look around and compare and I considered myself lucky. At least I could power my own wheelchair without having to rely on someone else. No matter how bad I felt there was usually someone else worse off than me and this taught me to stay positive.

Diary Entry: 21ˢᵗ June 2002

The fact that I know that I am going to get better is a great comfort to myself although I know that this will only happen with the continuation of the care and exercise to my legs and of course the positive attitude.

Four weeks after my return home I was admitted back into hospital. The two parts of bone in my right leg had married up and sealed strongly enough for the next part of the process to take place. The bone would be broken in the good part and then the extension procedure could start taking place. Although I was back in my old ward, all of the patients had moved on. The only familiar faces were those of the nursing staff and practitioners.

"Change into these please Mr Judge," the nurse said as she drew the curtains behind her. I stripped naked and put on the attire that I was supplied with, which consisted of a disposable gown and some sort of hairnet. I was collected by the stewards who pushed my bed down to the required department. I felt a little bit breezy under the gown but I lay there with my hairnet on, uncomplaining. The operator came out to me with a clipboard to run through the standard questions of who I was, name, date of birth, hospital number. She then said, "Right, we need to just check which leg we're doing" and with that she swiftly lifted up my gown to view which leg had been written on for confirmation. "Oh my goodness..." she screamed, "you're naked!" Her eyes squinted as she stared at me and then said "Mr. Judge...why have you got your pants on your head?"

I woke up six hours later with additional pain from my leg and also three extension ratchets fitted to my cage. In my dazed debrief it was explained to me how it was my responsibility to twist the ratchets a millimetre a day to extend my leg length to 100mm (four inches) or thereabouts.

From that I took it that in a hundred days my leg would be the right length and then I could start walking again. I must admit that I didn't really hear the next bit of the plan or maybe I didn't understand. What was said was that once the leg had been stretched to the full 100mm it would just leave a gap in the bone. The bone would then have to grow back and that could take many months although in reality this process would take over a year. I was going to be in for a big shock further down the line as my goalposts would be constantly moved, further and further apart. This amount of leg lengthening was highly irregular. Only half the distance, 50mm, is recommended as a maximum length. Because of this there were many questions, queries and doubts as to whether the process would be successful and there were by no means any guarantees of solid results.

From the start I found it a big challenge to keep count and remember to turn the three ratchets four times a day every three hours to equal 1mm in total length. If I turned them too many times then the calcium line may not stay connected and the bone would not grow back. Turn it too few times, no problem, except that would just prolong the agonising torture of having this damn metal contraption on my leg. The pain of extending my leg was a tool of torture that I was subjecting myself to over and over again. The pins of the

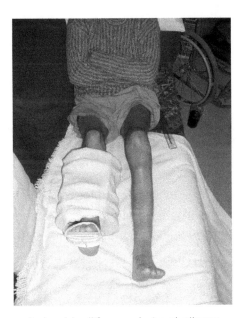

A sizeable difference but a challenge where there was no choice.

cage were slowly ripping through my skin and stretching my muscle and ligaments. I was on a high dosage of medication with pain relief and antibiotics which together made me feel sick and lightheaded.

After turning the screws blood would weep from the insertions and there would be a dull ache coming from my leg. The weakness that I felt made me feel angry and impatient. I was actively working towards my goal with grit and determination but having to quash the temptation to speed up the process. I desperately held myself back so as not to crank up those screws to maybe 2mm or 3mm a day. I couldn't afford to take short cuts as this might very well send me backwards. I used my impatience to get the job done to ensure that I did everything correctly, as instructed, like an engineer…just 1mm a day.

I liked the responsibility and the satisfaction of being competent enough to use the spanners on the nuts and bolts of the cage. As the days and weeks progressed my cage got longer and when necessary I held my breath as I kept my leg completely still while I slid out one of the connecting rods from the outside of the cage and replaced it with a longer one. I secured the nuts tightly before I allowed myself to breathe again and smile.

Thoughts, Feelings and Reflections
July 2002: Thank You

Thank you Lord for saving my life
Thank you Lord for my loving wife
Thank you Lord for helping me believe
Thank you for giving me the power to achieve

We had been planning our wedding since the spring of 2000 when I had proposed to my girlfriend in Paris at the top of the Eiffel Tower. I had got down on one knee and produced a ring with a heartfelt monologue ending with the words "Will you marry me?" We spent the rest of the romantic weekend planning our special day and now it was just months away. Despite suggestions of postponement I was adamant, probably through my stubbornness, that we were not going to move the date.

Our planning was meticulous in every detail although the accident did cause one or two unforeseen issues. The honeymoon to Crete had to be cancelled, and I had to appoint a second best man to help me with the additional duties and medical equipment. All our family and friends would be there and it was a perfect opportunity to show my progress and for me to prove that the accident was not going to hold us back. We were getting married in our local church and within that vision was me standing at the altar. This was a big drive for me to stand again but more than that, I had a deadline. The physiotherapist was pleased with the progress of my rehabilitation, and in my June appointment she gave me a Zimmer frame to take home and start using.

As instructed, I would bring the frame up to my wheelchair, and rock myself forward. Using the momentum and my arm strength I would lift myself up and lock my arms with my hands gripping the top of the frame. Fighting with my brain over dominance. I eventually released the weight through both of my legs although realistically mainly through my left. Petrified, I slowly shifted the weight over to my right leg where the pins took the brunt with a burning sensation through my muscle and bone. There would be an audible 'click' and a 'clunk' from my ankle as the dull pain shot through me, making me cringe. I counted to 8…9…10 and then quickly pulled back the weight. I gritted my teeth and squinted my eyes as I lowered myself back into the chair with short gasps of breath. With sweat trickling down my back and tears rolling down my cheeks, I sat there recovering. Building myself back up and repeating the process another two times was exhausting both physically as much as it was mentally.

As the wedding date approached, it became evident that I was going to struggle to achieve my goal of standing at the front of the church. Although I wasn't prepared to give up on this vision I was going to have to come up with a new plan and another way of doing it.

The plans for my stag do also had to be re-evaluated as it was clearly going to be impossible to spend the weekend away with my friends mountain biking and paintballing. In the end I conceded to an evening and night at my mum's house where we would drink and play games in the garden before everybody slept over in tents. Three days before the weekend I was rushed into hospital for an emergency operation on my left knee. There had been a continuous 'discharge' from where a screw was holding down one of my ligaments. This had finally got infected and so the operation involved them drilling down, removing the screw from my bone and then sealing my knee up again. As I was released from hospital I was handed a bag full of antibiotics to prevent further infection and given strict instructions to keep off any alcohol…Great! Fifteen friends came over as well as my brother (the newly appointed second best man) and we ran a few games for everybody including tug of war and wheelchair racing (which I won), and finished off the evening with a fire at the end of the garden with pizza and hotdogs.

On our wedding day I looked very smart in my wedding outfit with my tailor-made trousers. Up to this point my mum had adapted many of my underpants and shorts so that they had a Velcro strip down the right hand side, enabling me to wear them over my cage. For my wedding outfit she had taken me to a tailor as the trousers not only needed to have an opening at the side but they also needed to be wide enough in the leg to wrap round the massive cage. I guess they were a bit like a stripper's pair of trousers. The ones where they quickly rip them off to show their flesh…but I wouldn't know anything about that!

Bruce and David ready to help me while I'm ready and waiting with my 'stripper' trousers on.

I had a big smile on my face but I could see from the reaction of friends and family that they were shocked to see me looking so gaunt and skinny in my wheelchair. I guess I needed to increase the number of fish finger sandwiches that I was consuming. Entering the church I whizzed down the aisle and took my position at the front next to my two best men, David and my brother Bruce. I'd known David ever since I had moved up north from Hertfordshire when I was nine years old and we'd been best friends from then onwards. There was a lull before the organ piped out the Wedding March as my fiancée entered and walked down the aisle. At that moment I rose from my wheelchair using the Zimmer frame and once I had risen David removed the wheelchair while Bruce passed me a shooting stick: a metre-long stick with a seat on the top which I shoved underneath my bottom and sat on. The congregation's view was of me miraculously rising from my chair and standing. Many people told us later that there was a beam of sunlight shining down through one of the side stained glass windows onto me. My future wife shone with her own beauty as we secured our love for one another. 'Through richer or poorer, in sickness and in health.' It's fair to say that it was a very emotional wedding ceremony with not a dry eye in the place. I remember my friend Andrew saying how incredible it was for him to see me stand and how proud he felt at being my mate.

The shooting stick was used a couple more times for the wedding photos but mainly I was seated next to my wife on a wooden bench that Dave had brought over from his house. The wedding reception was difficult as I couldn't mingle very easily. Getting round the tables or even chatting to people was hard. For the first dance I once again rose from my wheelchair in the middle of the dance floor but this time my new wife was there to support me. I stood there surrounded by our friends and family watching on dutifully as our song played. I was putting as much weight through my left leg as I could while gripping my wife's arms a little bit tighter than she may have well liked. It was a special moment for everyone in the place but as the song finished I was ready to collapse. My leg was beginning to spasm and about to give way and my wheelchair was returned to me just in time. Ten minutes of deep breathing and regaining my composure and then I was ready once again to enjoy the evening.

The night finished with me being physically carried up the stairs to the honeymoon suite by two of my strongest mates as the quaint hotel had no lift installed. Not quite the tradition of the groom carrying his new wife over the threshold! It wasn't quite the romantic night we had envisioned but it was certainly memorable. We had achieved our goal of getting married as planned. Sadly there were consequences from the exertion of the day's events. I suffered badly with muscle pain, aches and exhaustion for the next three days. But I did believe that it had been worth it.

Thoughts, Feelings and Reflections
September 2002: I get up

I may be strong but the pain knocks me down
I may be determined but the lack of sleep knocks me down
I may have set goals but bad results knock me down
Although I want to achieve, my lack of energy knocks me down
Although I am persistent, my fatigue knocks me down
Although I am committed I wonder how many times I can get up,
And fight back after being knocked down
I get up.

Physio was my life; it was my job. I was now in a strict routine of what I had to do and I was very committed to following it. As a patient I was thinking of everything possible to improve and soaked up the information like a sponge.

What more can I do?
What more can I do?
What more can I do?

I was hungry for input. Was I doing everything right? Were the results looking good? I was spending over four hours a day on physio exercises which included the repetition of over twenty different exercises as well as regular physio visits at the hospital each week.

I got annoyed when the pain drained me and meant I couldn't do my physio. Some of it was hard work and some felt pointless, such as staring at my left foot and 'willing' my static toes to move like I was some sort of 'Jedi Knight' guru freak. With all my efforts there was no result, however I would do it over and over again.

Diary Entry: 10th June 2002

Physio on left foot...looking while I'm doing it my foot doesn't move but the fact is that I know if I keep going then one of these days there will be movement. I know that and I have to stay positive.

My wife's commitment to looking after me was incredible and where possible she would take me out on trips into the countryside or to see friends and family. This involved her wrestling the heavy wheelchair into the boot which she managed to do somehow. We went to the theatre where I used to act and also to our local church. It was nice to get out and people were always so lovely to talk to. My mum also took me out and once we went an hour up the road to Bradford to watch Bruce as he represented the County of Hertfordshire in the Inter Counties 10K Road Race series. It was great to support him from the pavement and cheer him on. Watching all the athletes sprint past pushing themselves made me realise that they had goals that they were working towards just like me. Theirs were clearly different to mine as with anybody. My situation was different to theirs, my health, my life. That's what affected my desires and ultimately my drive.

Mum and me supporting Bruce because sometimes actions speak louder than words.

I became increasingly aware of and frustrated by how difficult it was to get around on my own in my wheelchair with the high kerbs, steps and narrow doors. I needed to get out of this wheelchair but I also had other incremental goals before that. Reducing the drug dosage that I was on was a high priority as it made me feel sick and sluggish which inhibited my physio agenda. I had to control my pain, accept it and deal with it from within.

"I think you're ready to try something new today" said the physio as she brought over a set of crutches. Inside I knew this was progress from all my hard work with the Zimmer frame but I was scared, if not petrified, as I looked over to my mum who was there. My physio showed me and explained in detail how to use them and then handed them over. I lifted myself up from a seating position, stood, composed myself, and balanced. I was frozen; my brain wasn't allowing me to walk or even move my feet. After five months of not walking, had my body forgotten how to? I took deep breaths, trying to compose and prepare myself for the ordeal. I lifted my chin up, looked ahead and broadened my shoulders as I clicked into 'logical mode' status. I knew what I had to do and so I would just 'do it'.

Using my right leg I took my first step. I held my breath behind clenched teeth. The sharp pain screamed and a wave of thunder shot through my body. I rapidly took another step using my left leg and transferred the weight over as I sucked in air. Breathe, breathe. I moved forward again, like a robot. The pain was now making me lightheaded as beads of sweat trickled down my back. I wasn't sure how long I could keep it up but I kept going. One foot rigidly in front of the other. Mind over matter, squeezing the sticks so hard that my hands hurt. The physio was at my side and saw me starting to wobble as fatigue and exhaustion set in. I just had enough energy to efficiently choreograph my final manoeuvre, using my crutches to lower myself down onto the chair and then…slump.

Drained, my head hung down as I breathed in and out, gasping for air with the crutches slack in my hand. I looked back at the ten metres that I had accomplished. I did it…I was smiling and I was shaking…I was spent…I was sweating, but I'd done it, I'd walked! I looked up to see my mum who was beaming with pride and excitement to have seen me so tall, strong and able. My smile quivered as it started to turn. She bent down to me and I hugged her. I couldn't hold back the tears of joy, of pain, of emotion. As I squeezed her I whispered, "I did it Mum…I did it." Following my dad's advice I'd been the best that I could have been. I was so happy and fulfilled from the experience of achieving my goal which gave me the inner strength to sit up and breathe…breathe.

On that day I was awarded my long-awaited crutches. I held onto them like a trophy, like a new toy that I was so proud to go and play with. Getting rid of them would be my next goal but for me that was a long way off, as little did I know that in eight months' time I would be swapping them back for a wheelchair!

CHAPTER 5

Living with Consequences and Regrets

Still searching for that independence, eventually we went looking for a car to buy. Before the accident, I had considered myself a good driver (don't we all!) and I was fairly confident about getting back behind the steering wheel again. My main stipulation was that we got one which had an outstanding safety specification. After a little searching, we viewed and bought a second-hand Volkswagen Golf TDi.

The car was an automatic, so I wouldn't need to use my left foot. We sent the car off to have hand control adaptations fitted which would result in me not needing to use my right leg either. Picking the car up a week later, I instantly attended a driving lesson specifically for converted cars. Proving my confidence and ability in the car park, the instructor then promptly directed me out onto the busy streets of Leeds city centre. Half an hour later I returned, skilled in the use of my new controls although a little bit sweaty and drained from the ordeal. There's nothing like going out of your comfort zone to get the job done! I had passed and my newfound freedom would give me more independence, more control and less need to ask others for help.

With the crutches my initial goal was to walk at least the ten metres from the door of my house to the car. My desire for this fuelled my courage as day after day I practised until I was ready to go outside. The gap from the steps of my back door to the car seemed an eternity but reaching it and sitting in the driver's seat resulted in the biggest smile on my face. The dashboard lit up like a time machine and I was ready to go forward into my future.

Driving around, window down, sunroof open, wind in my hair and some great tunes blasting out of the radio, I was free, free to go wherever I wanted. On arriving for my hospital appointments there was even further to walk with the super-long corridors but that wasn't going to stop me. I saw it as a challenge. I set out on the theory that the only way I was going to get there was to not leave enough energy to get back. I always found the inner strength within me to push myself and achieve what I set out to do. Attending the hydrotherapy sessions at the hospital gave me the first feeling of walking unaided although I was initially very deep in the pool.

As the weeks passed, I progressed into shallow waters where it was harder work but the results were more beneficial. I was always the first one in and the last one out in the two-hour session. As I stepped out of the sanctuary of the pool and used the crutches on the wet tiled floor it brought back to me the petrifying reality of my situation. The fear drained me of my reserve energy and I would sit in the waiting room before setting off on my perilous journey back to the car and then again catching my breath while I sat in the driver's seat before driving myself home.

Diary Entry: 26th September 2002

The physio is so hard and I get so tired after hydrotherapy and my right leg hurts so much. Maybe I push myself too hard but I have to. At times it becomes very emotional as I just feel that I am trapped in a worn out and useless body or at least one that cannot keep up with my needs.

On the way home I would extend my independence by visiting a drive-through establishment seeking a well-earned energy and 'carbo' loading feast. By the time I got home I was 'zonked out' and although my legs would be twitching from the muscle exertion my eyes would close and I would fall into an exhausted sleep with a valiant smile on my face.

Due to bad circulation and lack of movement the swelling of my right foot was beginning to make it look like a purple balloon and consequently inhibited its mobility. To release the swelling a good massage and a swift 'cracking' of the bones did the job. This task was initially carried out by the physio but once I leant the technique I could administer the treatment myself. Bad circulation is not good and I would attempt to wiggle my toes or move my foot but it was almost physically impossible. With the trauma, the injury and the cage pins stuck through my leg and ankle my efforts were little more than pathetic. I begged my physio, "Is there anything else I can do…anything?" "Well," she said, "there is one thing…"

I entered the supermarket on a mission to find some mop buckets and hoped that I wouldn't have to walk up and down too many aisles on my crutches to find them. The physio had explained to me that by filling one of the vessels with hot water and the other with cold then I could alternate plunging my foot into them. The difference in temperature would encourage active blood circulation and aid the reduction of the swelling. 'Worth a try,' I thought, but I needed some oval shaped buckets for my foot to fit in.

Luckily aisle two held the house cleaning equipment and I used my crutch to slide a mop bucket onto the floor for me to pick up. It looked to be the right size but just to make sure I looked up and down the aisle before I subtly lifted my foot up and placed it in the bucket. Perfect, a little tight but that's because my shoe was on and with a bare foot it would be a good fit. I smiled. 'Job done.' As I lifted my leg up to retract my foot, the bucket lifted off the floor.

"Damn!" I muttered and tried again but again the bucket lifted up. It was stuck! Trying to vigorously shake my leg just looked like the action was being played in slow motion and had no effect whatsoever. My frustration was making me perspire and some of the other shoppers were giving me sidelong glances. Using my right crutch I tried to push the bucket down while lifting my foot up. My crutch slipped on the side of the bucket and went spinning across the floor. The action sent me off balance.

"Whoa…whoa…whoa…" I tried to steady myself with my other crutch while clonking down the aisle with the bucket still wedged firmly on my foot. Keeping momentum to stay upright, I walked in a big arc, eventually returning to my fallen crutch. "Everything alright, sir?" asked the security guard who was holding my crutch and looking down at the shop's bucket that I was stomping around in.

"Do we need a hand, sir?" he asked with raised eyebrows. I looked up at him and without thinking just blurted out, "I… I just wanted to see if it was the right size."

It was now six months since the accident and we set up a desk downstairs so that I could use the computer. My diary was evolving into more of a progress record. I started taking more photos and video clips and even wrote down my feelings by way of poetry or prose. It was a great way of expressing my feelings as well as monitoring my progress. I had also come to an agreement with work that I could do some data inputting from emails that they sent to me. I was on sick pay and I wanted to show them that I was thinking about what I could do rather than what I couldn't do.

The data inputting work was so boring but it gave me a purpose and the feeling that I was needed. Setting goals for independence was a huge drive, although it still came with limits. I remember the day when I was able to use my two crutches to precariously walk into the kitchen, shuffle around and make my own cup of tea. I looked at my accomplishment with a proud smile and then I realised…Bother. I can't carry the damn thing, not while I'm using two crutches. I laughed at how ridiculous the situation was and then stood up straight, shoulders back and said, "One day! One day, Steve, you WILL carry your own cup of tea." I'd learnt to tell myself that it wasn't failure, it was just feedback and this encouraged me to work towards the next goal of walking with just one crutch. I had no idea that achieving this almost simplistic progression would actually take a full year.

I was still learning about the consequences of pushing myself following one escapade leading up to Christmas. I took myself shopping for family and friends around the huge complex of Meadowhall on the outskirts of Sheffield. A full day of mingling with the hustle and bustle of shoppers as I powered myself around on the shopping centre's wheelchairs. They were built like tanks and just as hard to manoeuvre.

For the next two days I suffered from muscle ache, fatigue and exhaustion. My rehabilitation schedule could not be adhered to so the results suffered and this had a negative impact on my progress. The consequences of my actions vexed me to the max and filled me with regrets. This was my health and my recovery that were the consequences and I didn't want to do anything that would jeopardise this progress or undo all of the hard work that I had put in. I had to be wary of external factors that might cause me to stray from what I wanted the most. It was more than balance or priorities, it was choice. I had to take control, ownership and responsibility. Only I could do what had to be done and going forward I didn't want to have any regrets.

By my calculations time was nearly up. I had been twisting the ratchets for coming up to a hundred days and I was excited about the prospect of not inflicting pain on myself, and getting this damn cage off. I enquired at my next appointment when exactly I should stop lengthening my leg and received the rather flippant reply "When it's the right length". 'Well I know that, but when will that be?' I thought. I was hoping there was some extremely accurate and precise way of measuring my bone because as an engineer I was not happy with the statement "Just stop when it's the right length".

There was no methodical system presented to me and so I took matters in my own hands at home. Sat on a chair in the kitchen, I rested my bare feet on the floor about 15cm apart. I then placed a spirit level on my knees and noted the position of the bubble. As crude as it may seem, this is what I used in the last couple of days of extending my leg. Eventually the bubble was there, resting exactly in the middle of the two gauge lines. I punched the air in triumph and consequently ceased twisting the ratchets. I had done it. It had been tough and extremely painful, but my leg was all the way back to the right length. Wow, it had been an amazing feat of engineering and human body tolerance to succeed in such an incredible achievement. My wife and I celebrated with some well-deserved champagne for stretching my leg a full 100mm.

At my next hospital appointment, I was grinning and proud of my success. I could see the light at the end of the tunnel. Without the manipulation of leg lengthening things would settle down. I could get this cage off, get some sleep, get my strength back and get walking properly again. My first jolt back down to earth was when I eagerly asked when the cage could come off, to which the surgeon's assistant replied flippantly,

"When the bone has grown back!" I was a bit confused because I thought my bone was there in my leg! "No Steve," he said, "at the moment there is no bone. You have a 10cm gap in your leg which is being held together with the external fixator."

My heart sank as I heard him say, "The fixator will be removed once your bone has fully grown back which we will check with the x-rays periodically."

Periodically? What did that mean? "How long will that take?" I asked in desperation.

"It's unknown but it could take up to four months," was the reply.

My whole being sank and the life drained out of me. "Four MONTHS!" I wanted this thing off my leg NOW, not in four months' time. "Can I...erm... speed up the process at all or do anything?" I enquired.

"Mr. Judge, it all depends on how quickly your bone grows back. A healthy diet will help but mainly you have to use it. The more active you are the more it will encourage your bone to grow." I exhaled. Ok, got it, a gauntlet laid down for me. "I'll show you four months!" I muttered to myself.

If the great philosopher and singer/songwriter Chesney Hawkes taught me one thing it was that I am 'The One and Only' and everyone is different. Don't start comparing me to others or 'the average'.

I left the hospital with my white tiger growling from within, contemplating how to channel the frustration into action. Let's do this! I was on a mission. I've always said that anger is not a bad thing, so long as you use it in the right way. I was ready to work hard now and do whatever it took to get this damn cage off my leg. Little did I know that despite my best efforts and dedication the length of time the cage would be on my leg would be double that previously expected! And the cage itself...well...that would also be extended.

My pain and suffering was about to enter a whole new level and I was completely unaware of it.

CHAPTER 6

Don't Lean on Your Excuses

Due to my progress through my rehabilitation, at my next physio appointment I was booked in at the gym. Seeing all those machines with their moving parts made me apprehensive and protective towards my legs. "How on earth can I use them?"

With guidance and instruction, I mainly used the cross trainer and the stepper machine. I would always start off by cheating and putting as much weight through my arms as possible. Slowly I would be courageous enough to release my body weight onto my legs. The pain I subjected myself to would make me sweat even more and grit my teeth, so that I stopped breathing, which was not ideal. I learnt to breathe through the discomfort which enabled me to control the pain and work out for longer. I knew that this was the route that I needed to take to get fitter and stronger and grow my leg back.

Working out with the other patients in the physio gym reminded me of a story that my dad told me. He had had physio treatment following a dislocated shoulder from a rugby injury many years ago. During the session the physio was called away from the gym. All the patients relaxed and eventually stopped their exercises and one of them turned to my dad and said, "You can stop now, they've left the room." My dad said flippantly, "I'm not doing it for them, I'm doing it for me!"

Thoughts, Feelings and Reflections
January 2003: Jealous

Jealous of the runner pounding the streets
Angry at those who are too lazy to run

Jealous of people who dance
Angry with those who are too shy to dance

Jealous of those who play in the snow
Angry with those who say it's too cold

I started seeing the machines as a playground for me to explore and develop on but the sessions were very infrequent – it was only once a week for 45 minutes. I had a very basic exercise bike at home and asked the physio if I could start using it between my sessions at the hospital. It had been used to build up my dad's fitness during his cancer treatment and I'd used it throughout my past physio sessions from running injuries. The physio replied, "Of course not, Steve. Every time your leg goes round the external fixator will clash with the frame of the bike." I thought about it for a while, cringed and shrugged my shoulders as I conceded that she was right. Later that week I was sat at home in my wheelchair, staring at the exercise bike and pondering. The engineer in me just felt that there must be some sort of solution.

Work bench of a grease monkey. Cementation mining, Doncaster, 1996.

I take after my dad in many ways and followed in his footsteps as a mechanical engineer. When I left The Hayfield Comprehensive School I was happy to get an apprenticeship as a maintenance fitter engineer working in the coal pits of Yorkshire. I would build up the huge mining machines from scratch in the workshop and send them down the pits to carry out the work. If the machine broke down then we would get the call and my job was to go down the pit and get it up and running again. Arriving at the coal face, I would be confronted with a situation that was nowhere near the explanation that we would have received in the workshop. What those guys did to those machines down there was beyond me. Anyway, I knew what the end result had to be and so I just needed to work out how I was going to achieve it. The pressure was on and at times I had to be ingenious to get the result. Sometimes I 'robbed' parts from other broken down or 'abandoned' machines. Whatever it took to get the machine up and running because there could be no excuses.

Staring at this bike, I just felt like there must be a way – just because someone told me that I couldn't do it. Was that true? I thought about it in a different way; I thought about how I could do it! The end result was to get on the bike and pedal so I asked myself, "What do I need to do to achieve it?" 'I need to bring my leg out by two inches,' I thought. "So…I need a big pedal…with straps on it," I said. Suddenly I felt a rush of excitement through my body. "That's it! I need to make myself a big pedal."

I purposely kept my idea to myself so as not to be dismissed by anybody and immediately went about measuring and sketching out my requirements. I took myself out to the garage using my wheelchair and crutches. It was like an Aladdin's cave of equipment and possibilities and I searched for the necessary tools and materials I would need. Meticulously working on my project brought me so much joy and excitement. I was not only independently using my skills but I was actively working towards my goal. The euphoria helped me push myself and by the end of the day I had produced a big wooden pedal. It had support brackets and a Velcro strap for my foot and an adjustable nylon strap for fixing it to the bike. I'd even proudly rounded the corners off and smoothed them down. I fixed it onto the pedal and enthusiastically climbed onto the bike, securing my foot in the straps.

My homemade wooden pedal that gave me the ability to not lean on excuses. Cassette tape player rigged up for the pumping tunes.

I started to move the crank round. Slowly lifting my knees and pushing them down, I was building up my momentum into a rhythm. Sitting tall on the bike,

I gasped for air, feeling the adrenaline building up inside me. I went faster, feeling a strong urge of power inside me whispering "Go…go for it" as the endorphins were released. I stared down at my legs. 'Wow… look at me…look at what I'm doing' I thought as I accelerated smoothly. I caught myself in the moment and acknowledged my achievement as I smiled for the first time in a long time. "I did it!" I said through gritted teeth. "When others said that I couldn't…I did it."

I told myself that in future when someone tells me that I can't do something or even if I tell myself that I can't do something I must ask myself, "Is that a fact, or an excuse?" If it's a fact, then fair enough… however, if it's an excuse then I've got to turn it round. I've got to make sure that I don't lean on my excuses and instead turn my excuses into challenges.

The lyrics of one of my favourite training songs from Rocky V, 'Go For It' by Heart and Fire, rang true. In life things can hold you down and that's when it's time to fight back even harder. Grabbing my crutches, I climbed off the bike and as I stepped away I turned and looked at the new lease of life that I had created. I realised that my future days of physio had just entered a new era and would be a whole lot more fun from tomorrow. I smiled to myself. 'I need to get some music rigged up, things are going to get sweaty!'

"You need to get that leg straight," said Simon, my consultant. He threatened to install an extension to my cage that would force my leg straight. The thought horrified me but I knew that I was to blame. I hung my head in shame because I knew why my leg was not straight. Quite simply it was because it had been bent for months. It was a comfort thing. As I lengthened my leg the ligaments were stretched tight. When lying on the sofa it was more comfortable to bend my leg rather than keep it straight, especially with the big cage on it. I had been enjoying the mobility of my wheelchair as I sat there with my legs bent rather than lifting my leg up or propping it up. At night while I slept I couldn't help but curl up, bending my legs. On top of all of that my physio time had been spent on other aspects of my body. Yes, I was guilty of all of this and now the consequences faced me.

"Mr. Judge, if you are unable to straighten your leg then there will be repercussions. For one you will walk with a limp for the rest of your life!" Hearing this bombshell made the blood drain away from me and my stomach felt empty. My goal was to get back to normal, standing and walking and blending into society. If I didn't, people would see me as different. They would surely ask me why I was limping and then a flood of questions after that. I did not want to have a limp – absolutely and definitely not. I wanted a straight leg and I needed to get it sorted. I certainly didn't want another cage on my leg and I didn't need to ask for help! I promised my consultant that I'd get it sorted. I'd had a similar issue with my left which I sorted out, so I was damn sure that I could get my right leg straight. 'I've got this!'

The first thing I did was buy myself a protractor from the stationery shop. I made some technical additions to it (using tape and cardboard) so that it could be fixed securely on the top of my cage and I could measure the angle of my knee. I needed to get a benchmark of where I was so that I could accurately measure and monitor my progress. From my running training I knew how important it was to have a visual goal written down to work towards. A fifteen-minute warm-up on the bike was followed by moving myself down onto the floor in preparation for the session to begin.

I sat there with my leg outstretched and my ankle resting on a roller. I placed my hands on my knee and, using all the strength in my arms, pushed down with great force. I could feel a burning pain below my joint as my hamstring was being stretched and strained with the pressure. Pushing harder and harder and then holding it there while I slowly counted...18...19...20!

The pain made me feel faint and my arms hurt from pushing. And I knew at some point I had to release my knee and then the pain would be much worse. Cautiously I would release my hands from my leg and

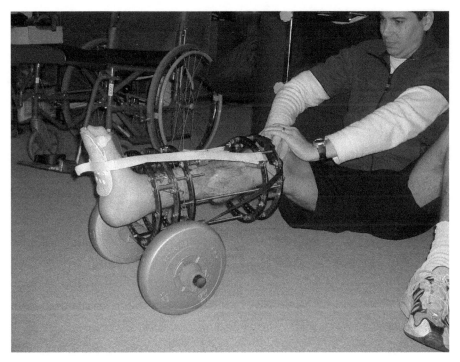

'Bring on the pain!' as I prepare myself for another physio session. An interesting alternative use for my weights.

that's when the pain would hit me like a hot flush surging through my body. I screamed in silence.

After numerous sessions when I could feel fatigue setting in my shaking hand would grab the protractor, securing it in its fixed position. I would use only the muscles in my leg to straighten one last time; that was the rule I had set myself. Looking for the figure, for the results of my pain and suffering. Quickly writing it down before collapsing in an exhausted state and suffering the aftermath of the session.

Thoughts, Feelings and Reflections
March 2003: The Aftermath of Physio

Frown, hard, really scrunch your face up and hold it for the next five minutes.
Squint your eyes so you can hardly see through them.

> Clench your teeth, not too tight but hold them together like they are glued.
>
> Hold your breath for five seconds, release it with a sighing grunt and quickly take another breath.
>
> Flinch your head like you have a nervous twitch as the pain from the aftermath causes you to go temporarily insane.

I would relentlessly enter the results into an Excel spreadsheet so that I could see my progress. At my hospital appointments my physio would ask me, "How is the leg straightening going Steve?" and I would say, "It's going well...I've got a graph!" My dedication and commitment was not going unnoticed and from all of the hard work my leg was getting straighter. Little did I know that all of this time, effort and pain would end up being in vain but until then I carried on pushing forward.

It had been nine months since I had been putting weight through my right leg and encouraging my bone to grow. I would stand using the Zimmer frame with just my right leg on the weighing scales to view my efforts. With help from the 'drive-through' and a well-stocked kitchen I'd put on about three stone, bringing me back to my normal weight of twelve stone. Walking normally would mean putting my full body weight of twelve stone independently through each leg and so this was my goal. Subjecting my right leg to this much weight would also massively help in encouraging the bone to grow back.

My results, meticulously entered into a spreadsheet, resulted in the graph increasing: 8 stone, 9 stone, but then the graph flattened off at 10 stone. Time after time I tried but failed. I couldn't put any more weight through my leg before it buckled and I collapsed onto the Zimmer frame. Gritting my teeth I would try again, but it was no good and seemed just physically impossible. Why? Why couldn't I do it? I was frustrated and feeling defeated.

I had come so far and now I was so close. I explained this to my physio and as I showed her my efforts she firmly placed two of her fingers just underneath the kneecap of my right leg in support. Oh my gosh…it worked! I could stand on one leg. As she let go my knee gave way. The realisation of what a difference this made was initially enlightening and then my heart sank. I couldn't stand on my right leg without help, my knee COULDN'T do it. 'My knee needs to "lock out"! I can't do this with a bent knee. No wonder I can't fu@king do it…it's a waste of time. I NEED a straight leg!' As well as my weight bearing my standing posture was also affected. "Put your bum in, Steve!" the physio would constantly tell me as I attempted to stand up straight and tall.

Thoughts, Feelings and Reflections
March 2003: Bottom Annoyance

"Stick your bum in Steve"
"See if you can put your bottom in"
"Your bum is sticking out a bit"
"Can you push your bum in a bit more?"
"That's good but just push your bum in a little bit more"
"Bit more, your bum is still sticking out"
"Your posture is OK but you really need to push your bum in"
"Can you squeeze your bum in a little bit more?"
"Squeeze…bit more"
"Just a little bit more Steve"
"Give me a straight leg and I promise you
My bum won't stick out."

Bad posture would also have consequences on other joints like my hip and even my back. My walking ability was also affected as I couldn't walk in a Reciprocating Gait Movement (RGM) since my right leg would give way. Without maximum weight going through my right bone, the speed of the recovery of the bone growth was inhibited which consequently meant the cage couldn't come off. And then there was the time… Bloody hell. The amount of time and pain that I was putting myself through every day, three times a day. I feared my sessions of physio that I subjected on myself; I hated them. I would end up in tears at the end, punching my knee for giving me poor results. Not shifting and not being fu@king straight. I was coming to the end. I just wanted a straight leg...NOW!

Thoughts, Feelings and Reflections
March 2003: I JUST WANT A STRAIGHT LEG!

Fu@k me!
A straight leg
That's all I want
After all this time
After all my effort
My persistence
My pain
A straight leg – just give-me-a-straight leg!
My posture
My weight bearing
My walking
My balance
All my progress is stuck on this leg
I'm sick of it
Bored of it
I just want a straight leg

The realisation of the consequences hit me hard and initially I threw myself into the conflict of a defeated boxer swinging frantically in the last round. I doubled the amount of heartbreaking and torturous physio sessions but if anything it had the opposite effect. I suffered so much from the pain I subjected myself to that I couldn't sleep at night due to muscle spasms. The lack of energy and weariness resulted in being unable to continue any physio the next day and thus going backwards with the results. It was a catch-22 situation and it tore me apart as reluctantly I finally had to admit that I had failed. I was getting nowhere and I was falling apart.

Thoughts, Feelings and Reflections
March 2003: Waiting

I wait
Tick Tock
Tick Tock
Into the depth of the night
I lie here,
Awake and waiting,
Suddenly my teeth clench as my body spasms with the pain
While my body jerks I wait for it to finish
After a while it leaves me, exhausted.
Tick Tock
Tick Tock
Into the night
I wait for the pain.

I sat on the floor in my living room and looked at the depressing score on the protractor through tear-filled eyes. My heart felt so heavy and low. I was desperately trying to convince myself that after three months of subjecting myself to pain it hadn't been in vain but instead I had tried something that just hadn't worked. There's no such thing as failure, only feedback, I told myself. But the feedback I was getting was that I had wasted my time and put myself through hell and the only next step forward would be even worse. The way I saw it, I had no choice. I needed a straight leg. I was struggling to achieve my goal, but at no point was I going to consider changing the goal and so I needed to change the plan. I knew what this meant.

"No…No…NO!" I cried. "I don't want another cage!" I punched my leg over and over again and pushed down on it as though some miracle would happen but instead the pain screamed out, forcing me to let go and buckle with it. Curled up with my shoulders shaking and the agony now surging out in pulses, I knew I was defeated, totally and utterly done in. There was only one thing left for me to do and although I feared having another cage fitted I had no idea exactly how deep it would drag me down.

The post came through the door and I collected it in my wheelchair and brought it back to the desk. Recognising the logo on one of the envelopes, I knew that it was from work and so opened it up curiously.

> *"Dear Steve, It's coming up to a year since you had your accident...*
> *We have been able to support you over this period....*
> *With regret we will no longer be able to continue this support...*
> *...end your employment with us in April...*
> *Regards..."*

My stomach felt empty, completely hollow. I was frozen like a statue, just staring at the floor. I didn't understand...but...does that mean...no job or that I have a job but no sick pay?

I read it again..."*end your employment with us*"...it was clear. I put my head in my hands and closed my eyes, trying to shut out the reality. The room was spinning around me. My brain categorising all of the events and the situation and calculating the consequences, all swirling round in my head. "I don't believe it...FU@K...I can't believe this shit!" I rubbed my eyes with the palms of my hands, harder and harder. Not breathing as the emotion built up inside me. I squeezed my head tight while I sucked in a long breath of air. My hands came down now, covering the whole of my face. My body started jerking, my shoulders moving up and down, but I wouldn't let out my emotions. I held my breath behind my gritted teeth. My face screwed up and my mouth like a gargoyle's. The blackness now spinning as I exhaled while spluttering. As I sucked in air, the floodgates opened. I slumped in my wheelchair with tears rolling down my face, thinking it would stop...but it didn't. I was drained and empty. Eventually I took myself over to the sofa and lay down. I hated this sofa. I had spent too many hours lying on it. I hated the physio equipment that I could see and the pain it inflicted on me. I hated these four walls that trapped me every single day of my life. The tears built up inside me to be sporadically released through my bleak and morbid thoughts. Again and again and again.

Diary Entry: 12th March 2003

> Double physio where possible. SO MUCH PAIN. I'm
> pushing the physio so much that I cause myself so much
> pain and then I can't sleep.
> I get very tired every day.
> Exhausting pain and no sleep.
> Very very low Wednesday onwards, made redundant,
> I feel I have no purpose.

The next three days were lost as I gave in to a world of darkness. My soul was beaten and my body weary from crying. I was nothing, I was empty, hollow. I was spent. I just couldn't do it anymore. On the fourth day as I lay on the sofa staring around the dormant room I caught a glimpse of my unused bike and physio equipment and a wave of guilt shivered through me. I saw that there had been no input to the table of results for the last three days. All that hard work I had been doing was just going to waste and I hated that. The fact that I had absolutely no compulsion to do anything made me realise who I had become and I hated that, I hated me. I was an unshaven and unwashed, dispirited waste of space doing nothing all day. 'I'm better than this. This isn't me!' The anger I felt sent a pulse of energy through me as I wiped the tears away. I started thinking about all the shit I had been through in the last year. I was sick of this situation. I wanted to get this damn cage off my leg. I wanted to get rid of this stupid wheelchair and get back to normal. But I was struggling, big time. I found it almost impossible to move forward and conceive my goal. Now, I had a new conception. Now my realisation, my goal and ultimately my drive was just to not be the person that I had become.

The following Monday at the hospital clinic I was a sad shadow of my former self. Downhearted, I admitted defeat and accepted the offer of a way out of this situation. I agreed to go through another operation to have another cage put on my leg. They scheduled it for four weeks' time. As I drove home I glimpsed the hospital in the rearview mirror as well as my bloodshot eyes, tired of crying. I was deflated, despondent and frustrated at my chosen fate and petrified at what was to come.

CHAPTER 7

The Torture of Progress

I woke up screaming.

As I regained consciousness from the operation the wave of pain from my right leg was overpowering. I screwed up my eyes and gritted my teeth to deal with the pulses of pain jerking through my body, intermittently letting out a vocal expression of discomfort. The grunts increased in pitch and frequency as I opened my eyes and reached down to grab at my leg. My hand clashed with the new metalwork that surrounded my knee, joining a two ringed top cage above to a new 'slimline' bottom cage below.

"Help me...HELP ME...owww," I pleaded with staff. "Take it off...TAKE IT OFF... Oww." Gasping for air, I was struggling to make it clear that something was wrong and I needed action.

My dad told me that when he had his dislocated shoulder operation in the seventies he woke up in bed with a clear imprint of a shoe on his skin. These surgeon guys are amazing and at times have to be ruthless and I would never question what goes on inside those operating theatres. What I did know at this moment in time is that they had gone too far with me. To give me a head start on my leg straightening ordeal, after securing the new cage to my leg they had then cranked up the connecting nuts and bolts. This had wrenched and stretched my ligaments to an incredible level with no objection from me and my body...until now. Over the next three days in hospital I was on a high dosage of morphine while they monitored my sleep, movement and pain threshold. I was eventually released and sent home with a big bag of pills.

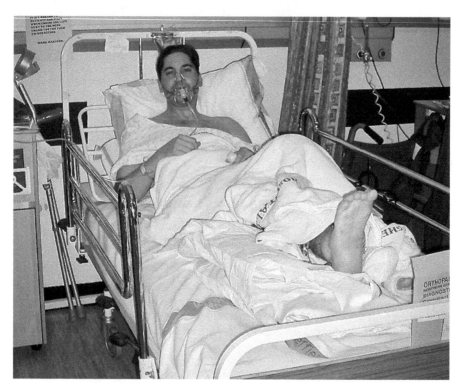

Far too many days and nights spent in this place but it saved my life. Sheffield Northern General Hospital.

On my first night at home my cries were so bad that the doctor was called, and increased the dosage of pain relief to give me and my wife some sanity. The new addition to my life was here to help me but my initial feelings were far from accommodating. One of the biggest and most important accomplishments since the accident was my independence and now that was gone. With the weight of the contraption it was now impossible to get in or out of bed without assistance.

When my wife went on a pre-booked holiday to Crete for a week my mum would drive over every day to look after me. Late evening she would leave me in bed where I was stranded with a plate of snacks, a bottle of water and a 'pee bottle'. I hoped the medication would not cause me to confuse these items in the middle of the night as this could cause me discomfort on a whole different and disgusting level.

I could no longer transport myself up the stairs on my bottom without someone else lifting my leg cage in unison. My car sat redundant on the driveway; to be transported around I had to sit in the back with my caged right leg stretched across the seats. Fear shook me when the car door was slammed shut, given its close proximity to my foot...extremely close! Infections from the top pins stung as though fresh from the Sheffield furnaces, the sizzling agony emphasised with every slight movement.

Thoughts, Feelings and Reflections
April 2003: No Sleep

11.00pm
OK, here we go
Pillows positioned, body set, comfy!
My eyes close and I relax.
12.00am
Everything is ready
Everything is calm
1.00am
Soon, very soon

The sleep will take over...soon!

2.00am
The TV channels are searched
Help me relieve the boredom from my mind.

3.00am
The silence surrounds me
The discomfort controls me.

4.00am
This is just so annoying
I can't believe this

5.00am
The morning light is visible through the curtains
Time is nearly up

6.00am
Another night is over
Another day of suffering begins.

Another birthday came and went with me sat in a wheelchair while my friends and family disappeared on the car treasure hunt that I had meticulously set up weeks before. It was a great turnout to celebrate my 30th and a lovely event but in my head, if I can't take part in the celebrations then it's not really a birthday...I'll bank it for some other time. (That's two now...but who's counting.)

Thoughts, Feelings and Reflections
May 2003: This is me

I'm so bored
I'm so tired
I'm in so much pain
I'm so frustrated
I'm so unhappy

My first week in this phase of hell was living through the torture, discomfort, restrictiveness, exhaustion and deflation. My diary entry on the 27th May showed that I was clutching at the positive when I wrote, "I guess you need the bad days to appreciate the good ones". In the second week I was able to gather my strength which enabled me to proceed with my physio. By turning the connecting bolts on the cage with my spanners I would wrench my leg straighter. The speed and ferocity of this action was up to me. What a delightful decision I had to make every day. Hmm…how much pain shall I subject myself to today, one twist or two? I created a spreadsheet on my computer so that I could record my actions in regards to how much I turned the bolts each day. I consequently monitored the results through comments of the pain level within my knee. Some days were worse than others which came with the temptation to ease off but I never did. With grit and determination I kept twisting the bolts day after day with the driving force to get my leg straight.

Once again Chesney Hawkes with his lyrical wisdom told me not to drag myself down and even though it was 'Gonna Be Tough', I could do it…with or without support.

After initial issues with my ankle adjustment the weight bearing results became a lot more progressive. In just over a week of activity I finally managed to put my full body weight through my right leg for the first time since the accident. As I looked down at my leg and all the metalwork wrapped round it I questioned my methods: was this not cheating? 'No, Steve, this is not cheating!' I would convince myself. I had tried everything and this was all that was left. This wasn't deception; this was the next step, progression. I'd made damn sure at every phase of development that I had 'no regrets' and because of that I would accept the pain along with the good results. Having no regrets was a powerful source of stability and pride that I carried with me to hold my head high.

Thoughts, Feelings and Reflections
June 2003: How Good?

How good do you want to be?
How much time are you willing to give?
Training
Practice
Endurance
Persistence
Commitment
Time
Time, time, time
Give a lot and you will receive,
How good do you want to be?

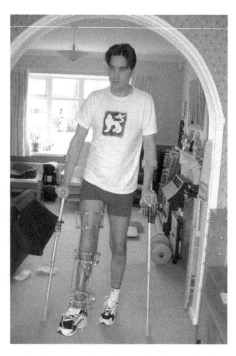

Smiles were lost through this period!

With full weight bearing through each of my legs my crutch walking improved tenfold and I was now using the RGM technique properly. I desperately buried the fear of falling over on my crutches along with the possible associated consequences of twisted metal and torn flesh. Courageously I carried on with all of the rehabilitation exercises that would lead to me getting better. Straightening my leg daily with the spanners caused the pins to gradually tear through my skin and the infections were being subdued with more antibiotics. My sleep suffered but as a compromise the physio results improved. After three weeks I went for a consultation at the hospital to discuss the removal of the top cage. The conclusion was for it to remain on for another four weeks.

I sulked and moaned that the practitioners "didn't understand". A further four weeks of sleep-deprived pain and suffering was endured before my return trip to the hospital and another consultation. I waited with bated breath until they eventually made the decision that the top cage could be removed. This would just leave the bottom cage on until the bone had healed more. I exhaled through my beaming smile and inside I was punching the air in triumph. "If you go into the treatment room next door, Mr. Judge, we'll get it sorted out." "What do you mean?" I asked. "Book an appointment?" "No, Mr. Judge, we'll take the cage off, immediately." Wow, this was awesome.

Next door I lay on the treatment bed waiting for the anaesthetist but instead my consultant turned up. "Grab yourself some gas and air," he said, "and I'll start loosening off the bolts." "Do we not need an operation to remove it?" I asked, thinking that he had clearly got me confused with someone who just needed a splinter removed. "Not at all, we'll have this off in a jiffy, I'll just go and get some spanners," he replied. A wave of sweat swept over my body and I quickly grabbed the mouthpiece for the gas and air...it was empty... "Shit!"

I reached for my rucksack and took out my set of spanners, frantically starting to work on the cage. Loosening off the nuts and bolts, if done incorrectly, caused a sudden jerk and so this bit I wanted to do myself. The consultant returned and was surprised to find only the cage brackets left to remove which then left the protruding long thin metal pins. "There's no gas and air," I said. "We're nearly done now," said the consultant. I was unsure what that meant as I anxiously waited, wondering how the pins would be removed. Snipping one end of the rod with a pair of pliers, he then grabbed the other end with the pinchers. With wide eyes I watched him swiftly yank the rod out of my leg as though pulling Excalibur from the rock.

"...OooooWWw. THAT REALLY HURT...OOOoWWw."

In a flash I realised that two pins had been removed. My teeth were now clenched, dealing with the immense pain and preparing for the next pin to be withdrawn.

"Let's go...GGNNNNE."

One more...just one more left now.

Come on, COME ON!

Let's get it done.

"UUMmph."

With my teeth still clenched the noise was retained but the pain was like a burning rod of steel, sending a flood of lava through my thigh.

Tighter I clenched my teeth and squeezed my eyes shut...breathe, breathe, it's all over now, I know it is, I know it is, breathe...breathe. The heat receded but not the memory. Oh my goodness, the mental thought of the pins being wrenched out through my bone will last for a lifetime. The whole experience left me exhausted and drained like a spaced-out zombie over the next couple of days.

Eventually getting back into my routine of physio, I gleefully measured my knee joint only to find that it still needed work on it to get it fully straight. On top of that, due to it being clamped for over six weeks I now struggled to bend the damn thing fully. "Are you kidding me!" My exercise bike was just sat there in the corner of the room collecting dust until I could sufficiently bend my knee. My painful journey began with my goal being to get back on that bike and do some proper exercise. The double cage had, however, managed to get me 'over the hill' with regards the straightness of my leg and now I felt that the end was in sight. The reality was that it was a spot on the horizon of a laborious six-week slog through a minefield of tearful turmoil and activity. As I sat on the floor once again, pushing myself through the pain, I started to wonder if I would ever get it straight but I wasn't willing to give up yet. 'Let's do this.'

Diary Entry: June 2003

The knee straight exercise is really hard and has made me start crying again. I'm sick of it. I did a lot this week and was tired because of it. I can't wait to get back to normal.

Two weeks after my top cage was removed I had two of the bottom rings removed from my lower cage. This still left me with three rings from the original cage tightly wrapped around my right leg and although this didn't make a massive difference it proved that things were moving in the right direction. As the pins were removed from near my ankle I was hopeful that I would receive more movement but I was disappointed in the outcome. It was bluntly explained to me that because my ankle had been held in its position for well over a year the joint had seized up and there would be near to no hope in getting the ankle to move any more than ten degrees. I encouraged myself not to quit with this information and to hold on to some small prospect that the more I used it the more chance there would be for greater movement. I'd already learnt how amazing the human body is and that boosted my optimism although the pain I received from forcing my ankle to move was off the scale. So I continued.

Over the last year I'd been modifying my shoes to accommodate my right foot throughout my rehabilitation and now I had just finished my third which was the best one yet. My toes were clawed due to the tightness of my ligaments and so they constantly dug into the ground with my increased walking activity. I would buy cheap pairs of shoes and then modify them at home with glue, screws and Velcro. My past shoe designs included different stability methods as well as a simplistic but non-slip creation that assisted me into the hydrotherapy pool. The latest modified shoe had a tilted sole and a trench for my toes to sit in at the end. A large Velcro strap secured my foot in position and it even looked fairly good too. I was pleased with my work but I also knew that this was not the answer; I needed my toes straight. My weird and wonderful clamps and creations of torture that I had invented did nothing but... torture me.

I visited a chiropodist who took one look and promptly referred me on to a private physio. Once a week he was given the instructions to ignore the rest of my body but instead concentrate on my right foot and specifically on my toes. Crunching the static bones free loosened off the swelling and then down to the toes where this six-foot physio used his technique and muscle to work on each individual toe, stretching and bending them straight. Our enjoyable conversations would end up being one way as I was forced into silence due to my clenched teeth. I would drive home hanging onto the steering wheel through exhaustion and weakness but I needed these toes straight so whatever it took I was prepared to endure.

 I felt that people had given up on my left leg; it looked OK and the nerve pains had simmered but for me I wasn't finished. I still couldn't move my foot much at all and had very limited feeling. I researched and booked myself an appointment at an acupuncturist. A strange concept, paying someone to stick many needles down my leg week after week in order to bring back some kind of sensitivity. The pain endured in this technique was deep within my body's nervous system. The torment sent shudders through me once again, causing my conversation to become stilted as my eyes rolled upwards and my inner being shuddered. I kept my optimism glowing with the possibility that 'maybe this week something will ignite', believing that some sensation would come to life but in the end I always drove home bedraggled and despondent.

It wasn't just pain that brought me to tears but emotions of what I couldn't do anymore. Hearing great tunes on the radio would remind me of how I loved to go out clubbing and dancing until the early hours of the morning. Now stuck here in the wheelchair and crutches, I wondered if this would ever be possible again and if so then when?

Diary Entry: 19th July 2003

The weeks are so busy with all of the various exercises but using the bike and getting fit makes me feel that I have purpose. I walked with no crutches this week which was amazing and went swimming which was really hard work. The x-ray review at orthopaedics was disappointing as another 2 months to go as the bone is not strong enough yet.

Thinking about what I could do rather than what I couldn't do made me think about what I had already achieved through hydrotherapy. This gave me the confidence to venture down to my local swimming pool. My heart was beating fast and my breathing shallow as I dared to walk along the wet tiled floor, dressed vulnerably in only my trunks as my crutches 'clinked' with every brave step. I felt the eyes stare at me as I walked, petrified but focusing intently on the wall heading to the shallow end. As I sat in the chairlift one of the attendants cranked the handle, lowering me slowly into the holy water like an Egyptian emperor being paraded in front of his disciples as they looked up. I felt the warm water on my toes, feet and then legs as I was submerged and then finally my cage of wonder was out of sight. The gathering of people dispersed and got on with their swimming routine and I squatted, looking around. I blended in to the mass of heads and shoulders and found that people were ignoring me. They weren't staring, pointing or intrigued with me but instead just passed by. It was brilliant. I felt normal in my surroundings and also mischievous as they couldn't see what I was hiding underneath the water.

I turned and gazed at the vastness of the pool in front of me as if it were an open highway. 'Let's see what I'm capable of!' I broke into a front crawl stroke, rapidly powering my arms through the water with a new lease of hope and determination, just managing to swim all the way to the deep end of the pool where I held on to the edge and gasped for air. "Wow...I...am...shattered." I shook it off, turned and focused on the opportunity that I had given myself. Pushing myself off from the side using my left leg I paddled hard, grabbing the air from side breaths as I released my caged tiger and let rip. As I neared the end of the length I was spluttering and splashing. Conscious that the cage was uncomfortably close to the tiled floor I slowed down, and waded to the end. I was panting, my chest heaving up and down, feeling a mix of pride and disappointment. 'Flipping heck...I'm done in. Is that it? Is that all I can do?' I rested and went through my actions in my head. I knew that this was my first time swimming again but I couldn't believe that I was so unfit.

I wondered about the effect of the cage on my leg and asked one of the lifeguards to pass me a kick float. I waded to chest height, launched myself with the float held in front of me and kicked. I kicked profusely, with both legs splashing around. I noticed my lack of progress and streamlined my head by sticking it in the water, bringing my legs up and letting rip. Exhaustion was setting in now as I gasped for air before one more final thrust of action. Eventually I was done and I looked up. I put my feet on the floor as I focused on the side of the pool, breathing in.

Are you joking? I looked behind me in disbelief and then to the side again. I hadn't moved...at all! I was puzzled and after a short rest I launched myself again. Head down, float out in front and pumping my legs. Taking side breaths as I kicked, eventually becoming erratic. I was brought to a halt by exhaustion and dared to look over at the side. Grabbing short gasps of air, I felt that I was beaten. I returned the float to the side of the pool and contemplated the results of my session. 'Nothing, absolutely nothing.' I shook my head. 'They're useless, flipping useless, especially with this stupid cage on my leg.'

Before I quit I did a few more lengths of breaststroke, knowing that more than ever I was going to have to build up fitness, especially in my upper body. Before I signalled to the lifeguard that I needed 'out' I looked down the length of the pool at the gauntlet that lay in front of me. I took a deep breath, filling my chest, and whispered to myself, "I need to get some goggles".

Don't Lean on Your Excuses | Steve Judge

CHAPTER 8

Uncaged

Some time in the early nineties, after enduring a particularly horrendous chemotherapy session, my dad was given the all clear from the doctor that he could start walking again, although he should take it easy. My dad's response to this green light was to take himself out the front door and then onwards. The resulting fatigue caused by his exertions made him fall over and cut his leg as his skin was incredibly thin and fragile. My mum, unable to lift him, had to call on the next door neighbour to get him into the house and the doctor was called out as an emergency due to his state and blood loss. On patching my dad up the doctor said, "What on earth were you doing out there Roger?" "Well you said I could start walking again, so I did," my dad said emphatically. "I meant walk around inside the house, Roger, not go on an expedition!" In my eyes my dad had done nothing wrong and had simply interpreted the instructions as he saw fit and I believe he knew in his heart that he was capable of more.

In fact a couple of years later my mum and dad successfully walked North England's Coast to Coast challenge from St Bees to Robin Hood's Bay. An astonishing 192 miles achieved and that was before heading off to Alaska for more adventure. Having this kind of attitude seems to be quite typical for our whole family.

Thoughts, Feelings and Reflections
August 2003: How do you do it?

How do you get there?
By not leaving enough energy for you to get back.

Walking around the block on my housing estate was limiting me and I needed somewhere with more scope for my walking training. I packed my rucksack and drove down to Rother Valley Country Park, which consisted of two big lakes with a flat five kilometre path circulating them. I parked my car and sat there, contemplating if I was really going to do this. It gave me the same apprehension as walking into a desert of the great unknown without a map, compass or water.

I knew that I had to do this although my brain was telling me otherwise. I had to push myself out of my comfort zone. I reset my pedometer to zero and started my stopwatch as I left the safety of my car and walked using the correct and very slow method of RGM. As my stepping got into a rhythm I was able to look up at the beauty of the park, the lake and the sky. Breathing in the air of liberation brought a smile to my face and a deep pride that I used to help me with the next step and then the next one. After ten minutes the pain was now setting in and my rhythm was getting out of sync. Grunting on each step with my right leg became a real slog. The dull pain was now draining my energy and as I gripped the crutches my vocal efforts became louder. After twenty minutes I found it increasingly difficult to cope which consequently drained me further. I was struggling and looked up for salvation. Ahead of me in the distance there was a park bench. It was quite a way, but it was closer than going back to the car.

I wasn't ready to turn back, not yet. And with that note I took a step forward. "Oww." The pain was really ramping up now. I squeezed my crutches hard and took another step. "Oww." Through my breathing I forced myself into a rhythm. The yelps of pain were weakening me as I slowly stepped closer and closer to my goal. Wobbling as I approached the bench through fatigue and apprehension, I finally reached my destination. I composed myself, turning, positioning and with my last strength slowly lowering myself down onto the seat. My crutches dropped to the ground, my shoulders sloped and I breathed… just breathed. I stopped my watch at 31.06 minutes. I was panting. "31 minutes!" I looked at where I had come from and then looked at my pedometer which said 0.28 miles. "What?" I said with a mocking smile and laugh while still catching my breath. I shook my head in disbelief with a cynical grin, staring at the path that I had travelled down. Then a wave of memories came flooding back to me as my face scrunched up and my lip started quivering. Running, sprinting, marathons, 10Ks. My legs used to be so mighty and strong with muscles that powered me through life. Not even half a mile…"HALF A MILE!" I looked at my watch again and put my head in my hands. The tears ran down my face as I let myself cry. It was justified. 'What a waste of time…' I was exhausted, demoralised and my legs were throbbing. I was despondent, furious and disappointed. 'What's the point?'

After a couple of minutes, I breathed in deeply and pulled myself up straight. I looked at the cage on my leg and saw that some of the pins were bleeding. The blood was trickling down my leg and soaking into my sock. I couldn't have done any more, not this time. My dad's words to me before he passed away jumped into my head: "Keep doing what you're doing and always be the best that you can be". Well I'd certainly done that here. I couldn't have walked any further as I was physically exhausted. I had been sweating but now I started to feel cold. I needed to get back, I needed to get home.

Step by step as I work towards my goal at Rother Valley Country Park. At least it's flat! Note CD player on my belt.

Grabbing the crutches from the ground I levered myself up, reset my watch and took the first step. A wave of heat flushed through my body as the pain awoke. Unable to scream out through my gritted teeth, I grunted as I used my reserve energy, digging deep. I looked up at my goal ahead of me, the path that led me back to my car. I used my grunts and deep breaths as a rhythm to push me forward one step at a time. When I finally reached my car I stopped my watch before sinking into the seat and closing the door so that nobody could see me cry this time. I wiped my eyes, started the engine and drove home. I entered the house and closed the door with shaking hands. I just managed to get to the sofa where I collapsed, pulling the blanket over me and curling up in a shivering mess. I had a sleepless night with muscle spasms, and spent the next day recovering and tending to my wounds. Then the following day I got up, packed my rucksack and drove back to Rother Valley Country Park.

Thoughts, Feelings and Reflections

August 2003: Get up

You are strong
Determined
Set on your goals
Committed ready to achieve
Persistent
But just how many times can you get up after being knocked down?
You get up!

Sometimes I fell and many times I cried but eventually I made it past that first park bench and onto the next one and after that the next park bench. Eventually I made it around the top of the lake and to the next bench. It's quite a good story about 'benchmarking' if you think about it. With the aid of my CD walkman playing such songs as Kenny Loggins' 'Danger Zone' I was able to push myself continuously out of my comfort zone and then onwards. On every session I was the best that I could be and I knew that my dad would have been proud of me. Eventually over the next three months I managed to get all the way round the lake and I achieved my goal.

Thoughts, Feelings and Reflections

September 2003: RGM – I know

I know it's Bench Mark
I know it will get better
I know it will get quicker

I know it's a great achievement
I know it takes courage
I know it takes persistence

I know it will help my progress
I know it will encourage bone growth
I know it's good for fitness

I know that I compare to how I used to be
I know that I get very emotional
I know that it makes me cry.

With progression and new development came new physio exercises. Every time I went into the outpatients physio I was given more challenging exercises. They would fill my routine up and push me physically with numerous activities, twenty, thirty, up to forty exercises. It became increasingly important for me to enquire more about the physio exercises and why I had to do them as I had moved on from just doing as I was told. The balancing would help me as I attempted to walk on two legs again. The hip exercises would help with my posture and stability. My thigh strengthening would help me with support when moving my legs. I was building up my physical tools one by one that would help me to achieve my goal and walk again. At the moment that was my job: that's all I had to do, that was my goal and that was my life. I understood the need and the requirement and asked for more. I equipped myself for the challenge that lay ahead of me, being the best that I could be and having no regrets. Bring it on!

Thoughts, Feelings and Reflections
October 2003: Because They Care

"Pain is your friend"
"This may hurt a little bit"
"You may be sore after I've finished with you"
They do it because they care

"How many have you done? Do ten more"
"I know it hurts but keep doing it"

"Try and do it here, where it's harder"
They do it because they care

"When you've finished, do them again"
"Try harder, push harder"
"Keep your posture straight"
They do it because they care

"Just five more, quicker this time"
"Do it faster than that and straighter"
"Really try and use your muscles"
They do it because they care

"OK, have a rest and then we'll start again,
I've just thought of another exercise for you to do."

Being independent was critical for me; it gave me purpose and took away the need for other people like my mum or wife to help me. They had enough to do and I didn't want to inconvenience them or pressurise them to help me. I revelled in the week when my wife went on holiday leaving me home alone as I saw it as a test. Between my physio and exercises I cooked and cleaned, tidied and even put some shelves up. Limping around, lifting and taking calculated risks gave me a buzz as well as pride in my efforts.

After the success of one-crutch RGM walking and finally being able to carry my own cup of tea came the next massive step in progression. Walking with...Wait for it! No crutches. And even the possibility of carrying two cups of tea. The process started in the living room taking shallow breaths as I courageously took a step away from the wall and focused on the sofa ahead of me. The thought of it scared the living daylights out of me. One step and then another, breathe...breathe, keep the posture, focus. The lack of support felt like standing in a vast openness of fear and space. My brain whizzed round in my head calculating my balance and how to correct it using multiple nerve and sensory readings connected to the necessary muscles. Another step and another until finally I could reach out and grab the safety of the furniture. A deep sigh followed by an intake of breath as I turned and smiled at my four metres of accomplishment. Wow, I did it and it actually wasn't that bad. I sat down on the sofa arm and set my sights on the television which was a whopping five metres away. Back straight, chin up as I walked with bold determination step by step until I could place my hand firmly on the television. I turned round and thought, 'Right, where next?' From that day onwards my short explorations could be mapped by hand smudges on the furniture as I 'ping ponged' around the house. Taking this to the next level and doing it outside would be a couple of weeks down the line.

September, and sleep was still my nemesis. I was waking up frustrated at the pain and sleep deprivation that had formed an unwanted nightmare routine. Religiously doing my physio exercises and conceding to the positivity of gaining just one degree more of a straight leg... Great result! I wanted to go out in the fresh air and have some fun. I used to do so much before I had the accident and I couldn't help but think about the millions of things that I could have been doing if it hadn't happened. It was when swimming that I could release my exasperated caged tiger as I ploughed up and down the pool, now scoring a total of fifty lengths per session. Standing tall in the shower afterwards, feeling satisfactorily pumped and exhausted, I would inevitably be subjected to whispering, staring and nudging from the local school kids.

Eventually the reluctant young 'spokesboy' would be shoved forward. "S'cuse me mister, what happened to your leg?" I already got comments from various people who stared at my leg and would say things like "Ooh! That looks painful" or "You're not going to be doing the marathon next week then?" I guess people felt uncomfortable and felt the need to say something which I guess was ok but after a while it became annoying.

With the kids down at the pool I enjoyed giving a short account of my story to the group who stood there with their mouths open in wonderment, listening intently. The car accident, growing my leg back and the achievement of standing, walking and swimming again. After a couple of weeks I felt like a change. Instead, I would explain in great detail the events of the crocodile attack in Northern Australia. How I was dragged under by my clasped leg and hurtled into the death roll. By relying on my instinctive reactions I unleashed my sheaf knife and plunged it into the beast's eye socket to release me to my freedom. I even explained that the crocodile tooth I wore round my neck (retrieved from my travelling souvenirs in the loft) was dug out of my mangled leg and that I wore it as a reminder of that fateful day. You may deem it wrong to tell this yarn to naive pupils but I didn't care. It brought me a joyous and mischievous release and most importantly it made me smile and those were hard to come by.

Thoughts, Feelings and Reflections
October 2003: Three Point RGM – Realisation

What was a slope, is now a hill
Considered smooth ground, is revealed as rough
What was so near, is now so far
Where steps assisted they now obstruct
Every stone, is now a boulder
Each hole, is a crater
Every crack, is now a crevice
Every twig, is now a log
What was so easy, is now so hard

I was getting really bored of doing the same thing every day. Progress was in the form of the bolts being loosened on my cage and I also knew that the more pain I could put up with the better…but it was hard. I had to believe that it would go, maybe the next day or the day after that. If I didn't believe it then it would break me. Until then I had bad pain in the day and terrible pain at night but I kept on picking myself up. I knew through rehabilitation that 'pain is your friend' but sometimes, I just wanted to be alone. People would ask me if I'd be glad to get my cage off and I'd hesitate. It had been a good friend to me as it had held my leg together and regained my leg length. It had protected me and still did. We'd had teething problems between us but through time we had learnt to accept one another. "Will you be glad to get it off?" they would ask. The best answer that I could give was "Once I get it off…I'll be glad".

I sat with my legs out straight on the surgery bed looking at my cage for what could be the very last time. The x-rays had come back and my consultant had given the 'all clear' to have the final bits of the cage removed. A wave of happiness and excitement washed over me and I beamed in accomplishment. There was also a hollow sensation of excitement in my stomach as I breathed in the joy with the thought 'Wow…really…is this it?' I had tried not to be too excited when I drove to hospital with my mum as I'd had many other consultancy visits where I had been given the rotten news of "Just four more weeks Mr. Judge!" or "Just two more weeks Mr. Judge!" My mum was with me on this hospital visit because if the result was positive and the cage was removed then I knew that I would need assistance in returning home. For both of us I think there were also less practical reasons than that, something to do with emotions and caring and stuff.

Either way the decision had been a good one as the nurse came into the cubicle room with a clinical toolbox which she opened. I can't deny that although I had wanted this damn cage off for a long time now, when they finally said that it was going to happen a little part of me thought 'Are you sure?' This cage had been holding my leg together for a year and a half and taking it off was a one-way street. If they had miscalculated the solidity and strength of my bone then all of the treacherous months of hard work would be in vain. My bone would simply bow and snap as I attempted to stand on it. The cage couldn't simply be put back on. I buried my thoughts and fears and once again put my faith in the skilled professionals that had done a sound job up to now; a little bit more trust would be suitably justified.

I knew 'the drill' and assisted the nurse in loosening and removing the nuts and bolts around my cage. As the sections were detached it just left the pins sticking out either side of my leg like leftover cocktail sticks at the end of a party. These were then snipped with the pliers in preparation to be removed. I dreaded this bit (again) but this time I felt an inner strength and a glow that made me quite nonchalant. I had dealt with more pain than this and on top of that I could see the cusp. I was coming to the end of a chapter, to the light at the end of the tunnel, to freedom and deliverance, and I was eager.

One by one the static pins were wrenched forcefully out of my leg, through the skin, muscle and bone that had held them fast for way too long. The sharp pain sent my adrenaline through the roof and I knew there would be a comedown within the next half hour. All the pins had been successfully removed which just left one 4mm bolt that was screwed into the actual shin bone itself and sticking out of the leg by 3cm. It had no bolt head on it so the nurse gripped the round rod with the pliers and attempted to unscrew it. The grip slipped and the vibration streaked through my bone and made the rest of my body shudder. I closed my eyes and with clenched teeth sucked in deeply as her second attempt again resulted in failure. "I'm going to have to get some help," she said.

I opened my eyes and scanned the room like James Bond looking for a solution. I'm not having any delay, nothing's getting in the way today, I've got this. "Can you pass me those mole grips?" I asked without hesitation. She looked in the box, picking up various tools. "These?" "Yep, that'll do fine." I adjusted the jaw on the device to just less than 4mm. Bending forward I reached down to the end of my right leg, steadied my hand and clamped the mechanism onto the rod that was protruding out, solid. I gritted my teeth as I slowly squeezed the pressure to release the seal and turn in an anticlockwise direction to unscrew the rod from my bone. I didn't think about what I was doing too much but just knew that it had to be done. Round and round until eventually it was out and I felt euphoria. Handing the locking pliers and the bloodied rod to the nurse, I lay back on the bed while the mess was mopped up and the wounds cleaned.

My adrenaline rush had passed and the wave of exhaustion forced me to lie back and look at the ceiling. We'd done it; the cage was removed and I lay there smiling while they fixed a temporary fibreglass plaster cast which I would need to wear for about four weeks. It offered support as well as mental acceptance of the leg's new state. With no cage anymore I wondered what a difference this would make going forward. Physically in sleep and in my exercises and also, at last I'd finally be able to wear a pair of jeans.

I was relieved and a stage closer to reaching my ultimate goal of getting back to normal. It would only become apparent to me over the next year that the goal that was my constant drive was in actual fact non-quantifiable, non-achievable and non-existent.

CHAPTER 9

Let's See What This Baby Can Do!

I woke up from my first good night's sleep in a long time. My left leg was not clashing against the hard metal anymore and instead it snuggled up next to my right leg. There was no pain...wow! No pain from the pins, no pain from the discomfort and weight of the cage. I smiled as I took in my new and improved situation. After a year and a half the consistent buzzing of pain had finally been turned off. I lay there in a relaxed and tranquil state soaking in the pleasure that we all so often take for granted.

My brain was now in overdrive at the potential and possibilities. My white tiger woke up, yawned and stretched but remained lethargic due to the ordeal of having my cage removed. I was forced to take things slowly over the first week as I built up my energy and then gradually ramped it up. I gained so much confidence in walking without the visible restriction that had been physically and psychologically holding me back. Wearing long trousers, I looked normal and so therefore I felt I should act normally and consequently walk as normal people do.

I did a lot of walking using my one crutch down at Rother Valley. It was draining and physically hard work but I was pushing myself and working towards new goals. But by week three I couldn't walk anymore. My ankle was in agony. I could only naturally move the joint about 10 degrees and I was now forcing it to move more than that with my full body weight on it.

My clawed toes dug into the ground on every step, and the toenails had dug into the skin surrounding them, causing them to bleed. The wounds had got infected, sending out a sharp stabbing pain that made me wince with every step. Patching myself up with plasters, trips to the chiropodist and munching on some antibiotics, I continued on my progression until my hip joint flared up, halting me once again. The dull pain forced me to rest and recover. My white tiger snarled with frustration. This was not the plan.

Once the lightweight fibreglass cast was removed I took myself down to the swimming pool and with the lifeguards poised used one crutch precariously to walk around the pool and was able to lower myself independently into the water. Pushing myself off from the wall I smiled as I felt the water soar between my legs. My legs were now able to brush past each other in recognition of their presence and position.

Without the drag of the cage, I skimmed through the water, the freedom and liberation of the pool once again filling me with euphoria and courage. Eagerly I grabbed a float and secured my goggles. It was time to do the kick test. Giving myself a slight push off from the side, I plunged my head down between my outstretched arms and kicked. I turned my head for air and kept kicking and kicking. I sneaked a peek during my side breaths and it was not good, so I kicked harder and more frantically in desperation and then in frustration, which soon turned to anger.

I kicked and I kicked and then I stopped. There I was, frozen in the shallow end where I had started. Nothing, absolutely nothing! I was ten metres from where I had pushed off. I waded back to the edge of the pool and replaced the float before turning and plunging into the water again. I was now pounding up and down the lengths as planned, only now I was just using my upper body and dragging my useless legs in my wake. I would have been better off without any legs, as they were actually causing drag as opposed to propulsion.

This is when I had to accept what deep down I guess I'd already known. I was just hoping that I was wrong. Hoping that my legs would give me something, anything! What a joke! It was like farting in the wind. Zip, zero…nada!

I held onto the showerhead for support as the water cascaded over my body. My chest heaved up and down and my muscles flinched with adrenaline but my head hung low. I was downhearted. This was not how it was supposed to be, but this is how it was.

I wasn't going to give up but I was going to have to tame my tiger. This was going to take longer than I thought and once again I was going to have to use my impatience to do anything and everything to move things forward. I had to start thinking again about what I could do, rather than what I couldn't do. As my legs were almost a hindrance I had to start thinking about how I could use the rest of my body in the most efficient way.

The positives were there as it was great getting out and about and going to friends' parties. I even ventured out to witness the victory parade of the World Champions England Rugby Union team. This was down at Trafalgar Square in London where I spent the day with my protective brother and his wife by my side. Walking and standing with one crutch and dealing with the hustle and bustle was exhausting but it was worth it.

There were amazing patriotic scenes as the crowd cheered and saluted their amazing success as an elite team. Nobody could have imagined (especially me) that in ten years' time I would be the one standing there in Trafalgar Square on the raised platform, medal round my neck and with the crowds celebrating my momentous achievement for my country.

The new year was seen in with drinks and dancing with rediscovered liberation, looking towards the future of the year ahead. My immediate future of the morning after was always aches and soreness as my left knee, right ankle and toes would always be throbbing and pulsing from the exertion. In the end it came down to a pleasure–pain scenario. As long as there was enough pleasure in the activity that I had done then I would be willing to put up with the consequences over the next couple of days. Dancing was fun and I was willing to put up with the pain. But shopping not so much; I hated shopping. The physical aspects of standing and walking, stopping and starting put a massive strain on me. The next day...I'd have pain, unjustified agony, the worst there is. It wasn't worth it for the things I didn't really enjoy.

I was concerned about the lack of movement and the discomfort in my ankle but I had faith. The body is an amazing thing and mine had done its fair share through my recovery and I knew it wasn't going to give up now. My theory was that the more I used it the more it would ease up and start moving and reforming. It was an aspirational goal based solely on optimistic hope and a sprinkling of fairy dust. However my main present for Christmas was a set of walking poles enabling me to throw the crutches into the garage. Maybe the fact that I never returned them to the hospital was me admitting deep down that I had inner doubts.

In preparation for the pain that I was going to have to endure from all my walking I knew that there would be times when swimming would be my saviour. After discussions with Bruce over Christmas we came up with a plan. In mid-January I registered a team into the relay event of the London Triathlon for July of that year. The gauntlet was laid down and the goal set. I would be swimming 1500m in the Docklands area of the River Thames before handing over to the cyclist of the team for the

40K and then onto Bruce for the 10K run. The fact that we didn't have a cyclist we considered as a minor issue and something we could deal with nearer the time...a lot nearer as it happens. I had learnt that I needed a goal to focus on and to improve my fitness and pain resistance and the London Triathlon was the perfect antidote.

With my physical movement and ability increasing I was ready to give myself more aspiration on the mental side and get back to work because:

1. I wanted purpose. I wanted to do something. I had a desire to use my brain and actively do some work with it. I had kept myself as busy as possible at home but in reality it was no comparison to getting out of the house. I wanted to push myself and have the direction and the responsibility of having a job.

2. On top of the inner urge to venture out, mingle with others and give myself a function there was another reason. Over the last couple of years the mockumentary sitcom The Office had been running and I couldn't help but feel that I was missing out on fun in the working environment. I wanted to be part of bizarre goings-on in the work place. I wanted to have a laugh, hear the gossip, go on work nights out and Christmas dos. I wanted to play pranks and mould people's staplers in jelly. I wanted to get a job and I wanted to start working again and everything that goes with it.

For the second time in my life I took myself down to the Job Centre and 'signed on', explaining in great detail my situation, which took some time. I used my positive vibe to look for something or anything preferably part time just to get me into the swing of things. My qualifications initially took a back seat on my CV as I was keen for any kind of opportunity that presented itself.

Another time that I'd had to find some kind of work was seven years previously, in 1996, when I arrived in Australia initially after travelling through the USA and Canada. I remember how I went to a charity shop and bought a second-hand shirt and tie for job interviews. I obtained a variety of work placements including door to door selling, working in a hospital, bar work and even fruit picking, albeit in the burning midday sun. With the added finance I was able to fund my continued excursions backpacking around the rest of the country and through Singapore, Malaysia and Thailand.

On my return from my world trip and with no job I signed on for the first time. I used to get up early and cycle to the nearby town to buy the job papers, immediately searching and applying for an array of opportunities. Making that prompt phone call or getting the application in early gave me a head start against my competition and an added advantage of success. I'd regularly be following up on possibilities through to midday before spending the rest of the day enjoying the weather and keeping fit. My dedicated routine eventually paid off, initially with part-time bar work in The Crown Hotel in Bawtry and then at a more permanent job in Sheffield within a couple of months.

My current morning routine now mirrored that from six years previously with the added bonus of using the internet and computer for job applications. I created lists of possibilities with regards location, hours and physicality i.e. I wanted to be able to sit down the majority of the day. My first job as a receptionist was perfect until a more permanent job with slightly longer hours of an admin clerk moved me onto another company.

Having a job was brilliant as it gave me purpose, structure and of course some money coming into the household. As the weeks passed my frustration built as my intelligence and initiative was being quashed by stubborn internal procedures: "We've always done it this way" and "I don't think the boss would like it if we did it differently". Up to that point I'd not considered myself insubordinate or rebellious but when I'm instructed to do something just for the sake of doing it, I always question why. I love thinking out of the box and continuously improving to strive for better solutions but in these jobs I had my hands figuratively tied. My days off from work saw me down at my local gym in Eckington building up my upper body strength to aid me in the swimming. My biceps, triceps and shoulder deltoids gained some real power and structure, making me feel confident as well as stronger. I also worked on cardiovascular exercises like the rowing machine which was a good all-over workout although the lack of flexibility on my ankle was frustrating at first. Walking on the treadmill was good to build up my confidence in a safe environment but being next to someone who was running became ever so frustrating.

Thoughts, Feelings and Reflections
January 2004: Reflections

As I walk on this treadmill of recovery
I focus on my reflection in the mirror
Concentrating on my posture,
My balance,
My foot position,
My rhythm,

Poker faced through determination
Persistent, I look ahead…
Through my tunnel vision I can't help but see past the wall of concentration.
My neighbour's reflection.
His whole body flowing with speed and agility
His athletic motion pounding the treadmill
And I wish (just maybe for five minutes) that I could change reflections.

My time on the static bike felt ridiculous as I had a real bike at home and I was finally compelled to use it. Where I lived there was nothing but hills so it's not an easy chore to just jump on the bike; however, I felt I was ready. Digging out some old football shin pads from the loft I placed them over my injured legs for some protection if the pedals swung round and bashed me on the shins. My skin was paper thin and the slightest impact could cause a big mess. I ventured out and straight up the mile-long hill through my village of Eckington, selecting the appropriate gears to ease my movement on this quest and support my goal of getting to the top. My fitness was pushed to the limit as my lungs dragged in the oxygen with sweat running down my face and the winter freshness chilling my cheeks. I kept my eyes to the horizon as it slowly, very slowly got closer and closer. My thighs were powering along with the muscles that had been built up but sometimes they struggled, causing a wobble in balance. I finally reached the top of the hill which has a beautiful vista looking outwards towards the Peak District. I pulled my bike off the road and stood there breathing shallowly, amazed and proud that I had achieved it. The view meant so much more than when I'd seen it from the car window. Now I had earned the right to gaze around at the magnificence and I felt at one with the environment. I looked around over my shoulder before sucking in the chilly air and then giving an almighty yell: "WWooooooo – HHHOOOoo!"

I was liberated and I wasn't gonna back down, just like the motivating and powerful lyrics of 'You Can't Take Me' by Bryan Adams and Hans Zimmer from the film Spirit.

I smiled at the release of the energised whoop and the amazing feeling of accomplishment of cycling up the hill. Eckington Hill, that's a tough one for most people, but I did it. I DID it! I looked around the fields and woods that surrounded me and saw a feast of exciting possibilities…but not for today. "One step at a time", I said to myself, but in my head I was already working out future ventures. "First things first, let's get down this hill." I set off on the gradient, at times holding on for dear life, dodging the potholes and drains as my wheels powered along on the tarmac. The wind, the adrenaline, the speed, the buzz and the excitement. I hadn't felt this rush for such a long time, for years. I was trying to breathe through a gormless smile and tears caused by the gusting air beating into my face. 'You get what you give', I thought to myself and although it had been a slog getting up the hill I put my bike away in my garage with hands that were shaking from the adrenaline rush and excitement of the milestone I had just achieved.

"That…I need to do again," I panted. Over the year my cycling improved which enabled me to go out with my friends and wife on various excursions.

Thoughts, Feelings and Reflections
March 2004: The Positive

How do I put up with it?
By being positive
By knowing that at least I am able to walk from A to B
Yes, there is pain which is the negative but the positive is so much greater.
Why do I put up with it?
Because there is no other way that is apparent at the moment.
It may seem strange that this is the best option – but it is…

My fitness and health were improving incrementally with my mental ability. Although I accepted the disability that I had I also challenged it with a positive attitude and I decided that I was again ready to move up a level. Before the accident my job had been in Quality Management working with tests and procedures within the laboratory of a company. This is what I enjoyed and my CV was adjusted to enable my job searches to take a different direction. I eventually landed an interview for a full-time job with amicable pay as a Quality Management System Officer. Standing tall with sweaty palms I shook the interviewer's hand as she led me away from the reception desk. It was necessary for me to acquire the job based on who I was and my qualifications and experience. I wanted employment because I was the right person who would bring new ideas and initiative and drive. My disability didn't stop me from doing any of these things and therefore I didn't feel it necessary to share it. I did a good job of not limping as I squeezed my thumb and forefinger together to deal with the pain from my ankle.

"This way," she said, "just up the stairs." My eyes grew wide as I looked up at the stairs that we were about to conquer, spiralling upwards at a rapid incline. I took a deep breath to prepare myself for the exertion and also just in case the air was thinner up there. They could easily be compared to Mount Snowdon, Kilimanjaro or even Mount Everest. Not that I've ever climbed the latter two but from what I knew about them these steps were equal in comparison. Gripping tightly onto the thick banister and using my upper body strength I wrenched myself onwards and up the flights of stairs, smoothly and showing no apparent concern. All the way up the various levels until we reached the very top and came to the office with the door open. I sat down proudly and wished that the stair climb had been part of an initiative test for the job as I waited for the questioning to begin.

At no point during the interview was there any need for me to divulge the details of my disability so I skirted round various questions but I was also aware that there was a massive gap in my employment history. Inevitably the question came up of what happened from 2002 to 2004. I'd been rumbled and much as I tried to give a brief answer about the circumstances over the last couple of years. I found it difficult to abbreviate. I wouldn't lie and now that it was out in the open I was proud at what I had achieved. I played down my current restricted mobility which was easily justified by my positive outlook that things would get better and I believed it. I got the job and settled in nicely to the role and the company. My natural drive and enthusiasm soon saw me through my probation period and on to higher status roles.

Before I started my new job we finally had our well overdue honeymoon in the Dominican Republic. A marvellous location to relax in the sun and for both of us to have a well-earned rest after the hardship that we had been through. This was true for the most part although I had the London Triathlon coming up in four months and I hadn't had any 'swim time' in the wetsuit that I had bought for the event, even though my training was going well. Taking the suit with me on the holiday meant that I could grab the opportunity of swimming in the sea with it and getting some more training sessions under the belt. I'm not sure my wife was quite as ecstatic with the idea as I was but she seemed quite content lying in the sun reading her book while I sneaked off and changed into my suit.

I quickly realised two things about the wetsuit: firstly, wow, the buoyancy that I got from it was amazing. It lifted my legs up ever so slightly making me more slipstreamed and consequently efficiently faster. The second thing was the almost impossibility of getting the damn thing off my feet. I hopped around on the beach, falling over like a comical clown and getting covered in sand, but still I couldn't get the tight rubber suit over my unbendable ankles on either foot. Eventually I sat in the sand, sweating and grunting as I slowly eased the suit millimetre by millimetre over my feet using all of my upper body strength. I was aware that you should include transition training in your preparation but I wasn't aware how exhausting it was going to be. I was in a catch-22 with regards the suit or maybe a love-hate situation. It was a cross between swimming like a dolphin and then struggling like an upside down turtle. It had been a definite learning curve.

Once back at home I searched the internet for a solution but I eventually made the brave decision and took my brand new expensive wetsuit into a local clothing adjustment shop. They were a little shocked with my request but after convincing them that it would be ok they complied and carried out the job. They cut upwards by about 20cm on the seam at the back of each leg and then sewed in two big chunky zips. This then gave me great allowance when removing my ankles from the suit. Job done… but I needed to test it out.

I found that the Sheffield Triathlon Club met up and swam in one of the reservoirs north of the city and one evening I drove up there after work. Gliding through the tranquil unbroken water with the buoyancy gave me sleek efficiency in both speed and rhythm. I stopped to catch my breath as I gazed around at the amazing scenery of the surrounding hills. Over the sound of my panting breath I could hear the distant splashing of the other swimmers and the bird chorus singing as the sun was beginning to set. I calmly breathed in and out as my smile broadened and my eyes widened. Treading water in this openness and having the readiness, skill and spirit to move myself in any direction I wished brought me true liberation. I set my sights on the land and set off effortlessly with high elbows, pulling through with my strong arms, my firm core capably twisting my hips in unison with my shoulders dragging my legs behind me. Out of the water and wetsuit unzipped from my neck line as well as from my ankles. I peeled the suit off my upper body with ease and then rather than toppling over I voluntarily sat on the ground and managed to slip my left leg out of the rubber fairly easily. 'Result.' The right ankle was a bit more troublesome and required assistance from my inner chimp but still, it was a damn sight better than it had been. It had been a good session and among the things that I had learned was that the seal on my goggles leaked a little when I smiled too much. I sat on the grass gazing out across the water with the last rays of sunlight shimmering across the surface, my chest moving up and down with complete satisfaction at what I had conquered but then more so. I had been 'at one' with it ...and my white tiger purred.

My job was going well and I settled in very quickly. The building was large and old and had various levels all connected with stairs so moving around was always a task but I saw it as constant physio. Squeezing in swimming training into my day was difficult but just about manageable during my lunch hour.

12.30: On the dot I grabbed my swim bag and route marched out of the building and down some back alleyways to accurately bring me out at the gym which had a pool in it.

12:37 I would move swiftly through the changing area, shedding my clothes and diving straight into the water.

12:44 Sixty-four lengths of high intensity front crawl easily overtaking the other swimmers that were having a cool down after their steam room or sauna (sorry about the splashing).

1:15 (ish) Quick shower, dry (sort of), methodically get changed, grab bag and out of the door.

1:24 Rapidly eat sandwiches while briskly walking back down the alleyways while checking my watch for precision and sitting down back at my desk for 1:30pm. Job done…again.

On the warmer days of the year my hair was dry by the time I got back but my sweatiness was more visibly apparent. In preparation for the London Triathlon I had searched for, found and entered two other relay triathlons (as well as roping in some friends to assist me). The first was in Stratford in May. I completed the 400m swim in a pool before handing over to my friend Jim to complete the 20K bike section and then onto Bruce who sprinted the 5K run. There was a lot of discussion about how to efficiently hand over to one another and all went according to plan. My swim was good and the 'hobble' to transition was bearable.

The next relay triathlon was the Ironbridge Triathlon in July and this time it was a 1500m swim in open water. The swim was tough and with a mass start you soon find your place with people overtaking you and swimming off into the distance. I held my own and dug down deep, pushing it all of the way on the 'there and back' course, fighting the current of the river before dragging myself out of the exit and slipping on my trainers that I had left waiting. I grabbed my walking poles and hobbled the 150m as fast as I could towards transition one (T1). I couldn't help but be frustrated as some of the swimmers I had beaten in the water were now sprinting past me. Our friend Steve pushed hard on the 40K bike before passing on to my friend Theo who ran the 10K to complete the race. In both of the races we had been in fifth position out of the other relay teams but it was more than that. It had been exciting and it had been fun as well as nerve-racking. There are so many technicalities in triathlon and so much to think about that it had been amazing bringing it all together.

Email circulated to all Sheffield Tri Club members July 2004 'Clarkie'

Ironbridge Tri
This is a tough course, swim was up and down a deep river with good current, mega hills and six laps on the run…

...Steve Judge was there with two mates. Steve sustained serious lower leg injuries in a car crash but can swim/bike so he's a good guy for relay races...don't forget this... this guy has got more bottle than the rest of us.

I had been building up to these events for a long time with dedicated training but at the end of the day without my friends helping and participating it wouldn't have been possible. I appreciated that so much. Finally the big event of the year was here, the London Triathlon. This was the biggest mass participation triathlon event in the world so you can imagine the vastness and size of the transition area. Held in the ExCeL exhibition centre, when we arrived we saw numerous rows of racked bikes. My wife and I had driven down to London and met up with Bruce and his friend Russ and we discussed and clarified the transition handovers before I had to get suited up and work my way down to the mass start in the water. In our 'wave' there were 200 athletes and we all got into the water and swam over to the start line. I considered my ability in comparison to the other participants and positioned myself somewhere in the middle of the pack. I'd learnt that swimming is very much about getting into a rhythm and so I didn't want to be stuck behind someone but equally I didn't want someone tugging at my feet.

We were all hyped up with a chorus of "Oggy oggy oggy – Oi Oi Oi" before we all patiently waited for the start, treading water with an air of tension and anticipation. The horn went off and there was a flurry of flying arms and legs. I put my head down and powered my arms. I turned my head to get air but there was a wave of water instead. I turned my head the other way, now gasping, and got kicked in the face by someone's feet. Eventually I grabbed some breath just before someone literally swam over the top of me as there was no room either side. It was both daunting and exciting and reminded me of being in a rugby scrum from my days of playing for Doncaster Rugby Union. Head down I vigorously thrust my arms with certainty, determined to get into a rhythm as I headed towards the first buoy. After ten minutes the pack had 'thinned out' and I was able to get into a good flow and glide through the water. Another ten minutes and I was now heading back towards the exit pontoon, lifting my head to 'sneak a peek' to ensure I was heading in the right direction. Twisting my body in unison with my forcible strokes used every ounce of effort and I swiftly overtook a few swimmers nearing the end.

Unbeknown to me at this stage there had been an emergency with regards one of the other swimmers just ahead of me. Lifeguards had plunged into the water to rescue a fellow triathlete who was struggling and had submerged. As they pulled him out to desperately resuscitate him, none of the onlooking crowd knew who it was. My wife and brother were eagerly waiting to see me exit the water safe and sound. I reached the floating pontoon and placed my feet on the solid surface in an attempt to stand up. I grasped for air as I put one foot in front of the other. Grabbing the rails to hoist myself up the first steps, I then saw Bruce frantically waving and calling my

Swim done, next challenge to get this wetsuit off. London Relay Triathlon just two years after my accident where they told me that I may never walk again.

name. I hobbled over to him and unzipped myself before sitting on the ground. I removed my wetsuit as practised and put on the trainers he had waiting for me. Then I half jogged off up the stairs with wetsuit in hand and into the massive arena to pass over to Russ for the bike section. I was exhausted but buzzing from the experience as we supported Russ on the bike section. Just after an hour on the bike Russ handed over to Bruce who went off like a whippet, completing the 10K in 34:55. It was an amazing effort from all of us, which gave us the very satisfying result of 24th out of a total field of 272 relay teams.

I was so proud of all of us in our efforts and not only the swimming for me, but there had also been a lot of standing and walking throughout the day. I stared at the finisher's medal that hung round my neck, amazed at what I had accomplished in just two and a half years after my accident. From being told that I might never walk again I had continually set my sights on goals and worked towards them and achieved. I started thinking to myself 'What's next?', but actually I already knew. My wife and I had been working on a goal between us and seven months from now we were expecting our first baby to be born into the world.

It wasn't just me who had been swimming hard to achieve a goal.

CHAPTER 10

The Foundations of a New Life

I'd always wanted kids. Meet the right person, settle down and have one or two children. When I was in hospital with my legs trashed my vision of playing with the kids in the garden became very blurred. Much as I'm very positive in my outlook I couldn't help but have some negative thoughts flying around. Like my mum and dad did with me, I wanted to play with my kids on the lawn, teach them how to swim and how to ride a bike. The thought of not being able to had sent me to sleep crying at times but also these very same thoughts propelled me forward. I wanted to get better for many reasons. I would channel those feelings of tension and compulsion into my rehabilitation and into doing something, anything, as long as it was taking action. I wanted to be well again and fit and healthy and yes, I wanted to walk again for me, for my wife and for my future kids.

I knew how demanding it would be to bring up a kid. Well, I say that. I had some sort of idea that it would be pretty demanding bringing up children and I wanted to be ready, both physically and mentally so that I could help and support my wife who would initially have the biggest duty. Just short of three years since the accident and now here I was fulfilling my duty as a husband and a father, although it did get off to a staggered start. Even before Robert was born he showed signs of being like his dad. Due to his fidgeting and excitable state of impatience he took action and was born four weeks before his due date. It caught us a little 'off guard' but we got this!

Bath times for me were a chance for me to familiarise him with water so that I could take him swimming at the earliest opportunity. I was keen on advancing his crawling skills so that we could move on to his toddling and walking capabilities. I checked out what the earliest recommended age was to take babies out in bike seats. I was excited myself when my son and I could venture out on trips, initially along the bridle tracks.

Going out for family walks with the buggy and baby carrier was lovely but it was still difficult for me, with the main pain coming from my right ankle and toes. To encourage me to go out and push myself I generally needed a challenge or a goal, if not then I would be tempted to stay at home and not inflict pain on myself. Our calendar at home was of the beautiful scenery of the Derbyshire Dales with a different location for each month. I would use this to take us out on a quest to go to that very picturesque spot but then more. Our purpose was to find exactly where the photographer had stood when they took that very photo. I'm not sure my wife revelled in it with the same excitement I did as we climbed over fences and scrambled up the side of hills to seek out the exact position. Those dedicated photographers must have been hanging out of trees for some of the shots but either way we did our best to find the exact spot. We would then take a selfie of ourselves at 'the spot' before celebrating with tea and cakes at a nearby café.

I saw a 5K charity event advertised with the statement 'Run, Walk or Crawl'. 'Perfect' I thought, and signed up for the event. Using my walking sticks I powered myself round the undulated course. I was pleased how I overtook some of the other people although, to be honest, they were just enjoying a nice pleasant stroll...but...in my head...I beat them!

Work was going well and there was the obvious fun side as well as I readily looked forward to April 1st to play some practical jokes which over the years included:

- Fake CCTV 'accidentally' leaked to office staff.
- Fabricated sound effects coming from the toilet cubicle of a mysterious constipated employee.
- A talking photocopier which puzzled a range of personnel for over three weeks.

Every day I refrained from complaining about my discomfort and I certainly did not expose my limitations to others. At the start of the working day the pain would not be too bad in my right ankle and the flexible shoes that I wore accommodated the limited ten degrees of movement that I had. But as the day progressed so did the pain. I was now alternating between walking and swimming in my lunchtimes. The swimming was always good and although I had no set goal in this discipline at present the sensation of the gliding freedom with no subsequent pain was enough for me to want to carry on. On the days where I forced myself to walk I'd complete a good couple of miles even though it hurt a lot. My thought process was still of the mindset that the more I did it then eventually the joints would adapt and loosen up and progress could be made, no regrets. In fact the opposite was true and due to the pain my afternoons at work would see me squinting with agony every time I got up for the photocopier or walked to the toilet. Before I got up from my desk I would always ask myself, "Do you need to? Do you really need to?"

I discovered that there were three ways to combat the situation (that's if I didn't include not walking altogether).

1. The first way was to take small steps with both legs kept very straight to limit ankle movement. This didn't get me very far very quickly and also made me look like a tin soldier walking round the office.

2. The second way was to twist my right leg by 90 degrees outwards which caused an obvious limp but the pain was eradicated. The problem with this process was that it made me look like I was doing a very bad impression of Kevin Spacey's character in Usual Suspects. "In the morning I'm Steve Judge but come the afternoon I am the crime lord Keyser Söze."

3. The third option was to deal with the pain. By accepting the pain as it hit I could carry on with the ankle movement until I smoothly moved over to the left leg…and repeat. Easier said than done as pain is there for a reason. To push through my pain was not only mentally hard but physically it was extremely draining. I would pinch my forefinger and thumb or clench my teeth together as a way of distracting myself to aid pain management.

Moving around with no form of discomfort or limitation was my goal. I didn't want or need anybody's care and attention and I certainly didn't want anybody to ask me how I was. Most people with the slightest bit of common sense would probably encourage me to rest or even to not do the activity that hurt me or caused me discomfort. It hurt when I walked and I wasn't about to give that up. It was hard for me as I hid my discomfort and frustration when helping to move boxes in the archive area or just generally standing for long periods of time while out on site visits. I didn't want to admit it to my colleagues and I was probably in denial to myself. I was not going to give in. This was not going to beat me.

Once in the early afternoon the pain was excruciating to such an extent that I felt so weak and my breathing rate had increased. I realised that this was abnormal for me and promptly hurried out of the office, down the street, past the pharmacy and into the newsagents. Back at my desk

I quickly consumed the Chunky Kit Kat and can of Coke, wanting the sugar rush of energy to get me through the rest of the afternoon. Ten minutes later things had escalated – now my heart rate was pounding and I felt dizzy. For the first time in my life I had to leave work during the day as I was not well. I was weak and shivering and extremely emotional. As I slumped in my car I burst into tears, exhausted from the effort of trying to hold it all together. I needed to get home and fast. It's funny how it's never the doctors or the hospital…the first stop is always home. I gripped the steering wheel in a feverish state with my weak hands and finally made it home.

What happened next is a little vague but needless to say I ended up in hospital for the next couple of days with a life-threatening dose of septicaemia. My right leg was bright red and had ballooned up into a swollen state. By the end of the day I was hooked up to an intravenous drip and feeling a lot better but it had been close. I must have developed some kind of infection on my right leg which could have possibly come from something like athlete's foot. This may have been my fault through not drying my feet thoroughly before rushing back to work after swimming. The blood circulation, damaged glands and general complications with my right leg meant that it was unable to fight off the infection. This episode made me aware of just how susceptible my right leg was and showed me this was something I needed to be aware of in the future. It most certainly wasn't going to stop me from doing things but my body had changed from how it used to be and now I had to adapt to accommodate these changes. On my discharge from hospital I bought some antibacterial spray and implemented a new after-swim regime with closer monitoring.

I finally secured an appointment with Mr. Blundell, a smartly dressed consultant with a smooth and relaxed manner. I needed answers with regards my ankle and toes on my right leg and this was Mr Blundell's area of expertise. After his lengthy examination it came down to three options.

1. Seize the ankle through surgery so that there was no movement and thus no pain. The result would also restrict my ability to walk which seemed very extreme, seeing as most of the time I could accommodate the pain.

2. There was a procedure of going into the ankle and loosening it off by somehow scraping the bone and joint with some sort of surgical grinder. This operation contained many unknown factors until they opened up the joint and had a poke around. There was also the risk that the joint wouldn't be able to support itself afterwards which would lead to more complications. Again I wasn't too keen on this unknown, experimental 'jiggery pokery' and waited for the next option.

3. The next choice was a replacement ankle. 'Now you're talking,' I thought. Technology was moving so fast nowadays and I was keen to hear what robotic marvel they could secure into my joint to make me 'bionic'. My vision didn't quite match the reality, though, as it was explained that the only thing they could do was to replace my joint with a ceramics part embedded into my bone.

"Tell me more," I said.

"The operation is a fairly standard procedure with good results and your joint would work well and give you good movement…but…"

"Yes..?"

"Well, Mr. Judge, you are very active and keep yourself very fit."

I smiled with pride. I had relayed to Mr. Blundell all that I had already achieved and how committed I was to being healthy and strong.

"Well, because of your activity you'll probably wear the joint out."

I nodded with raised eyebrows at the correct assessment from my consultant but also realised that this might be my downfall.

Seeing the mixed feelings on my face he promptly said, "But…if you do, we can go in and fix another joint in."

"Oh…" I raised my eyebrows again as my smile returned. Once again I was warming to this option.

"But," he continued, "you'll probably wear that one out too."

I nodded with pursed lips as I waited for the next part.

"Well," he said, "after two operations it's really not advisable to do another. And also there is a possibility that your bone may have worn away which could lead to major complications."

"Err…like what?" I asked.

"Well the worst case scenario is that it may lead to having your foot amputated."

"Wow…" That escalated quickly. There were a few ifs and buts in the scenario but it was hard to keep positive about the potential consequences…

"And then…" Mr Blundell continued.

What! There's more? I thought we were finished. What do you mean 'and then'? I must have looked at him with a puzzled expression with my mouth slightly open, as I was intrigued as to what was coming next.

It was explained to me in great detail that due to the fragile state of my skin, when they wrapped it around my 'stump' it might not perform very well and it could easily get sores, abrasions and infections. Worst case scenario could mean that they would then have to amputate above the knee which was on a whole new level. As I sat there listening to the possible consequences of trying to sort out the pain from my ankle, my heart sank and I came to the quick conclusion that there was no guaranteed quick fix.

Next on my list were toes. "Ok, what about my toes, can you sort out my toes for me and make them straight?" Mr. Blundell assured me that this was a more simple operation but would result in me not being able to use my toes ever again…but they would be straight. "Lots to think about" I said as I booked in for a meeting the following week. There would be a group of consultants and my situation could be raised as a topic for discussion. As I drove home I realised that up to now, most of the big decisions had been made for me. This time I had the information and it was my turn to ponder the consequences. I had to decide my fate that would affect the rest of my life.

After the consultants had deliberated the various options and outcomes I interjected and staked my claim. "Let's start with the toes" was my decision. My thought being that with straight toes I could wear more accommodating footwear that might not ignite the pain from my ankle so much. I was thinking that more operations could be considered further down the line but for now, let's start with the toes.

Months later I was sat in the hospital ward just about to get ready for my operation when the thought occurred to me that I could just grab my bag and go home instead. I could just carry on with my active life as it is. If I go for this operation I can't do anything for the next six weeks. I'll be in pain and I'll be encouraged to rest and put my foot up and do nothing for SIX weeks. The scenario was very tempting but I had made my decision and this had been a long time coming. I told myself not to think about it anymore and instead just go through the motions, get changed, get ready…don't put the pants on your head!

Diary entry: 29th March 2006

Went under 1.26pm, came round 2.50pm.

Excruciating pain in the toes of my right foot that felt like someone was squeezing each one with a pair of pliers. Spasms of pain were causing me to clench my teeth. I was given morphine which eventually calmed me down. I did some deep breathing as I was wheeled back to the ward.

Each toe had been sliced across the joint and individually wrenched straight before a sharp needle-like rod had been forced down the length of the toe with the end protruding out. This sounds like some sort of medieval torture and it was true in every way especially with the amount of pain. It looked like I was trying to grow blades out of my body like the X-Men character Wolverine or even Freddie Krueger but...erm, from the foot rather than the hand! I was told to rest and put my leg up for six weeks which I nodded and agreed to but inside I was thinking of ways to get around these instructions. At home I mutilated an old pair of walking boots by cutting the toe section off and adding an inch-thick sole to the base. Inserting my foot and strapping the laces tight up to my ankle gave me confident support. The height lifted the pins clear of the ground enabling me to manoeuvre, walk and even drive. Stubbing my toe was not an option or even a thought that I wanted to deal with and so I had to be careful.

There were a few incidents, bumps and snags which caused me a lot of discomfort but I always knew I had been through worse. On one occasion I woke up in the night feeling very lightheaded and in a lot of pain. On close inspection I could see that one of the rods had been pushed deeper into my toe. I grabbed it and slowly pulled it out by about 2mm. The pain subsided and I was able to get back to sleep.

I had to quash my energy and urge to do things and instead force myself to take it easy. I still did jobs around the house and an upper body fitness routine but I also had a list of films to watch to force myself relax. It was like having a ball and chain round my foot that I'd opted to wear but in six weeks my sentence would be up and then I would be free.

Once again my birthday came and went with me unable to enjoy or celebrate it. I'd seriously lost count of how many I was due now. And my birthday always coincided with a Bank Holiday weekend which really started to grind on me a little bit, hearing everybody talking about what they were going to do. Going to the seaside or the park or maybe seeing their friends and having a few drinks. It was frustrating thinking of all the things that I couldn't do including playing with my one-year-old son. I was really starting to hate these bank holidays and so instead I just sulked.

I felt that I was watching my life pass me by, and I was just counting time until I was better. I sat there in frustration, tied down, enclosed in boredom and cloaked in depression. Metaphorically I was down on my knees but I would look up with determination. I'd imagine myself shifting my posture like a sprinter with one knee up, leaning forward and placing both of my hands in front to stabilise myself. I would be ready for the 'Go'. Could I hold the pose for another two weeks, patient and poised on the starting blocks? My white tiger was clawing at the cage. I was ready to be unleashed, ready for freedom and liberation. Ready for life's opportunities that had passed me by. Ready to catch up and to push it! The race would be ON!

After six weeks of agony the pins were finally removed and I could start my rehabilitation and start walking again properly…well, up to my standard. I knew what to do for rehabilitation; I'd been down this road before. I did the physio as often as prescribed, I frowned to compensate for the agony and gritted my teeth through the pain. I squeezed my thumb and forefinger to control the anguish of screaming out. I walked when I didn't want to and pushed myself through barriers just to get me back to where I used to be. I couldn't believe how much pain and discomfort there was as a result of the procedure and just getting through my first day back at work was a challenge, but I did it.

However, I couldn't help but continue to sulk. I knew that sulking wasn't really helping me and nobody else was sulking but at that moment in time that's what I wanted to do. I knew I'd 'snap' out of it at some point, but until then I wanted to sulk…just a little bit longer.

Trying to pretend that the pain wasn't there didn't work and so I had to admit how bad it was. I had to limp more to reduce the pain I would otherwise force on myself. In the evenings I would work out what modifications I could make to my shoes to help me with the discomfort that was draining me. I had to take the recommended medication to help with pain relief and swelling. Lastly I had to rest at the end of the day and put my feet up. Inside I didn't want to; my spirit was like a coiled spring ready for action but in reality I was still broken. The torture from my toes being straightened eventually subsided and the discomfort of introducing my foot to walking again eventually adjusted. The ongoing pain from my ankle was still there and in the end I conceded to the fact that it always would be there, every day.

Thoughts, Feelings and Reflections
June 2006: Every day

Every day I have pain
Every single day of my life I will have pain.
Every day I will have to squeeze my thumb and forefinger together to attempt to redirect my pain
Every day I will have to grit my teeth at some point to bear the pain from my ankle
Every day I will have to think twice before I make that walking trip from A to B
Every day I will ask myself "Is it worth it?"
Every day people will ask me "How are you?"

Every day I will water down my response "Yeah, I'm fine, how are you?"

In the summer of that year we went on holiday to Portugal to relax and bask in the sun. It was great to spend some fun and relaxing time with my wife and son but I still had some built-up energy. I felt like a coiled spring with over six weeks of tension ready to explode. I started doing a good number of lengths in the pool, twice a day. I hired a bike and explored the local area during siesta time, coming back soaked in sweat before diving into the pool. My tune of the holiday was New Radicals' 'You Get What You Give' and by the end of the holiday I had relaxed and enjoyed myself with food and drink but more than that. I felt fitter, stronger, leaner. I was doing what I had promised myself, catching up on life and making the days count and it felt amazing and I felt awesome.

On my return I wanted to keep up the momentum and researched bike orienteering, something that I never really knew existed because I always thought orienteering was connected with walking or running. I'd taken part in a few international mountain marathons with my dad when I was eighteen years old and in Venture Scouts. In fact I have fond memories of a particular event that reminds me of the closeness of our family. It's also enlightening to realise how the many strengths that got me through my ordeal were forged from my past life experiences.

My dad and I soaked to the skin and drained after a two day mountain marathon but still smiling. Somewhere in the North Pennines, 1989. (A year after this my dad was diagnosed with cancer.)

There was a two-day orienteering event in October running up and down hills collecting points and sleeping in a field next to a river in the middle of nowhere. My sister and brother had previously completed these gruelling events. Bruce went on to excel at the event, doing numerous other ones around the country year after year. I'd just turned sixteen and was taking part in my first one with my dad as my partner and Bruce was also competing. The conditions were so tough that it had forced over 50% of the competitors to drop out or retire. My dad and I were not going to give in but at the end of the first day we were struggling and lay shivering in our tent.

We were in a field which could only be described as a sea of tents and yet Bruce managed to find us.

He went down to the river, collected water for us and got us cooking our essential hot meal. To this day I still don't know how he found us in a pitch black windswept field with so many similar looking tents with the rain beating down...but somehow he did.

The next day the rain had not eased up yet we got up, packed up and set off to finish what we had started. I remember at one point on the route looking down at the slope and I suddenly thought that maybe it's not such a bad thing to set off on my bottom to reach the lower path. I got to the bottom, turned and saw my dad also whooping and giggling, doing the exact same thing as me. I managed to get my camera out in time to catch him sliding down with his legs in the air, full of life. And yet just one year later, Dad

What's the quickest way down the mountain?

was severely struggling with what we now know was the start of his seven-year fight with cancer.

So I was familiar with the concept of orienteering but to do it on a bike was going to be very different. I started training, pushing myself on the local hills, and I brushed up on my map reading skills. The event came and I was 'pumped' and giddy like a school kid. The hills were tough and the distance travelled was extreme and after the allocated three hours I returned to base camp with my lungs burning and legs shaking. Due to my late return the 220 points that I had collected were all wiped out and I stood in last position on the leader board. I panted through my smile as I looked at the results. "That was awesome," I gasped. I had absolutely loved every moment of it and I was buzzing. I felt like a complete and utter novice grinning ear to ear. It was the most fun I'd had in a long time. I had loved the training and the preparation as well as the tactical pressure and the competitiveness of the event itself and I eagerly wanted more.

Thoughts, Feelings and Reflections
December 2006: I'm Glad

Someone caught me smiling to myself the other night and –
I asked myself why?
I'm glad to be here tonight
I'm glad that I can put up with the pain in my foot
I'm glad that I can have a few drinks
I'm glad that I have got a job and that I am at the Christmas works do
I'm glad that the people at work are so friendly and so much fun
I'm glad that I can stand and walk and dance – I love to dance
I'm glad to be here tonight
I'm glad I didn't die on the 26th April 2002
I'm glad I put so much dedication and effort into my recovery
I'm glad to be ALIVE!

Some time over Christmas after a few pints with the lads it seemed a good idea to agree to cycle across England. Not there and then but some time in the summer of 2007 when the weather would be pleasant. The Coast to Coast (C2C) is a recognised challenge setting off from Whitehaven and ending up in Whitburn Bay, Sunderland. The route covers a distance of 135 miles through the beautiful undulated and hilly area of the Lake District and North Pennines. Five of us signed up for the challenge: Theo, Jon, Scott, Mark and myself, and training began. We decided to raise sponsorship money for the Blue Bell Wood Children's Hospice. This charity consequently went on to do a lot of amazing work in supporting our friend David and his wife and their severely poorly child Daniel.

There were a few weekends where we met up and cycled a good distance as well as chatting about how we were going to cope not only with the distance but the endurance of cycling day after day. We eventually calculated that splitting the trip into four days would be a realistic but still challenging expectation. With a focal point my training increased and I would spend many evenings pushing myself around the local hills building up my strength, power and endurance. Cycling into work when I could got a little bit dirty and sweaty but it was time efficient.

I loved taking Robert out on the bike seat in the evenings and weekends. It would give my wife some rest time and give Robert some fresh air and the chance to see the surrounding countryside. For me, the extra weight would push my heart and lungs and pump my leg muscles to the extreme. The sweat would drip off my nose and down my back as I panted up the hills, climbing higher and higher. At appropriate viewpoints I would grab a breather and enjoy the view with my son. We would share a banana and some water and then push on. Sometimes unbeknown to me Robert would nod off and so to my surprise when I returned home shattered he would wake up and then want to play. I concluded that this was the endurance training.

We started the Coast to Coast challenge in June of 2007. This was a particularly wet one with flooding all over Britain and so waterproofs were most definitely packed. Day after day we cycled through the land and celebrated our achievement handsomely in the evening with food and drink and a bit more drink. My training had paid off and I found the cycling, distance and terrain fairly relaxing. As we proceeded on our quest the hardest thing for me was getting up in the morning after the night before. On the last night we were sat in the hostel's restaurant area having our last supper with a few empty bottles of wine on the table. Just as we were reminiscing the challenging events of the last three days and planning the next dubious day ahead the doors of the restaurant burst open.

Photo taken minutes before the true coast to coast heroes gatecrashed our celebratory evening, June 2007. From left to right: Theo, Scott, me, Jon, Mark.

The perilous wind and rain blew in two fatigued, drenched figures. Closing the door behind them they politely panted their request for some water as they caught their breath. As they were wearing cycle helmets we asked if they were doing the Coast to Coast. "Yep," they replied, "nearly done." "Wow, you're...finishing it tonight? When did you set off?" "This morning and we've got another 22 miles to do to make it in under 24 hours."

I held my breath and just hoped that they didn't reciprocate the question. We ended up swapping a few stories of our related quests before they turned and braved the elements for their final assault. My friends and I finished our meal and drained the bottle of wine before heading off to our cosy beds. We had a momentous day ahead of us, albeit slightly marred now by our encounter.

Completing the C2C in four days and getting the glory and accolade from friends and family made me feel guilty. Some of my training sessions had pushed me harder than the event itself. I needed something more, an achievement that I could be proud of. I was always on the lookout for events and opportunities but I never thought of looking where I eventually found it and that was within myself.

CHAPTER 11

The Challenger Within

While sorting and organising the paperwork in my office the file tab 'Sport Times' jumped out at me from my filing cabinet. I have numerous pages of sports times and training results from when I used to go out running, cycling and even swimming. Some of these were written on the back of the race number from the event but the majority were on a continuous handwritten table dating all the way back to when I was a teenager living at my mum and dad's house. Our home was next to the main road on the outskirts of Bawtry and was surrounded by fields and woods. Most times I would take our little Jack Russell dog, Sugar, out with me when I went for a run. Our cat was called Spice and together as pets they were very nice. Although Sugar's legs may have been small it was always a challenge to keep up with her.

My most enjoyable exploits were running cross country at high speed through the woods and comparing it to the 'speeder bikes' scene in the film *Return of the Jedi*. I knew every twist and turn and tree and bush so well that I even ran through the woods in the late evening in pitch darkness. Beyond the woods was the quarry where I would 'beast' myself running up and down the sand hills, sometimes until I was physically sick, before jogging back home. The more controlled and serious runs were along the path next to the main road. The distances were as accurate as possible as my dad and I measured them out using our bike milometers. I'd have a set routine of listening to my particular 'Run' tape compilation that I'd put together. Enya's 'Far and Away – Book of Days' had a 'key change' moment which, combined with the uplifting lyrics, would hype me up so as to give me the inner ability to visualise the run in great detail before I opened my eyes and set off to 'smash it'. After each run I would regimentally write down all of the information necessary: date, distance, times and comments.

I took out my training record from the cabinet and sat on the floor to scroll through them. Most of them were running times. Reading them and taking in the comments that I wrote to myself took me back in nostalgia. *"Fantastic run, good pacing fast sprint at the end. Beat that Steve"* laid down the gauntlet for the next time I wanted a challenge. I sat there in silence reading through my notes as the tears welled up in my eyes before they burst their banks. I missed running so much, the control, the power and the propulsion. I missed the thought process of the tactics and the competition in events but mainly, I missed the personal rivalry. Like in the song 'Open Road' by Gary Barlow the person that knew me best…was me. I used to push my body so hard against the wind, against the clock, against myself. Chin up, knees high, pumping my arms towards my next PB (Personal Best). Without running in my life it felt empty and as if I was missing something. I'd accepted the concept that I would never run again but I had to keep thinking of what I could do rather than what I couldn't do.

As I scrolled through the sheets of results I came to the ones with swimming times on them and then some with bike times. Most of the entries were when I was living at my mum and dad's but near the end there were a few that I had entered from when my wife and I had moved into our new house on the outskirts of Sheffield. My last entry had been three weeks before my accident when I cycled the undulated route all the way over to my mum's home. I'd noted down the distance, the time and most importantly in the notes it read *"…fast, training"*. I wiped the stale tears from my eyes and smiled. I saw the challenge and the gauntlet that I had laid down for my future self five years ago. Now I had a goal. For this I needed my road bike which was a lot scarier to ride than my mountain bike. I also needed to get the clip-in pedals sorted. This was petrifying as to click out of my pedals I would need to twist my ankle which doesn't twist. The thought of falling over on my bike and onto my leg sent shivers down me. I had to overcome my fears and think positively about what I needed to do.

Adjusting the pedals and practising as often as I could helped grow my confidence. My training progressed with longer and faster bike rides, checking out the route and building up my speed and endurance. The day eventually came and I set off, pushing myself as fast as I could down the slopes and up the hills. I'd made the decision to listen to music on my journey as I needed all the help I could get. I hoped that the traffic lights and junctions would be kind to me as I exerted all my efforts, racing my former self from five years ago who not only had no disability concerns but also had age on his side. I was determined not to lean on these factors as excuses as I changed through the gears, the music igniting my passion even though I felt my thighs burn on the gradients. After an hour of cycling I swept through the town of Bawtry where I'd grown up and attacked the last two mile stretch, eventually coming to an abrupt halt outside my old home. I immediately checked my time to see that I had done it…only just but I did it. I clenched my fist and gave a brief jab to the air with clenched teeth. I was shattered but I was proud. I produced a video of my many weeks of training which you can view on my YouTube page by typing in: Steve Judge 'Spirit'.

My mum had since moved down south to be near Dawn and her family and her old school friends so I leant up against the driveway post and turned off my music. I was proud enough to take a photo of this momentous occasion but there was no smile due to the exertion that I had put in. My wife had agreed to pick me up at one of the cafés in Bawtry but I only just managed to cycle the two miles back there. My legs were already stiffening up and I was struggling to turn the pedals. I was wobbly on the up hills and coasted down the other side with gritted teeth. In the café I precariously grabbed each chair for support as I walked over to where my wife and son were sat. As I finally sat down I allowed myself to accept my achievement. I had beaten my former self. I was officially faster than I had been before the accident. For me, this meant that for the first time the accident hadn't had a detrimental effect on my life and this was because I wasn't prepared to let it. I had a sort of anger inside me, a fire that was glowing and one that I wanted to stoke and inflame. I wanted to use this passion and fury. I wanted to find something else. It was vital that I fed this 'need' but I had to work out how.

A calming influence entered our world with the birth of Susannah. She was a perfect bundle of happiness and although Robert's arrival and presence had prepared us very well for baby number two entering our lives, things seemed very different. Susannah was definitely a quieter baby than our first and balanced out the yin to the yang or is that the yang to the yin. Either way we had a lovely healthy family, gorgeous in all ways. Our holidays generally featured a swimming pool and cycle tracks. Robert was already on his first pedal bike and Susannah took her place in the bike seat. On the gradients there were times when I would be pushing Robert up with one hand while my legs pumped furiously to power Susannah and myself. Great team work and formidable training for me.

Work was progressing nicely and I was studying and developing myself to gain relevant qualifications for my role as Health and Safety Manager. I was even having to do homework which I wasn't used to. In fact it was 16 years since working towards my last academic goal to achieve my HNC certificate in mechanical engineering which was extremely challenging. I had a one-day release from 9am to 8pm where my brain became quite literally full. On the other days of the week I'd have to take myself to Doncaster library so that I could study my notes to absorb and understand all of the information. For me, this level of commitment and dedication is what I had to do to achieve my goal. The hard work paid off and after two years my mum and dad were proud to witness me receiving my qualification at the graduation ceremony at the Doncaster Dome. I was just as proud of myself when I received my NEBOSH certificate in Health and Safety because it supported my ongoing progression and responsibility within the company that I worked at.

Meanwhile I was still on the lookout for that thing that would excite me and fuel my need. My friend Lee was getting married and on his stag do in Madrid we got on a coach to travel to a tiny airport where we had arranged for him to go on a tandem parachute jump. I remember looking up at the clear blue sky and feeling the excitement inside me. In the past I'd done a couple of bungee jumps but this

When cream suits were cool… have they ever been cool? Left to right: Nan (my mum's mum), Mum, me and Dad. Doncaster, 1993.

was going to be on another level. I consequently signed up and within a couple of hours I too was sat in a little aeroplane spiralling upwards to a height of 15,000 feet before plunging out into the Spanish skies. Jumping out into nothingness and freefalling was such a breathtaking experience. Breaking through the clouds and seeing the earth hurtle towards me took my breath away and then gliding down to the ground with such elegance and control from the parachutist was profound. It wasn't that I had grabbed the opportunity but more that I had created the opportunity. I saw the potential and I made it happen and it was an incredible experience.

I set about looking for some cycling events that would exert me and signed up for the 55 mile Cat and Fiddle Bike Challenge. The route went through the beautiful but very hilly Peak District including an infamous seven mile climb to the summit. It was great to train for the event and satisfying to complete it but once again it wasn't a race.

I found a British Heart Foundation charity bike ride called the Dark Peak Challenge, a forty mile route through the rolling and craggy area of Derbyshire. Once again the event wasn't a race and I remember hunting down a target cyclist in front. Focused on the horizon, I caught my rival and took him and as I gasped for air he turned to me and said "Good morning". 'GOOD morning? What the...?' No, No, NO! This is not what I wanted. I didn't want 'Good Morning!' I wanted him to fight back, to challenge me. I said "Good morning" back to him and pedalled onwards. Ultimately this was a charity cycle ride and people weren't there for battle.

My friend Scott and I carried on at our competitive speed until we got to one of the many pit stops where I stopped to fuel up on some juice and cake. "I'll catch you up" I shouted as Scott cycled off. One minute later I set off and then disaster! I had a puncture...back wheel. Without a second thought I jumped off my bike, turned it over and set about removing the wheel from the oily chains and replacing the inner tube with my spare one that I carried. I pumped the tyre up and got back on, all within about six minutes. With the inclusion of stopping time I was now roughly ten minutes behind my mate. 'Game on,' I thought as I could feel my heart racing. I set off like a rocket knowing that we were over half way round and that I probably only had just over an hour to catch him. Whizzing past other cyclists and sweating in the cold breeze, the chase was on and I was loving every minute of it. My white tiger was released as my eyes fixed on the horizon for the familiar figure of my mate and I pushed on. Blitzing it through the rolling terrain, pumping my legs and gasping for air, I eventually saw him. Pulling up behind him I caught my breath before I nonchalantly said, "Alright Scott?"

"Oh, hi Steve, where have you been?"

"Oh..." I panted, "I just got a puncture but it's alright now."

And that was it! Inside I was beaming with pride and outside I was covered in oil, grease and mud with a sweaty smile. I did it and it had been awesome. Within five minutes of catching him up we finished the event. I was buzzing from the experience even though my legs felt like jelly and I stood tall and glowed with a smile of exhilaration.

Leading up to the end of 2008 I arranged to go up to the North Yorkshire Moors to have a cycling weekend with my friends Theo and Jon. The weather was chilly and we woke up the next morning in our campervan with a thick covering of snow everywhere. The crisp white blanket beautifully covered the hills and roads and there was silence all around. Beautiful as it was this was not what we had planned and there was no chance that any cycling was going to take place. Our options were limited.

We either sat in the camper or we ventured outside and went for a walk. The thought of walking didn't ignite any excitement in me and worse than that was the thought of walking on the slippery and icy snow. I was unstable at the best of times and so actually making the conscious decision to go out in this environment seemed backwards. Looking at the map we found a local pub situated the other side of the valley which would be our focal point and our goal. The scenery was stunning as we trudged through the hills and valleys and my confidence grew.

Too much snow for cycling? I guess that means we're walking then! North Yorkshire Moors, November 2008.

I had no walking poles but I was padded out with layers of clothing and the thick snow would make for a soft landing if I was to slip. The local beer and the homemade meat pie was the perfect reward as we sat in front of the roaring fire. Seeing the snow start to come down again, we prepared ourselves and ventured off on the return journey. A mile into the whiteout and the tempest was hitting us full in the face in a concerted attempt to force us backwards. We weren't prepared to give in and we pushed forward. It was us or the elements.

I related our situation to the great explorers of this world like Captain Scott of the Antarctic and Sir Ranulph Fiennes. They too had pushed their body and mind to reach both the South and North Pole respectively. Clearly there was no such comparison as we were merely in North Yorkshire with a belly full of food on our way to our campervan, but you get the point. It brought out the adventurer and explorer in me. Man against nature, it stoked the fire inside me. Challenging me as I walked one foot in front of the other, out of my comfort zone. I never would have imagined that I would be out here doing this in the thick blizzard, yet here I was.

As the snow hit me I laughed in the face of this absurdity, how crazy and surreal it all was. I had broken free of the chains that had been tightly wrapped around me with every step that I took forward. Pushing myself against the wind and the snow that was sheeting down, and the gale that was attempting to restrict my movement and progress on my journey. I'd had enough of being held back and now it was time to liberate myself and see just what I could do. 'What else is there? What else CAN I do?'

I was hungry for a new challenge. I was ready to find that thing that would push me as a man and as a human being. What I eventually found not only satisfied my need but would also change my life forever.

CHAPTER 12

Coincidences, Karma and Good Luck

"So Steve, what's your challenge this year?"

It was a casual question at the end of a 'Happy New Year' email from my friend Phillida who I had met back in 1996 when travelling through Malaysia. I hadn't found a goal for the year ahead at this stage but because of the email from my friend I was compelled to go into the loft and look at some of my travelling memorabilia. I opened the small cardboard box and saw my luggage tag that had been attached to my rucksack for the whole trip round the world. There was a shell from a beach in Thailand and then I saw a very special gift that had been given to me.

I'd been travelling solo down the west coast of Australia when the floods hit and I became stranded for a couple of days with some other travellers in a place called Halls Creek. We later renamed it 'Hells Creek'! During our time in the hostel due to the floods we were advised not to venture out too far and I ended up helping a Japanese guy called Taka to improve on his English. As the days passed his written and spoken language improved and as a thank you he gave me a gift. The gift was a Japanese five yen coin called a Go-en. Translated this means 'good karma'.

He said, "Thank you Steve for your help. This Go-en will bring you good karma on your journey as long as you are aware of your vision and seize opportunities." Taka explained to me that you obtain good karma by receiving it as a gift but also by giving it, sharing it or passing it on. I thanked him and put it in my pocket. Later that day I set out on a trek into the outback on my own in search of a local landmark called the 'China Wall'. This is a natural vein of sub-vertical white quartz rising up to six metres in parts. During my journey my sandal broke, making it almost impossible to proceed on the rocky ground that lay ahead. I rummaged through my bag and as I'm always prepared for any eventuality I found a roll of tape from the asparagus farm where I had previously worked outside Brisbane. I bound my sandal up enough for me to limp on towards my goal which I had set out to achieve. Eventually I reached my destination, scrambled up the side and stood on top of the China Wall, arms aloft in celebration of my achievement. While I looked around at the vista I reached into my pocket where I felt my Go-en and I reiterated to myself: "Be aware of your vision and seize opportunities".

Over the next couple of months, to share good karma with others I set out gathering more of these coins and consequently presented them to immediate and extended family. I wanted to bring some positivity and 'good luck' into their lives. Although I knew the theory about giving the

Go-en, I could never have imagined how true it would end up being that I would receive good karma by giving it.

My camera was hanging in a tree from some string when I took this photo and it was in the days of having to wait for two months until I developed the film to find out if it was any good. Radio by my feet as music was always with me on my journey. China Wall, Halls Creek, Western Australia, 1997.

Back at my computer I was still searching for a new challenge for the year ahead. I wanted a race or an event with swimming and cycling in it. I searched for a long time and the result that came up time and time again was 'triathlon'. Swim, bike...and run. That was no good as I couldn't run and it started to become a little frustrating. I'd completed a couple of triathlons when I was twenty-one years old and they had been awesome. I'd trained for them during the summer by cycling to the swimming pool and sometimes squeezing in a 'cheeky' swim before work. In my first triathlon that I did with my brother there had been a fatality during the bike ride which everybody was distraught about, especially my mum who was at the event and unsure if either of her sons were involved. My dad had been receiving chemotherapy in the hospital on the first race but on my second race he was there in full support, noting down my times and cheering in support. In both races my swim was energetic and my bike was average but I excelled on the run.

A year later after my experience with triathlon I was travelling around the world with my girlfriend. We stayed overnight in San Francisco where I saw a poster for an event called 'Escape from Alcatraz – Triathlon'. It said that Mike Pigg was racing who was very well known in the triathlon world. At his peak, no one was better at the Olympic distance and he won four national championships. The next morning as I excitedly went down to the docks on my own there was the usual deep haze drifting over the water. I strained my eyes as I watched these elite athletes swim away from the redundant prison of Alcatraz. They powered themselves through the choppy water all the way to land where they grabbed their bikes and cycled 18 miles including over the Golden Gate Bridge and then ending in an 8 mile run. Watching one of my heroes run past me and grab first place was incredible and I wasn't shy about going to meet him afterwards. "Mike…Mike…over here," I said and as he came over I shook his hand. "I've been reading about you in various triathlon magazines." I beamed with childish excitement. "I can't believe that I'm meeting you," I said with a big grin on my face. I got someone to take a photo of Mike and me (selfies hadn't been invented yet) and hoped that it would come out ok when it was developed at the end of the film. I found the photo in one of my many albums and started to reminisce.

I grabbed a few other photo albums from the loft including one which was called 'My Life'. It was a compilation album that I had put together with a selection of photos from each year of my life. I came across a photo from when I was ten years old and I had just won Cub of the Year. I was there holding the trophy wearing my uniform with all its badges and there was a huge grin spread across my face. On my arm were the first three activity badges that I had ever received in Scouting and I leaned in closer to look at them. Focusing on the images that were portrayed on the badges, there was swimming, cycling and then running. I was gobsmacked at this discovery and stared at the photo in disbelief.

Cub Scout of the year and my first three activity badges ever achieved, symbolising swimming, cycling and running.

The way I view coincidences and my lack of belief in them is that millions of things happen every day and the fact that one thing is slightly connected to another thing is not that far-fetched. Even with the Go-en that I now wore round my neck I didn't think it would magically bring me good luck. Wearing it reminded me of Taka's words. To be aware of my vision and to seize opportunities that present themselves. For me it was also about being 'sighted' and in tune with my subconscious.

Back at the computer again I started to rethink about the possibility of doing a triathlon. I stretched backwards and looked at the ceiling. "Let's think about this," I said to myself. Maybe I could push it hard on the swim and bike and that would be my competition and then just walk round the run section using my poles. It wouldn't matter if people overtook me; my goal would be to finish, and complete the course. Something inside me ignited. 'A triathlon? Complete a triathlon? That would be cool.' I felt that a triathlon carried a certain 'wow factor'. Multiple disciplines, endurance and speed. As I took a deep breath imagining this achievement the oxygen fuelled the fire inside and I smiled.

My eyes widened as I stared at the search results on the screen: "Rother Valley Country Park"! As in the park with the lake where I'd done my entire crutch walking rehabilitation? There was an air of puzzlement and disbelief. How lucky was that? Or some might say "What a coincidence"… but I obviously don't believe in those.

The triathlon was being held in June and would be a sprint distance. This was a 750 metre open water swim, 20 kilometre bike and 5 kilometre run. As I read the information I scrolled down and when I got to the bottom of the page another title caught my eye, 'British Disabled Triathlon Championships'.

There was a thing called paratriathlon which was triathlon for disabled people; who knew? That seemed quite lucky for me or maybe another one of those 'coincidence' things? As I read more I discovered that there were different categories for the athletes. Intrigued, I clicked on more links which eventually brought me to a plethora of information on how the athletes' disabilities segregated them into the different categories. I was intrigued. Am I disabled? If so then do my disabilities categorise me into one of these classifications? Should I actually be doing this event rather than the able bodied event? I printed off the disability categorisation sheets and started wading through it all. There were nine categories altogether and it was clear that I was not suited for some of them as I was not in a wheelchair and had no visual impairment. The other categories I had to decipher as it depended on how many body parts your disability affected and to what degree. It was clearly more complicated than this but in my ignorance I was baffled by all of the descriptions and technicalities.

My initial task was to go down to Loughborough where the British Triathlon offices were for an initial assessment so that I could clarify which category if any I fitted in. The assessment was going to be a backwards step for me because for seven years I had been working towards having no disabilities and even disguising or hiding them. Against my past and present 'mindset' I now had to think about what I 'couldn't' do rather than what I could do. I had to be completely honest with myself and the scoring system otherwise I could potentially be put in the wrong category and give myself a disadvantage against the other athletes.

There were questions like "Are you able to get out of the water on your own or do you need assistance?" From what I'd been through and with my mindset I'd drag myself out of the water using my teeth if that's what it took but I couldn't say that! I had to think as a competitive athlete. If I got assistance would that help me achieve my goal? The answer was yes, I do need assistance.

I had to state how much pain, lack of function and disablement my right leg gave me. I had to stipulate the lack of movement, function and feeling that I had in my left leg from the knee down in conjunction with the 'drop foot' diagnosis. I had to explain to the assessor how my legs literally dragged while I swam and how I struggled with power and hills on the bike. My pain and limitations when walking and the complications I had in transition. Getting out of the water, wetsuit removal, footwear application.

I sat there as I pronounced the disability and restrictions that I have on this body of mine and it brought negativity and anxiety. I delved deep into the abyss of frustration and torment and brought it to the surface. It highlighted the gloom of my situation and my restricted future. My blind optimism was quashed, by myself! I had to let a massive emotional guard down which left me vulnerable and close to tears. It told me that I lived my life with this guard up, protecting me and enabling me to be positive and smile. Without this guard I felt exposed and scared and I needed to find my inner strength and courage so that I could live without it.

From the assessment and prior communications with British Triathlon it was confirmed that due to my disability I would be classified with a P20 scoring and could compete in the Tri 4 category as a para-athlete. I smiled as I clenched my fist. "Yes!" I said to myself. "I AM disabled!" For me this meant that I had no more excuses to lean on. I was going to be competing against people with similar disabilities. I'd been given the green light and now it was time to see exactly what I could do with this body. Now that I had a goal the next thing I needed was a benchmark and so I contacted the organisers for the results from the year before. They understood my competitiveness and sent them over to me. I looked down the list and found the Tri 4 category. My swim times looked pretty good in comparison and my bike time wasn't too bad but then the run section would let me down. But as I looked at the figures I couldn't help but get excited. Two out of three disciplines wasn't too bad but what was I going to do about my run? I hadn't run for seven years, not with my legs in this state. I remember being asked at the assessment if I could run and I looked at them and said "Not yet!" Now I had a goal.

I'd learnt that whoever won in their selected category would be crowned British Champion 2009. This possibility excited me and I was going to have to see just exactly what the limitations were on my ability to run. I was going to have to push myself way out of my comfort zone once again just to see what possibilities there were.

Packed in my suitcase for the family holiday to the Spanish island of Fuerteventura were, among other things, shorts, T-shirt, running trainers, and iPod with a fresh running playlist selected.

Since I'd last run, technology had changed. Now – seven years later – I was able to strap my tunes to my arm, earplugs in, equipped and ready to go. Early in the morning while everyone was asleep I set off out of the complex with a jog to just warm up the joints. As my pace increased my right foot seemed heavier on the pavement, sounding like a one-legged elephant coming down the road, but at least I was moving forward. I kept my chin up for posture but my eyes were fixed securely on the path in front, searching for any raised ground or imperfection on the path that could cause me concern.

My brain knew how to run but I couldn't quite get my legs to do what they were supposed to. My right leg stomped down and lifted up whilst my left leg was doing all the work propelling me forward. My arms were pumping furiously as though they alone were powering my legs with propulsion. I sneaked a peek at my feet and saw them working in unison one in front of the other. Wow! I was doing it! I was running. I couldn't believe what I was seeing. There was a rhythm and there was speed. It was beautiful. There was a fresh breeze in my hair and I looked up at the sunrise ahead of me. My heart began to beat faster and a wave of emotion caused my mouth to quiver and my eyes to well up. The feeling was incredible. Such a feeling of power and prowess as my arms swung in rhythmic alliance with my legs. I wiped the sweat mixed with the tears away from my cheeks. Eight minutes in and I saw the start of the desert coming up and wondered if I should take it off road. The words of 'The Garden' by Take That were playing in my ears. These were the cards that I'd been dealt with in my life and now it was time to open my eyes and start living...and believing.

Wow! I'm running again, and it feels amazing. That is until the pain strikes. Music now played via an MP3 player on my arm. Fuerteventura, Spain, 2009.

My white tiger roared as my caged frustration swept fire through my heart. My brain had a new controller now as my bottled-up anger exploded, driving me forward. I knocked it up a gear and turned onto the uncertain rocky ground of the desert. Now gasping for air with my senses heightened, I was scanning the ground in front of me and adjusting my course accordingly. I felt lighter, faster, skipping past stones and even launching off small rocks and skilfully landing on my left foot. A flood of memories and instinct kicked in from running through woods and over tree stumps. Faster and faster I went, lungs gasping, unsure of how much longer I could keep this speed up for.

Lack of oxygen eventually forced me to slow back down to a jog and cease my frolicking. Eventually I stopped and stood there, hands on my head catching my breath through my open grin. There was a vastness of space around me with the desert in front, the sea far in the distance to my left and the road directly behind me. "Wwooo Hhooo!" I screamed at the top of my lungs. The sound of my voice echoed in the crisp morning air. I looked down at my legs and felt proud of what they had achieved. "Wow…that was incredible…WOW." As I turned to look at where I had come from my right ankle buckled with pain. "Oww" I screamed as I nearly fell over in agony. It was throbbing every time I put weight through it. 'Got to get home,' I thought.

I had one more look at the view before I squeezed my fists tight and started to jog back. "Ow, ow,ow, ow." Every time I stepped down the pain shot through me. The rocks were now boulders and greatly obstructed my return journey. Getting to the road, my frown was squeezing my face tight as I attempted to get into some kind of rhythm. Chin up with good posture I breathed deeply and carried on. My thoughts were fuzzled and so I was relying on the muscle memory from my brain to my legs to keep me going. Using my upper body arm movement I dragged my legs home one after the other with great effort. It must have been hard for my wife to see me in such pain and I myself had mixed emotions. I was limping and moving by grabbing onto one piece of furniture and then the next and I was in agony but…I had run. I had run after seven years and it had been amazing…I did it…and I smiled.

Sat on the sun lounger, I reminisced about the euphoria that I had felt through the desert, the liberation and the excitement. It had been so much fun…apart from the pain bit. I limped around the resort, played with the kids and swam a lot in the pools. My wife and I hired bikes with kids' seats attached and we explored the island. After a couple of days the pain had subsided and I was able to have another go which was great, but the pain that I was putting up with took away the spark of enjoyment. Now that I knew what to expect there was an element of courage needed. I ran three times that holiday and it was amazing but it took its toll on me. However, I was willing to accept the pain and I was prepared to suffer the consequences.

After the holiday my training increased and I found that I was already running for training purposes rather than for fun. I was now cycling more on my road bike and even to work and back at least once a week. It only covered a total distance of twenty miles and commuting in rush hour traffic was not favourable but sometimes I would get up even earlier and detour into the peaks before arriving at work which was better. I swam a couple of early morning sessions at Ponds Forge which had an Olympic sized pool. The swimming was going well but I really needed to practise some open water swimming in my wetsuit. I was constantly reminded of how privileged I was and how bad things had been in the past. When I had pain from training I knew that I had had worse. When I felt tired I remembered the times when I literally couldn't get out of bed. I constantly thought about the things that I could do and therefore I did them. I suffered another episode of septicaemia and was immediately admitted to hospital but I knew it wouldn't be for long. I didn't belong there. My time for being hospitalised was in the past and now I had moved on. Apart from this stupid infection I was fit, healthy and strong and I needed to get out of my hospital bed and get on with my life. Time was slipping away and I had things to do.

One Saturday morning I had cycled down to Rother Valley and was running the whole way round the lakes completing a total distance of 5K. To my amazement I saw some people actually swimming in the lake. I'd considered swimming in the lake myself, maybe early in the morning, but when I had enquired I had been told it was unsafe to do so. After completing my run I cycled past the group on my way home. "Hi there," I said. "How come you're allowed to swim in the lake?" I asked, intrigued but also wanting to be polite. "Oh, we have agreement from the owners of the park," said one of the swimmers who I found out was called Clarkie. "Great…erm, how come, who are you?" "We're Sheffield Triathlon Club." I was gobsmacked and on hearing the name I also became excited. I had presumed that they still swam the other side of Sheffield which was too far out of the way for me but instead they were here on my very doorstep. Not only that but they swam here every Saturday morning in the same lake where in two months' time I would be competing in my first ever paratriathlon. I started to wonder just how much power this Go-en round my neck actually had with good luck, karma or coincidences. "Count me in," I said. "Where do I sign up?"

Thoughts, Feelings and Reflections
May 2009: Wow

FANTASTIC
Just went for a run
Did a good time, felt strong, good pace
I looked down at my feet and said Wow and smiled.
Pushed it and was able to
Did you ever think this would happen?
Did you ever think I would be running again?
Did you ever think I would be running like this again?
FANTASTIC!

And so the training continued over the six months leading up to the event and I worked out that I had a good chance of doing well in it. There were many external factors and unknown elements, however I took the positive and felt the fire burn and crackle inside me. My music playlist was once again updated, this time with the song 'Lose Yourself' by Eminem. I could do this! This was my chance and my opportunity. I believed it and I wasn't going to let it go.

I loved to run and to get it back after seven years was amazing. Now with a defined goal I would imagine myself running round the final stages of the triathlon, pushing hard towards the finish line. The enjoyment and adrenaline rush allowed the endorphins to be released which masked the pain that I was subjecting myself to. The consequences were the next day when I would be limping badly and so I would swim. I powered myself up and down the swimming lanes using my strong upper body to drag my legs in the wake, counting lengths as I visualised myself in Rother Valley lake competing against the other paratriathletes. The next day I would still be in pain with my ankle and so I would cycle. Pedalling around the local landscape I accepted the hilly terrain as 'great training'. Although on some days I would have appreciated it a little bit flatter. Hmm…those damned hills. The next day the pain would have subsided and so I ran again because I loved to run. And this was my training plan and this…was triathlon. Through my training I would always think about what I could do rather than what I couldn't do.

At last race day arrived, the 6th of June. This happened to be the exact same date that my dad passed away in 1998. A subtle coincidence in salute to my dad who was looking over me. I missed my dad and wished that he could have been there to see how fit, able and strong willed I was. He had always come to support and watch me in the past whether that was playing rugby union for Doncaster or doing a 10K run event. He'd cheer me on as well as monitor my performance and explain to me where I could make improvements. Eleven years to the exact day had passed since his death, and as I registered I received my race number. Number 11. I smiled as I looked upwards. I guess in one way or another he was going to be with me every step of the way through the whole event. I reached up and touched my Go-en.

My family were there supporting me along with my sister, her kids and my friends David and Claire. I was keen to see who my competition was but also nervous. My first impression was that everyone was so friendly. Paratriathlon was a new sport and rapidly growing so there was a massive air of encouragement and helpfulness. I loved meeting all of the athletes although I was unsure about asking them about their disability. Was it ok to ask them? Surely it was better than just staring at them and judging them. All of these people were incredible. They were my kind of people, individuals who weren't leaning on their excuses. They had turned their excuses into challenges and were doing a triathlon. Some of them had no legs and some had missing arms. Some of these guys were visually impaired or completely blind yet here they were just about to compete in a swim, bike and run event. I was intrigued how exactly some of these athletes were going to manage it.

When I had travelled through Canada in the nineties I had gone to see the statue of Terry Fox who was an athlete from the seventies that I had learned about and admired. I'd watched a film about him called The Terry Fox Story when I was just a teenager. Due to suffering from cancer he had one of his legs amputated but as a keen runner he acquired a basic prosthetic and set off to run across Canada raising money and awareness. He died from the disease, a true hero and an idol that hadn't let the condition of his leg stop him doing what he loved.

The transition area was full of different shapes and sizes of equipment. Wheelchairs, tandem bikes, prosthetic legs and arms lay on the ground. There was an array of equipment set up and ready for the race ahead. I racked my bike next to my main competitor James Smith, who was the current British champion. I had meticulously studied his results in preparation for the rivalry. James welcomed me to the sport of paratriathlon with open arms. We chatted openly and James informed me of the intricacies of the event from his experience over the last year. In return I exchanged details of the course from my training over the last couple of months as I'd got to know the park pretty well by this stage.

Through my planning and build-up for the event I had moved on from just wanting to finish. I now wanted to win and without James and the other athletes being there, there would be no challenge and consequently no achievement. Without the added pressure and drive there was no goal. The rivalry was what I needed to push myself further than I had ever gone before. That was my need.

I climbed into my wetsuit and zipped it up. Barefoot I limped over to the edge of the lake, waded in and then dived into the chilly water. I needed to get moving because I was starting to shiver or was that just the nerves? We grouped together in a vague line, treading water and staring across the lake. Our focal point was a big yellow buoy about 300 metres ahead of us. Breathing deeply and slowly, my heart was pounding as I waited for the horn to sound.

CHAPTER 13

Achievement Through the Cultivation of Time

The horn went off and we powered away, cutting through the water. When I got out of the lake I felt dizzy as I hobbled and limped on the stony ground into transition. James's bike was still racked so I knew I was in first place in my category. I then proceeded to take the longest ever transition time known to anybody as I struggled to get on my tight lycra vest over my damp head, broad shoulders and wet body. I put that down to a novice learning curve and after heaving, stretching and struggling

I eventually sprinted out of T1 and jumped on my bike. With the damp weather the compacted mud and gravel track became puddle ridden, creating a splatter hazard for all the athletes but we pushed on. On every lap I clearly heard my supporters screaming, specifically my sister who used to sing in cathedral choirs. Now her vocal chords were getting a different kind of workout as she shouted "Come on Steeeve". This made me smile but also dig in deep as I knew that I wasn't just doing this for me. After four laps of the lake I pulled into T2, through transition and with my trainers secured on my feet I sprinted off.

It was awesome hearing the words of encouragement and it made a massive difference, even the comments after the event like the ones from my friend David who said: "It was incredible as we thought that Steve couldn't run but then there he was…running and running really fast. I don't know how he did it." Remarks like this made me feel really proud of myself and it was great to know how much he cared and that he was impressed.

The change in speed from bike to running was agonising. My brain was saying 'Come on, COME ON!' and my legs were screaming out 'We need more power Captain!' I was giving it everything and the results seemed comparatively slower than the bike but I knew this was my maximum, and the adrenaline pushed me on. On the first kilometre I 'beasted' myself with stubborn determination before I finally got into a pace, holding my chin up and relaxing my shoulders. I couldn't give in to fatigue; I knew that this would have a detrimental effect on my whole body as the weight would fall onto my legs and especially my right foot. I had to be upright, eyes ahead, focused with a spring in my step.

Coming up on my left was one of the benches that I used to sit on when I walked around the park on my crutches. I saw an image of my former self slumped there in my world of pain. "That's not me anymore," I said to myself. "I've moved on." As I ran past the bench anger swept through me at the consequences of the accident. How it had dragged me down. How it had made me slow and weary. Not now though. I'd moved on; this was me now.

Looking straight ahead, one of the songs from my playlist popped into my head. 'Run for Your Life' from the band Bucks Fizz, and just the title alone motivated me to push on. My white tiger roared, my heart beating frantically, feeding my body with oxygen through all of my muscles to drive me forward. I swung my arms to power my legs in alliance. Two kilometres done now and I was on the long back leg of the lake. I kept the pace up with good speed and sucked in the oxygen.

Ahead of me I could see another runner in a red top, a long way off and in another category but I needed a goal. I needed to push myself on as I knew that my competitors behind me would be chasing me down. Three kilometres done now and I was struggling. I had no smiles left in me. I glanced behind me and saw a figure in the distance. It was no game anymore, it was just bare grit and determination. Looking ahead, the runner in red seemed a little bit closer. I was working towards my goal, pushing myself forward and equally away from my rival. The last kilometre and now I could hear the tannoy drifting towards me, calling me home. I looked over my shoulder again. It was all a blur but I saw James, closer than last time...definitely closer. My heartbeat raced. I tried to change gear and put the throttle down. There was nothing there. There was no extra speed. This was it. I was running on empty.

Closer and closer towards the noise of the tannoy, moving my arms and lifting my knees up to keep me going forward. Frantically breathing, gasping, my lungs burning. "Come on Steeeve!" Again I heard the familiar sound of my sister's voice. "Keep going," the crowd shouted. As I came round the corner I finally saw the finish line and I was smiling. I've done it! I've made it! I sprinted down the last fifty metres as I raised my arms in achievement crossing the line. Wow. I did it. I DID IT! I finished!

I felt shaky and grabbed some water next to the runner in red whose name was Kevin Flint and I shook his hand. As I turned round I saw James Smith cross the line and it confirmed to me that I'd won, I was first. I won. I WON! I shook his hand and said something like "Good race" but I can't remember exactly. I saw in the crowd my wife and two kids. Robert was in tears with his arms outstretched. "Daddy, Daddy." As I lifted him over the barrier my emotions exploded and in the midst of all the glory and celebration I burst into tears myself. I shielded my face with my hands and then buried it in my son's shoulder and squeezed him like a teddy bear. I felt a huge release and then went and hugged my crying wife who had put up with me through my endeavours and supported me in achieving this goal of mine.

A special moment in a special place. Robert and me after my first paratriathlon at Rother Valley Country Park.

Mum was ecstatically happy to see me so tall and strong and able. I bent down and as I squeezed her I whispered, "I did it Mum…I did it". Following my dad's advice I'd been the best that I could have been and I'd done it. My past physical achievements had been great but this was different. For the first time since the accident I was happy and felt fulfilled from the experience and sense of achievement. I loved this sport called paratriathlon and for me it satisfied my feelings deep inside, the desire to be the best that I could be. This attitude and mindset were my dad's parting gift to me. Now I was fired up and energised. My tiger was free and fearless. It was everything that I needed in that moment to have purpose and drive each and every day. To push myself outside of my current comfort zone, stretching and changing the boundaries and limits. Yes, I had found a way back from the accident.

I'd always said that the accident hadn't ruined me but just changed me and now I had found out how. This sport completed me and my need through happiness, achievement and pride. There was now a new world out there that I had discovered and I wanted to be a part of it.

CHAPTER 14

Seizing Opportunities

Chatting with James and some of the other athletes immediately after the race, I found out about the European Championships that they had just competed in and the World Championships in Australia that were coming up. It was information overload for me and I couldn't cope with the amount of possibilities that were out there...waiting...just waiting. One step at a time, I thought, let's see how my recovery goes. I was now limping fairly badly as the endorphins had drifted away. The prospect of doing another triathlon suddenly seemed quite daunting as I slammed back to earth. I was exhausted, in pain and beginning to feel extremely fatigued. I stood with my mum, sister and nephews Matthew and Jordan while I waited for the medal ceremony.

"...and in first place, the new British Champion for the Tri 4 category goes to...Steve Judge." A gold medal! My first gold medal that I had ever received. I waved to the crowd and hugged my big solid medal that was around my neck. All of the training over the last six months had led to this moment but realistically my journey to this moment had been a long seven years.

As I held the medal tightly I felt pride and responsibility within the team that I had joined. I felt compelled and instinctively took my Swiss Army knife scissors out of my wallet. As a former Scout I'm always prepared. I reached up to my neck and grabbed the shoelace that was holding my Go-en. I swiftly snipped it off and held it there in my hand. I looked at the coin that had brought me so much good luck or maybe just amazing coincidences, not that I believed in those things. Either way this Go-en that represented good karma needed to be shared. I turned to James and explained to him the story behind the coin, what it represented and why I wanted him to have it. He received it and I felt that we had an understanding of solidarity and competitive friendship through future rivalry. Further down the line this 'duel' between us would test our friendship but for now we shook hands as buddies.

The head coach came over and asked, "Steve, would you like to represent Great Britain?"

"Me? Represent Great Britain, wow! Would I ever."

He explained to me that later on in the year they were setting up an international event in London. Paratriathletes from all over the world would be coming to the UK to compete in Hyde Park. It made me realise that there are opportunities out there all of the time. I've got to learn to see them, hear them...smell them! But not only that, I've got to grab these opportunities with both hands and do something, take action. This was my chance and this was my moment and I was going to give it everything I possibly could. I was going to be the best that I could be and have no regrets.

That night with my family I drank champagne or something similar although it doesn't really matter as long as you can't see the label. The drinks helped numb the pain as I limped to bed with my gold medal. The next day I woke, turned on the computer and started doing some research on future races…I was hooked. In the background I heard the words to the song 'Something Inside So Strong' by Labi Siffre and I nodded in agreement with them. The barriers in front of me had been high yet I had smashed through them with such determination. While on the internet I also thought that I'd get me one of those 'tri suits' that everybody wore in an act of desperation to speed up my transition time.

The next race in the series was the Bedford Classic which was a standard distance rather than a sprint distance. My heart sank. I didn't know if I could physically do double the distance I had just done. 1500m open water…ok. 40K on the bike…tough but ok. 10K run…I didn't know. I seriously didn't know! After a couple of days of rest and letting my injury pain become more manageable I knew that I had to build up my running distance as a priority. I had to see just how far I could run and how much I could push myself. Only I could do what had to be done.

One evening when my wife was away with the kids I got home from work and took myself down to Rother Valley, pumped at the challenge ahead. Twice round the lakes would equal 10K. The time was not important but the style, posture and responsiveness was critical. I consciously slowed my pace down and thought about every step and breath that I took as I pushed myself. Lap one done and now I was running further than I'd ever run before with these legs of mine. Chin up as my eyes scanned the ground before me, kilometre after kilometre. I ran with pride in this solo achievement, down the side of the lake, eventually reaching my finish line. Wow, 10K…who'd have thought? My legs were a little shaky as I walked back to the car but my shoulders were broad and my smile beamed in confidence. I celebrated my achievement as I had promised myself with a bucket of chicken from KFC and a 'trashy' action film. Life was good.

Driving down to Bedford at three thirty in the morning, I still didn't know if I was physically going to be able to complete the endurance of the event. Training had been good on each discipline over the last five weeks but I hadn't put all of the sections together with the complete distances. To be honest I was still getting my head together on how much kit I needed to take to these events. My car was quite literally full to the brim with 'stuff'. The swim and the bike went well although my bum was really starting to hurt near the end of the 40K. Holding my race position on the bike for well over an hour caused backache along with my thighs feeling the strain. Onto the three lap run circuit and the main thing going through my head was 'Steady the pace and keep the posture...chin up'. As I continued around the course I realised something incredible. The paratriathlon course was intermingled with the able bodied event and I was running with them. Not only that but I was overtaking some of them. I started setting some of the other runners ahead of me as goals and amazingly I caught them and then overtook them. This was incredible and the buzz that I got powered me on further and stronger.

Amazed just to finish and ecstatic to win! Note to self: Must work on my arm muscles more. Bedford Paratriathlon, 2009.

"I can do this! I'm not going to stop. I'm going to give this everything I've got," I said to myself. My broad shoulders swung as both feet lifted off the ground and my confidence and prowess propelled me forward. Eventually I came round the last corner to see the finish line. 'YES!... YES! I've done it.' The smile spread across my face before every ounce of my body tensed in jubilation as I crossed the line punching the air in triumph with both fists. Just under three hours of dedicated concentration, energy and endurance. I was ecstatic about completing the 'standard distance' as well as coming in a good two minutes ahead of my closest competitor.

I staggered over to the transition area and found a pole which I leant on and held for support. I was spent, exhausted and suddenly felt very emotional there on my own. I went down on one knee as my shoulders jerked and the tears ran down my face. I didn't know why I was crying and I couldn't help it. I was so immensely proud at what I had done and so thankful for having completed it. I felt invincible and yet fragile. Kneeling there with my head down I shook it in disbelief at what I had just achieved. I'd given everything and left it all out there on the course just as I'd planned and now I was drained. I lifted my chin up and wiped away the tears as I took in a deep breath. I stood tall before limping over to my bike. It was an incredible accomplishment although the pain over the next couple of days from my ankle would bring me crashing back to earth.

After a couple of days of rest and recovery I dragged myself back into my training schedule as two weeks later the next paratriathlon race was at the London Triathlon event, the same one I had participated in five years previously when I had just completed the swim. I blitzed the sprint distance course to win first position and was now five minutes ahead of my closest rival.

Paratriathlon was still a new and developing sport which resulted in learning curves for athletes as well as the courses that hosted us. For me coming out of the Thames Docklands involved climbing up wet slippery steps in bare feet which was a nightmare as I hugged onto the banister for essential support and assistance. The athletes in wheelchairs had to use the small elevator which only held one person at a time so you can imagine the queue that formed of impatient athletes frantically pressing the 'call' button of the lift. Like I said, these were early days and it was a learning curve for all involved.

My win in London confirmed my status in the series as overall British Champion for the Tri 4 category but there was one race left in the year.

One of the biggest ever paratriathlon races was being held in Hyde Park, London with forty-two athletes from seven different countries. I was named on the billing as a "notable British athlete". I was excited, honoured and pumped but I was really nervous as well.

I was 'well up' for it and extremely giddy to receive and wear the official royal blue GB lycra tri suit to compete in. I'd told my family and friends about it and was keen for the crowd to cheer me on with shouts of "Go GB!" My kit bag was handed to me at the race briefing and I promptly opened it like a winner at pass the parcel. I looked and searched and then looked again but there was no kit. It was then explained to me that they had run out of my size and my heart sank. "Oh, that's ok" I said, but inside I was gutted. Instead I'd be wearing my 'all black' tri suit, quite literally like a shadow in front of the home crowd.

I discovered that competing at an international level was very different to anything I'd ever experienced before. In the past I had heard commentators make excuses for athletes stating that they had not had much international experience before. 'Surely that shouldn't matter?' I used to think to myself. 'If they're good then they're good.' The pressure, the thoughts, the fears, the responsibility and the crowds watching you. There is absolutely no leniency with any rules, which I totally agree with but it is stressed, over and over again. You will be disqualified. You will be taken out of the race. Your moment to shine will have gone. You will have disgraced your country. Hang your head in shame and leave through the back door! No pressure, good luck, have a good race. I left the race briefing like a startled rabbit and went off to try and get some sleep ready for the event the next day.

The day was long as we had to register our kit in at 6:30am in the morning but we weren't competing until 4:30pm in the afternoon. A good 10 hours to wallow in a sea of nervousness and anticipation. Finally we were queuing up on the starting pontoon and my face felt as taut as stone. The excitement and adrenaline mixed with the tight wetsuit on my lungs restricted my breathing and I stood there taking shallow breaths. "Wearing number 32…Representing Great Britain…Steve Judge."

And the little breath that I had in me got whisked away…

Email sent to family and friends:
The race was so tough and all I can remember is trying to get more air in my lungs for the length of the course. My swim was not its best, on the bike I pushed hard but was just a blur and my run I couldn't push any harder. Because I gave 100% I'm quite ok with coming 7th in my category.

I was physically and emotionally exhausted and it took a good five days to fully recover from my international ordeal.

Diary Entry: September 2009

Done it, I reached my goal, I did a triathlon! In fact I did a triathlon and won! I did three triathlons and won them all. I then represented my country in paratriathlon. In the process I near on achieved a miracle and started running again. I've reached a pinnacle, a height that I couldn't have dreamed of. The question is…what do I do now? I loved every minute of this year so what do I do next year?

Going down to my local running club Killamarsh Kestrels, some of the long-term members looked at me like they had seen a ghost. "Steve? What are you doing here? The last we heard about you, you were in a wheelchair!" Running the six mile distance wasn't necessarily the hardest thing on those evenings, it was combining it with the talking that nearly killed me. They'd simply ask me what I'd been up to for the last seven years and off I went. Panting up those hills while I was relaying my story put such a strain on my lungs but it was fantastic to share with them. For the runners with injuries I gave hope and for the joggers that wanted to improve I gave motivation.

At the end of the year I completed one more race called a duathlon (run bike run) which was a gruelling 'off road' course in Sherwood Forest. Straight afterwards it gave me great delight to run with my four-year-old son in a three kilometre event. We subsequently repeated our running together on Christmas morning across the frosty hills surrounding our village and through the woods. It filled my heart with so much joy experiencing this magical moment with my son. To do something like this had never been a goal of mine but merely a dream, yet here I was. Pushing myself out of my comfort zone this year had now enabled me to access other opportunities that I had never imagined possible and turn dreams into visions and visions into reality.

I had an appointment at the hospital which was just an x-ray check-up on my right leg to ensure that all was ok. I sat in the cubicle room waiting for my images and analysis, only for them to be brought in by my original surgeon Simon Royston. I couldn't believe my eyes as he walked into the room and proudly explained to his entourage, with a glint in his eye, the proceedings of my extensive injury and the physical results clearly displayed by me. I was bursting at the seams with all of the things that I had to tell him and blurted out as much as I could knowing that he was a busy man and time was of the essence.

Before we knew it he was being summoned to go to another patient but just before he left I said "Wait!" Since passing my original Go-en on to James I had replaced it with another one round my neck. Once again, using my Swiss Army scissors I snipped it off and passed it on to Simon, explaining the story behind it and why I wanted him to have it. It was one more thing on top of all of the 'thank you cards' and photos that I had already sent him but what I really wanted was more time with him. I wanted him to know how my life had worked out since our first interaction. How I was pushing myself to make the most of my life and how thankful I was for what I had and that I didn't take things for granted. I wanted Simon to know about everything that I'd achieved since he put his hard work, expertise and skill into me as a patient and as a person. I also wanted him to know that I would continue to do so and that I'd always be the best that I could be. Frustratingly, time to chat with Mr. Royston was something that I had struggled to get in the past when I'd made special trips to the hospital. For me this was an ongoing goal for the future and as with all my goals it was one that I was not only determined to achieve but one that I would eventually succeed in.

As I reflected on my year I also thought about the next one ahead and the prospects. I had entered a whole new world and I was very naive within it. I needed to step it up a gear. Triathlon satisfied my 'need' as I could dedicate myself to it mentally and physically and that brought me joy, satisfaction and achievement. My goal was to secure a place on the British Paratriathlon performance squad. To retain my British champion status. To compete in the European Championships. And I wanted a rematch at World Championship series in Hyde Park. These were goals that I had chosen in retaliation for the hurt and torment of the past seven years. As I visualised them I found myself smiling as my glowing heart spilt over with emotion. As it beat fast I felt the endorphin release but also the nerves in my stomach. A fire that was stoked with a burning desire to win that propelled me into action.

There was a hunger inside me that needed addressing, and competing in triathlon was the key. My white tiger could at last be uncaged but first I needed to train it. This wasn't going to be easy as I had a full-time job which on occasion required me to work around the UK carrying out site audits. I had a family with two kids and was passionate about my responsibility as a husband and a father. I now wanted to excel at swimming, cycling and running and compete in various races. I researched training methods and coaches that could assist and I took action. What I hadn't expected was to falter at the first hurdle and for my dreams of representing Great Britain to be put in jeopardy.

CHAPTER 15

Change the Plan, Not the Goal

Whatever it takes. Winter training through the beautiful local woods of Eckington (actually my hygge moment).

I did that whole 'winter training' thing through the freezing cold months. Instead of snuggling up and hibernating for the winter season I was out there in all weathers. Four layers of lycra and a cycling jacket and gloves that would be easily suited at the top of Mount Everest. Even then I'd squeeze in my thin running gloves just to add one more layer.

I realised that working towards my goals wasn't just going to be about the time that I had available but more about how I cultivated my time as to what I could achieve. My routine started the night before as I packed my swim kit and got my clothes and bag ready for work. I would load up the kids' cereal bowls, carefully placing a plate on the top of them and often leaving them a personal note to read before they added the milk in the morning. I would also make my sandwiches for breakfast and lunch, and I had an alarm set for 10pm every night to remind me to get to bed on time. My morning alarm was set for five thirty. When it sounded it was like a calling for destiny. It wasn't a choice, it was time to go, flick the switch, let's do this! It was now my time and I would use it wisely. With everything set up the night before it was a simple 'grab and go' with minimum effort and thought.

I would drive into Sheffield in the bleak conditions, the sleet hitting my windscreen and the street lights shining down on the desolate roads. I'd look straight ahead with bleary eyes, driving towards my goal and my vision. My music playlist selected 'Night Swimming' by R.E.M.

Ponds Forge had a superb competition pool with lane swimming early in the morning. Due to the fact that it was a facility for swim masters and training squads the temperature of the water was ideal for this activity or another way of putting this was that it was bloody freezing. I used to clench my teeth together in preparation for the icy shock as I dived into the water before thrashing up and down the lanes, if anything just to keep warm. After my session I had a slick, rigid and efficient routine through the changing rooms which enabled me to get to work just before 8:00am, ready to start my day. I ate my lemon curd and cheese breakfast sandwiches and drank a banana milkshake as I drove through the city streets.

Training notes November 2009: Make a decision!

Decide and follow through...please. Are you going swimming or not? Decide the night before and stick to that decision and DO NOT decide in the morning. If you plan to decide in the morning you will not sleep well. Shall I, shan't I? Shall I, shan't I? Your will power on decision making is weakest in the morning and if you do not go swimming you will feel guilty all day. You need to swim but you need to sleep so decide and follow through... PLEASE.

Some lunch times I had the opportunity to go for a run but I really struggled on the hills around Sheffield because only my left leg could help me up them. It was a constant quest to find a fairly flattish route and one that would preferably take me to a park of some description. Running over to Endcliffe Park and through the woods was exciting, or if I took the long slog over to Millhouses Park then this would be my endurance workout. For speed training I used the circuit of the Grade II listed General Cemetery of Sheffield which was ideal. I timed my laps of the perimeter working on pace, consistency and technique. The gravel pathways ensured that the frost didn't make the route too treacherous and the steep gradient added to power training.

As there were no showers where I worked I had to brainstorm for a solution. I considered various options from hosepipes to wet wipes and eventually invested in some towels, a sponge, a bucket and a bottle of body wash. I would sneak away from my desk at lunch time and disappear into a toilet cubicle. Moments later I would emerge, now changed into my lycra and ready for action. I'd lock the cubicle door from the outside using a coin and then covertly slip out of the building and off en route.

On my sweaty return I'd grab my small bucket, sponge, bodywash and two towels hidden in a cupboard near to the toilets. Filling the bucket with some warm water from the sink I'd then go back into my cubicle and strip out of my training gear. While stood naked on one of the towels I'd attempt to wash myself from head to toe the best I could.

When someone entered the toilets I would freeze and hold my breath knowing that there was just a 5mm plyboard wall separating us. As they washed their hands and left I'd give a sigh of relief but it was worse when someone came and used the cubicle next to me. As they sat the other side of the thin partition I would opt to carry on with my routine but in stealth mode which was almost like slow motion. I'd dry myself off using the other towel, change back into my trousers, shirt and tie and return to my desk, always within the hour, job done. In the summer months as the sweat continued to pour from me post run I'd direct the desk fan towards me to speed up the cooling process.

Cycling into work was an option and on a good day only took me just over thirty-four minutes which was nearly the same as commuting by car. The added hassle was the preparation and safety risk. Cycling through traffic in pre-rush hour meant complete focus on the job in hand. I stringently watched out for the opening of car doors and indicator lights as well as the lack of them.

The purchase of a Concept 2 professional rowing machine had seemed a rather extravagant one a few years previously but now it came into its own. The long machine was placed in the 'outhouse' which doubled up as my makeshift gym. It was a lovely environment in the summer months with a glass front but not so much during the winter. With no electricity, lighting or heating it was colder than cold with only a glow from the external streetlights illuminating my proceedings. The workout would start off with jumpers, hats and gloves until the adrenaline warmed up the blood pumping round my body.

Sessions on the machine were brutal. There were no excuses as I had complete control and consistency. No external factors affected my performance. It was just me the machine and the figures on the display screen. Not only did the sessions give an all-over body workout but they also gave me the opportunity to focus and visualise. Staring at the mirror ahead, zoning out into the depths of my eyes, beckoning, challenging and pushing myself as I powered through the metres and kilometres. Shoulders, arms and legs. Core strong, back straight. Mouth open as I frantically gasped for oxygen and my heartbeat rocketed up on every stroke. I would push myself to the point of collapse as I worked towards my goal. Session done I would eventually return to the serenity of the house, sweaty, pumped, endorphin-filled and music playlist still blasting in my ears. Time to shower, relax and then the bedtime routine instigated by my 10pm alarm to get me to sleep on time.

Reading became a good way to unwind before sleep and what better than to read the autobiography of Rick Hanson, a man confined to a wheelchair following a tragic accident in his teenage years. This man denied any excuses and raised money and awareness by powering himself around the world in his chair. As he entered the towns on his journey they would play the song that was specially written for him and his quest by John Parr, 'St Elmo's Fire (Man in Motion)'. It's a great powerful and uplifting song and listening to the words brought the raging passion out in me. This was not one that I would play as I drifted off to sleep but more in the morning to help me get out of bed. I felt the synergy and a connection with the lyrics of how I too was not prepared to stop until I'd won the battle. How I had to push myself onwards and do what had to be done. The accident had broken me but I was by no means defeated.

Joining the Sheffield Triathlon Club gave me access to training sessions, advice and knowledge. I signed up with the professional coach Bob Pringle and we had a preliminary session and assessments to evaluate a baseline. My eyes were opened about how technical and complicated training was to become. I learnt about cadence on the bike and the benefits of nutrition and training plans. The advice and qualified guidance was great. I trained when I could and I trained hard but I struggled to juggle this along with work and home life, especially to a specific and structured plan.

My goals for the upcoming year started with me filling in the application form for the British Paratriathlon performance squad. I found it difficult as it asked for PBs in each discipline for certain distances. I hadn't acquired this data up to now as all my training was from homegrown courses apart from my pool swims and even then it was a case of starting and stopping the watch myself.

The performance squad weekend arrived and I had a huge grin and wide eyes as I drove onto the campus of Loughborough University, seeing the students and athletes using the amazing elite training facilities where many past, present and future World Champions had performed. This is where the British Triathlon Federation (BTF) were based and the day was filled with focused training and constant assessing and mentoring on each discipline by the coaches and staff. The event finished with a formal interview before I jumped in my car and drove home with grinning confidence that I had been the best that I could be. Getting on the squad would bring much needed training, coaching, advice and expertise. I was so fresh to this sport that I needed as much help as I could get. There were also funding and sponsorship opportunities and of course the greatest honour would be that I'd be representing Great Britain in the year ahead.

I carried on with my training and started competing in a lot of club races run by Sheffield Triathlon Club, the aquathlons in the winter (swim and run) and duathlons (run bike run) in the spring. In duathlons my first run was always fast and try as I might to hold myself back my competitiveness and energy pushed me forward. Jumping on my bike I'd furiously pump my legs the whole distance at race pace before racking the bike at the end and setting off on the second run and that's when it hit me. I suddenly realised that I'd expended all of my energy and my tank was near to empty but I pushed on. I had to push through the pain exhaustion and discomfort to eventually complete the task. No matter how many times I did duathlons the second run was always tough. I knew it was, it always is and it always will be. For me it was a case of just shutting up and getting on with it. I found that the same was true with some things in life. Either at work or at home or just things in general, they would always be difficult. They always will be, no matter what way I look at them. It was about shutting up, stopping myself from moaning about them and just getting on with it, through the pain and the discomfort.

Competing against able bodied athletes was tough for me, mentally. I had negative voices in my head. No matter how hard I trained and how fit I was or how I pushed myself I could never be as fast as the majority of the athletes. There was no chance but I held my own and I never gave in. My goal was always to focus on the athlete in front and dig deep within myself to be the best that I could be. To cross the finish line completely exhausted and with no regrets, job done.

With the added exertion on my body there were bound to be one or two little 'niggles' and it was important that I dealt with them for two reasons. The first so that it didn't develop into an injury which would prevent me from training or competing. Secondly, having a twinge, soreness or irritation became mentally draining. It was always there, whispering in my ear. The main one I had was a shoulder strain from all of my swimming. My physio gave me numerous exercises to do, the main one being to use a big type of rubber band between my arms and to lift them above my head in a controlled movement very slowly. As stipulated I did them in front of the wall mirror to check for posture and synergy. This was until my wife banished me to the bathroom with accusations of narcissism and vanity. In solitude I would carry out my daily repetitive routine of physio as advised. The same happened at work where I sat in my toilet cubicle so as to perform my daily routine…of 'physio'…not the other one… although sometimes I'd do both at the same time…because it was efficient!

In late February the post finally delivered the letter from British Triathlon which I ripped open and read.

> "Dear Steve
> Thank you very much for your recent application…
> …we were pleased with your initial results in the sport but unfortunately we won't be offering you a place this time around."

What??? I didn't understand! I read it again and then read further. There was a list of areas of feedback:

"Lack of understanding and experience in the sport.
Need to implement more structure into your day to day training
Need to take the performance element more seriously
Attend more structured club sessions in swim and run
Etc"

I couldn't believe it. My heart sank. I sat down on the sofa and stared at the letter but looked straight through it. What does this mean? Since becoming British champion in my category last year I'd got better, stronger, faster, I knew I had. Does this mean that I can't represent my country? I had plans for the European Championships in a couple of months and the rematch in Hyde Park later on in the year. I needed answers because suddenly I felt very lost in the unknown. I congratulated my friend James Smith who had succeeded in getting into the squad but for myself I was still confused and my heartbeat was racing. Why didn't I get in? I really didn't get it. On making further enquiries I eventually learned that I could still represent GB... Phew! But I would be very much on my own with no support from BTF. This, however, didn't faze me. In fact, it fuelled me. I'd learnt from my experiences that when barriers or obstacles stood in my way; I'd stopped saying "Why me?" and instead I'd say "Try me!"

I became focused with my outrage in all my training. The years of being held back had built a fire inside me that now blazed. I had a clear goal of what I wanted...what was mine. Last year was a measurement, a benchmark, and now it was time for action. Each training session was an opportunity to retaliate. I woke daily with a burning desire to thrash out my rage in the pool.

I was angry that I hadn't been accepted but my goal was not going to change. I just needed to change the plan. I channelled my temper into my training sessions; I'd pull on all those disappointments over the past few years and give it my all. All those times when I had my hopes raised only to have yet another setback. No, this wasn't going to stop me. I would use this frustration, this disappointment to fuel me and fire me up. On the bike, my legs pumped until they scorched. This hill was NOT going to beat me. This goal was not going to beat me. When running my arms powered with impatience demanding that my legs 'keep up!' and 'move faster!' which released the tiger from within. I used every single muscle with controlled fury on the rowing machine to accelerate the metres per second. Mouth open, sucking in every molecule of oxygen possible to aid my progress. I challenged my reflection with daring animosity: 'You got this? Then let's show 'em. The non-believers, the people who ridicule. The people that say...No! Let's show them YES. Let's do this... yeah? So, let's SEE you do it!'

The song from the film Footloose, 'Never', written by Michael Gore/ Dean Pitchford pounded in my ears through my MP3 player. I was ready to fight, to be free, to fly. My tiger was released with such fearsome ferocity. Away from resentment, through the storm and towards my future, exhausting and expending its energy for it to limp back to its lair, weakened and drained in contentment.

Training Notes May 2010: Shattered

I'm exhausted. I've been training hard and training a lot. I'm supposed to be training today but there's no chance, is this just me? Do other athletes feel like this? I'm probably the fittest I've ever been but at the moment I just feel shattered and I don't feel like much of an athlete.

Even on our family holiday to Portugal I would still be up early to sneak a swim session in before anybody else woke up. I sacrificed my 'siesta' time for a run or bike ride in the blistering heat. The bike session inevitably and exhaustingly became longer than expected due to the lack of detail on the tourist maps that I was using. I'd return to the resort in a sweaty mess and literally collapse into the pool with the sound of "Ttsssss" as my steaming body was quenched by the cool water.

Training Notes May 2010: Too Much?

I feel terrible, fatigued, exhausted, tired. I have a hamstring injury in my left leg and my ankle hurts on my right leg. I'm struggling to walk and struggling to smile. I'm feeling that this isn't what I want and I'm wondering, is this too much for me? To achieve you must sacrifice and there will be pain and exhaustion on the way but how much? How much am I willing to give to receive? I just feel that I'm giving way too much.

In preparation for the European Championships in July I entered the Rother Valley Triathlon. Competing with able bodied athletes, I got the result of 229th out of a field of 451. The participation and completion encouraged me in my performance and the mid-range result kept me grounded. I was still recovering from a bad cold when I drove to Athlone in Ireland to compete in the European Championships. I knew it had been brought on by nerves, apprehension and possibly over training but there was nothing I could do about that. That was something I would learn to deal with going forward. I gave a fellow athlete a lift from the ferry port and dropped him off at the performance squad team hotel. My accommodation was in a cheaper part of the town on the outskirts of the city.

The next day at the end of the race briefing I was handed my kit bag which included information, my race number and…my GB kit tri suit! I peeked into the bag and touched it. My heart filled with excitement as I pulled it out. It was the new design kit that had the Union Jacks on either side of the waist and it looked awesome. I played it cool as I nonchalantly checked it over in front of the squad but inside I was trembling. The name 'JUDGE' was clearly printed twice on the suit, once on the chest and then also on the bottom. We confirmed a recce time for the bike course in the afternoon before I went back to my dwellings with a skip in my step as I almost danced down the streets. As I got in my room I turned to the mirror on the wall and with the biggest cheesy grin I danced a jig up and down, hugging the tri suit. I quickly stripped off and slowly, very carefully slipped into the crisp new lycra. It felt so good. I pulled it up over my shoulders and zipped up the back.

Done, I turned to face the mirror again. 'Wow. Look at me!' A wave of emotion welled over me with breathless excitement and giddiness. It looked awesome. I stood there tall with broad shoulders and the fire burning inside. My white tiger, startled at the image, began to claw at its cage. Now I knew how a superhero feels as they don the suit, ready for action.

The next day the familiar fanfare of the theme from Pirates of the Caribbean was blasted out of the tannoy system while our names were announced: "Representing Great Britain…Steve Judge." This was followed as usual by the customary pulsing beat as we lowered ourselves into the cold water "Boom, boom…boom, boom…boom, boom. On your marks…"

The swim was raw but I came out of it leading my category as I set off on the bike. After a couple of kilometres I was being overtaken by members from other categories and then Sebastian who was my German rival in my category Paratri 3 (the category number system had recently changed and I was now classed as a Tri 3 para-athlete). I couldn't keep up with him but I was still ahead of my British team mate, as well as the Spanish and French athletes. Off the bike I was chasing Sebastian round the undulated two lap course. After two kilometres my legs started to drag and I struggled to lift my chin up. Seeing Sebastian coming towards me on the loop of the second lap, our eyes met and through sportsmanship and friendly rivalry we both veered over to the barrier where we high fived. I struggled round the second lap on drained resources but eventually crossed the finish line and grabbed the silver medal. Completely burnt out and feeling weak, I smiled at my first international achievement. With the help of the traditional local drink of Guinness we celebrated and socialised and it made me realise how tense I had been leading up to the race. Getting to know fellow athletes including my competitors relaxed me. Swapping stories and tales and discovering them as a person helped me to realise that they were just like me. The newfound equality gave me a much needed confidence boost. I needed that boldness and I would use it in three weeks' time at the London Hyde Park event. My fortitude as an athlete had grown and I was ready for the rematch.

Summer training was best especially on a Saturday morning. With a full kit bag packed I'd cycle through the beautiful countryside to Rother Valley up and down the terrain to meet the Sheffield Tri Club at eight o'clock. Checked in and changed I'd then wade into the lake and proceed to complete my swim set. I would practise my powerful start and perfect my technique of slickly turning round the buoys before I settled in to some good solid swimming. The raw temperature of the water always made my left leg cramp up, causing a squeezing agony within my calf muscle. I'd learnt to accept the pain, discomfort and lack of mobility and just carried on powering away with my arms. With no requirement to count lengths or stop and turn round I could just swim to my heart's content. The morning sky above and the desolate park made these moments special, undiscovered apart from us swimmers. I tried not to smile too much or else my goggles would leak. On exiting the lake I would then carry out a speedy transition out of my wetsuit revealing my tri suit (not my GB one; that's for special occasions). Slipping into my waiting trainers I would then run round the park covering the 5K distance. Once my initial training was done I couldn't help but talk to my fellow triathlete friends about their training and future race events, always conscious of the time as back at home my prompt return would be expected.

Once home I'd have a supplementary breakfast of Weetabix while stood up in the kitchen and ask the kids "What do you want to do today?" I would more often than not then find myself back on the bike cycling down to the local swimming pool, Susannah in the bike seat behind me and Robert whizzing ahead on his junior bike. There was no rest in the pool, not down to swimming practice but more because of the game they loved to play called 'Tickle Daddy'. These usual hectic Saturdays just made me fully appreciate the relaxing evening that I would then have with my wife.

I was super fit, content and happy and full of confidence going down to London to take part in the World Championship event in Hyde Park. There was a spread of international athletes and although this was not the final the event carried huge gravitas. My family travelled down to support me which gave me a huge posse including my wife and kids along with my mum, brother and sister, her kids and my sister-in-law. The sun beamed on my face as I stood on the start line, smiling with no regrets.

No regrets with my fitness through the tough training regime six days a week.

No regrets on technique, equipment or diet decisions.

No regrets about knowing my competitors and carrying out extensive research on them.

No regrets about knowing the course and carrying out a preliminary recce the day before.

Ensuring that I had found a way to relax myself and calm my nerves.

With this inner confidence I stood there on the start line with the full knowledge that I had done everything and anything possible. I was race ready. I knew what I needed to do and I was itching to get into the water.

There were collisions in the swim and accidental punching and kicking that occurs but I must admit I gave as good as I got and had some slick powerful swimming areas to gain ground. Through the first transition where I could hear my family cheering as I set out on the bike and I was leading in my category. On various laps of Hyde Park I could hear my family cheering me each time I whizzed past them. "Come on Steeeve", "Come on Daddyyy!" Swiftly through T2 and then out onto the run. I sprinted off in front of the grandstand and then away from the cheers, finding my pace with swinging arms and feet lifted off the floor. A fellow GB athlete from another category caught me up on the run and as usual proceeded to overtake me but this time something happened. Something inside me said "No". A rush of belief surged through my body and registered with my brain. 'We've got more than this! Come on, let's go.' I turned up the speed and stayed with her and then realised that I was nearly clipping her ankles. I gradually overtook her back now, running swiftly and smoothly, focused on the road in front in an energised yet placid state.

Euphoria as I rip it up in London's Hyde Park, 2010. Photo courtesy of British Triathlon Federation

Around the top of Hyde Park, for the first time I took on water. Refreshed, I powered down the last kilometre still overtaking athletes from other categories. I was flying. I'd given everything that I'd got as I veered off onto the blue carpet of the finish lane. "Go GB!" "Come on Great Britain." With the blast of the crowd I lifted my chin up and I was now sprinting. The Union Jacks were being waved and people were shouting "Go on Steeeve". I suddenly saw my brother leaning over the barrier frantically waving his flag, beckoning me to take it. I reached out and grabbed it. With the last couple of metres I realised that the race was won as I raised my arms above my head. The flag was flying behind me as I crossed the finish line with the biggest grin of my life.

I'd done it and although exhausted and shattered the endorphin release lifted me up to the size of a giant. Later as I stood on the podium in my GB kit to receive my first gold medal representing Great Britain, I was beaming and lapping up the accolade as I waved to the crowd. A truly remarkable experience and included in this was being ushered away to have the obligatory drug test. I felt like a true professional athlete as I followed the protocol and procedure. This all then turned a little bit sour as I found myself sat in a marquee waiting in a queue to give my 'sample' while the celebrations were happening without me. I understood the reason and the need for the protocol and I was willing to comply one hundred percent without question. But it was frustrating for me as I knew the result already; it would be negative. Drink the water to hydrate myself so that I could pee. Not too much water else it would dilute the sample too much and then I'd have to start all over again...at the back of the queue. There were skills and techniques in everything to do with this level of the sport and I was still learning.

A couple of weeks later, flicking through the pages of the monthly triathlete magazine Tri News I came across a picture of me from the race. It was a truly iconic image of me in my GB kit, crossing the line with arms aloft and the Union Jack flag flying behind me. Wow, a picture that showed everything that I'd been working towards. I had done it. I had achieved. The completion of the other triathlon events that year reaffirmed my status as British champion. I was now crossing the finish line over

Susannah, my own special trophy after my glorious win at Hyde Park in London. Dawn looking on.

six minutes ahead of my closest competitor James Smith. One of my focuses and goals for this year was also to challenge other athletes from other categories. Kevin Flint who was the guy in the red top ahead of me from my first paratriathlon last year was one of those targets (although he didn't know it). Now that I was also consistently beating him I again looked ahead for future targets and goals. I regularly appeared in Tri News and Sheffield newspapers with photos and quotes about my achievements. I travelled down to Hertfordshire where I shared my story at my nephew's junior school following a request from my sister and I also spoke at a Sheffield School for autistic students.

I was proud and got a real buzz from sharing my story with the pupils by telling them about the inspiring messages that I had used to achieve my goals. I set up a website to promote the sport of paratriathlon as well as to share my journey and give out lots of useful information and links to help people participate in the sport. Passing my level 1 coaching course in triathlon also meant that I could give back to the Sheffield Triathlon Club. They had already done so much for me and I wanted to share my knowledge and experience to help others.

Unbeknown to me, through my accolades and temperament I had been nominated for Male Paratriathlete of the Year. This was against other athletes who I admired and who had achieved World Championship status. I was astounded to even be considered as this was a special award where only registered triathletes were allowed to vote. This meant that friends and family were unable to participate in the process unless they too became a fully fledged triathlete. But try as I might I failed to entice any of them to jump on board this bandwagon. The results were to be announced at the end of year's British Triathlon Awards night. On enquiring about attendance I was informed that as I wasn't on the GB performance squad I couldn't be given a complimentary ticket despite me being nominated. I was sent a link where I could buy my own ticket depending on availability and managed to secure tickets for my wife and me and I even hired a tuxedo for the prestigious event. The evening was full of glitz and glamour with amazing stories and recognition of people's achievements and accomplishments over the season.

Eventually the award for Male Paratriathlete of the Year came up and I sat there in excitement.

"And the award for 2010 goes to...Steve Judge."

And I won! Male Paratriathlete of the Year 2010.

Wow! I was so shocked. I couldn't believe it. Hearing my name announced sent a wave of vivacity through my body as I literally jumped up from the table and onto the stage to accept the award. My photo and name were on the big screen behind me as I raised the trophy above my head to rapture from the room.

Excerpt from Tri News:

> *A delighted Steven commented: "It's amazing, I am ecstatic. It's been a brilliant season. To find out I was nominated was amazing, and then to be voted on by the triathletes themselves, and to win, is just such an honour."*

Email sent to family and friends:

Over the last year I have got to relate, understand and admire the commitment and enthusiasm these top triathletes have for the sport. Last night I shared the glory with Alistair Brownlee who won Male Triathlete of the Year 2010 and chatted to his brother Jonny which was incredible.

These brothers were massive iconic representatives of triathlon and both achieved World Championship status. Alistair also went on to win the 2012 and 2016 Olympic gold medal in triathlon with his brother gaining bronze and silver respectively. Little did I know then that this wasn't going to be the only time that I would be sharing moments like this with the Brownlee brothers.

What I had learnt from this year was that I was right to believe in myself. By having a goal I could then work towards it. I realised that the clearer the goal then the more focus and dedication I could commit to the pursuit of it. On every race I was learning about triathlon as well as myself. I knew I was still fresh to the sport but with that came untapped potential. Over the next year I had to dig even deeper, explore and question everything even more. I was hungry for new challenges. I was ready and I knew what I wanted. I had a specific goal and I was ready to work towards it.

Just as I had done in the hospital eight years ago, I grabbed a pencil and some paper and started to draw my vision. I'd already experienced the power of being able to see my objective so that I could conceive it, believe it and achieve it. I drew a picture of me running down the final straight of the 2011 Triathlon World Championships. I coloured in the red, white and blue of my GB kit and my arms were aloft in celebration. The picture had a filled grandstand and the detail showed the crowds cheering me on. I drew a big smile on my face as I was crossing the finish line. The picture was my vision, because my goal for the year ahead was to become champion of the world.

CHAPTER 16

True Elite, True Achievement

I compiled a new playlist for the year ahead with the song 'One Vision' by Queen leading the way to wake me up at 5:30am every morning. As I listened to the lyrics while I was waking up my energy and focus became enhanced. One body, one fire, one passion and one ambition for me to proceed on my journey of feeding my need.

I'd had a very successful year in 2010 but at no point had I become complacent. I knew that there were other athletes from around the world in my category that were as fast as me or faster. Due to the variants, conditions and inaccurate distances of the swim, bike and run in other triathlon events it was near impossible to compare the times of other athletes that competed in them. I took the research on my competition with a pinch of salt but it gave me more awareness that I needed to get better, in all aspects. I was hungry for information.

After finally getting accepted onto the GB Paratriathlon performance squad in the new year, I was given a lot of input on what I could do to improve. Jonathon Riall was the newly appointed head coach of the British Triathlon Paratriathlon and worked hard to supply support in all aspects of our journey especially on the training camps. Once again we had the fantastic facilities of Loughborough University at our disposal and were allowed to use them like a playground.

As an elite athlete I was now thinking of everything possible to improve and soaked up the information like a sponge.

What more can I do?
What more can I do?
What more can I do?

I was hungry for input and learning from other athletes but not necessarily being led by them.

On our arrival we were informed of all of the training sessions and workouts planned as well as information and seminars laid on. The hotel was equipped to deal with our dietary needs and there was a bar for us to relax in if we wanted. It was our choice on what we did as well as what we didn't do. I was surprised as I thought it would be similar to a 'fitness camp' that my wife had attended where their timetable was provided for them including when to get up, when to eat and what to eat.

On the training camp it was refreshing mixing with likeminded individuals. We were all driven and committed to our individual goals as well as the overall goal of the Paratriathlon squad and Team GB. We encouraged and supported one another as well as having a laugh and swapping stories. Our hardest task was giving ourselves enough 'down time' so that we could 'go again' on the next session. Nutrition, strength and conditioning as well as mindfulness and personal development were all included and I came away with further tools that I needed to achieve my dream. I was videoed on my swim and then I sat down with the coach who analysed my every movement and gave me an improvement plan.

Being just 'good' at swimming wasn't going to cut it at this level and this was one area that I needed to massively improve on. I realised that I wasn't 'great' at it because I didn't enjoy it and I didn't enjoy it because I wasn't great at it. I needed to break the cycle and knowing that I couldn't force myself to like something, I had to choose 'plan B' which was to improve my swimming and so I needed to take action. It's generally said that it takes 10,000 hours to master something from new. I certainly didn't have 10,000 hours to play with and so instead of counting the hours I had to make the hours count. I realised that it wasn't a case of 'practice makes perfect' but more 'perfect practice makes perfect'. I had to make sure that I was doing the right thing first. Get some input and advice on my technique. Once I had that knowledge then I could go for it, practise practise practise.

Back at Sheffield I registered with a swim-fit class once a week where the instructor Richard Harland gave me specific one-to-one coaching on the various aspects of my performance. On my other swim sessions I coached myself through sets and repetition. Time in the pool wasn't always easy but I needed to make sure that I wasn't leaning on my excuses. I used the free weights in my makeshift gym as well as numerous floor exercises to carry out a multitude of workouts with strict discipline. In the cold early mornings and dark late nights I would build up the strength and conditioning of select muscle groups to optimise my body and enable me to excel in the disciplines of triathlon. I set up a pulley system with rope and some of the lighter weights. I could practise and demonstrate the perfect movement of my arm stroke and reiterate it many times over so as to build up my muscle memory.

I was very happy with Ponds Forge in Sheffield but I knew in my head that if there was an occasion or a reason as to why I couldn't train there then I would be very tempted to lean on that as an excuse. I jumped on the internet and searched out all of the local pools in the area especially

*What more can I do? Swimming with no water before
I hit the weights in my makeshift gym.*

the ones on my route to and from work. I found all of the other facilities, their opening times and equally important whether or not they did lane swimming. There was nothing worse than getting half way through a timed swim set and then having to stop for stray 'width swimmers', chatting with their heads above water and trying to not get their hair wet. Equally I'm sure they weren't keen on me splashing up and down with great ferocity and within close proximity. I think lane swimming was a must for both parties. Once I was equipped with this information then it joined my other stash of 'excuse busters'.

At six o'clock one winter morning, on reaching Ponds Forge the message was relayed that the swimming pool was closed due to boiler issues. I was already prepared for this very occasion and immediately slotted my car into gear and drove out of Sheffield to Graves swimming pool situated on the outskirts of the city. I'd done research on what other pools were available early in the morning and had them ready with my other 'excuse busters'. My spare trunks, goggles and towel sat in my car next to the spare trainers and spare bike helmet. For me to take action I needed to ensure that nothing would get in my way and all items were there as a proactive measure although some were from embarrassing past experiences...like the spare trunks! I parked, paid, changed and dived in to complete my planned training set for the day. At no point had it crossed my mind to drop the session. At no point had I conceded that this situation was out of my hands. Time was precious and I knew that there was no other available slot in the day for the swim to happen. The emergency swimming trunks...well that was a different story altogether.

Through the bleak months of winter my Saturday mornings bizarrely changed to an even earlier start.

I would wrap myself up and by the illumination of my bike lights I would cycle the forty minutes through the darkened countryside to a swimming pool that opened at 7am. Cycling home in the fresh, crisp early hours of the morning after my tough swim set was not for the fainthearted. Those hills never got any easier. I remember one morning as the hot shower massaged my face after my swim set I unconsciously slipped my trunks off and dropped them to the floor. It was only then that I remembered that I was in the communal showers...and these happened to be at the side of the pool. I quickly grabbed my kit and scurried away, clutching to the hope that my flash of inspiration brightened up the day for some of the other early morning swimmers!

To get better at cycling I needed to spend more time in the saddle, it was as simple as that. I couldn't afford or justify spending large amounts of our income on a new bike and so my trusty £450 Specialized road bike was fine. I did buy some second-hand tri bars to give me better aerodynamics but I knew the main way of becoming better was to work on the engine. Once again I needed to make sure that I was doing everything right and so I took up an offer from a physio clinic called Holywell Health who said they could help me. The clinic was set up above the running shop Accelerate where I always bought my trainers due to the expert advice and experience of the owners. In the physio lab Colin Papworth and his assistant set up a session on a Wattbike which monitored my power. I also had sensor pressure pads placed in my shoes to see how my feet worked in collaboration with the power. I was wired up like a lab rat as they walked around me with clipboards and pointed at monitors that were bleeping. From the results they were able to show me by way of a graph how my disability affected my cycling and consequently how to improve through some physio exercises mixed with some strength and conditioning workouts. On top of this there were a few suggestions and adjustments that I needed to do on my cycling style and technique and then I'd be a new and improved cyclist.

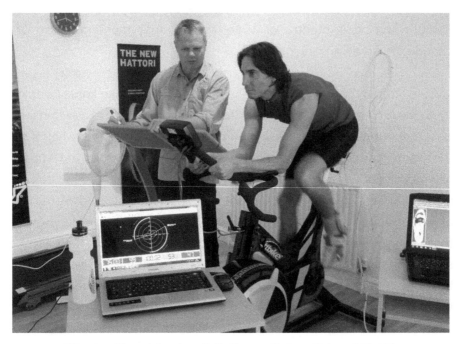

Wired up like a lab rat as Colin Papworth from Holywell Health helps me to find anything and everything to improve.

I needed to take myself out on some long cycle rides using the challenging and technical environment that surrounded me but I didn't have time for this. My time was already stretched to the max during the week and I couldn't get the support to take myself out on a long Sunday bike ride at the weekend. If I could grab two hours then I'd blitz it. If I only had one hour then I'd blitz it even more. Working to a deadline to get home continually pushed me. I didn't have time to appreciate the view or the achievement of the hill climb. I was on the clock, the road behind me had been an annoyance and the road in front was an obstacle. I wasn't looking at miles per hour, I was just looking at the time counting down. I wasn't out here to enjoy myself, I was out here training so that I could become a World Champion. On many an evening with my bike set up on the rollers of the turbo trainer I would sit in the darkness of the garage wearing a woolly hat and numerous layers, beasting myself through a workout. Transfixed on the speed, cadence, miles and pulse as I'd constantly be wiping the dripping sweat off the display screen. The music blasted out through my earphones, drowning out the drone of the wheels turning on the rollers. I cycled in a static state, intensely pedalling towards my goal.

The surroundings don't matter when you're focused on your goal.

Feedback on my running style was difficult as it was near enough a miracle that I was doing it in the first place. The lack of movement and flexibility in both of my feet limited the amount of work and improvement that I could make. Through more tests carried out by Holywell Health they discovered how I could make a slight improvement to my efficiency due to the fact of my drop foot. Wearing a 'foot up' strap on my left ankle would enable my style of running to be more efficient and less energy expended. However, I would have to calculate the time it would take for me to put this on in transition compared to the time I would improve on in the run.

My main improvement would come from building up my endurance and speed. Going down to the track training sessions with the Sheffield Tri Club was incredible. I felt like a true athlete on the track with the stadium lights shining down through the crisp cold air, illuminating the training ground before us. I'd already been swimming in the morning and worked all day plus overtime so that I went straight to the track for 6:30pm. I would start the session with my hat pulled down and my hood up. Fatigued, sombre and silent I would start my session. We all warmed up around the track, waiting for our adrenaline to kick in. As the sessions increased in pace and performance my tiger would yawn, stretch and defiantly wake up. I sprinted round the corners on the heels of the runner in front waiting for the straight. A song from my playlist, 'Explosion' by Eli 'Paperboy' Reed, played out loud in my head. Get ready…get ready…then POWWW! The sessions were like a video game for me but with real life 3D, surround sound and the pulsating adrenaline of true reality. I would change gear and pull down the throttle as I accelerated down the home straight. 'Up on your toes, up on your toes…toes, toes, TOES.' The voice in my head demanded obedience as I lifted my chin up and pumped my arms to power across the white line. I'd gasp for air with sweat now dripping onto the frosty ground. "Keep moving", I'd say to myself, "keep jogging…30 seconds then we're off again…focus…breathe, breathe."

There were times when track training was cancelled due to severe weather and so instead I took myself off to the Sheffield Cemetery. The sleet and snow inhibited my vision but not my progress. The speed and power built up in these wintery sessions gave me confidence and belief. The technique and experience was another tool that I carried with me and one where in an emergency I could 'break the glass' and release the explosion.

My outlook and action had helped me grow in confidence and boldness in all aspects. My injuries may still have been unseen most of the time but

I now had the fortitude to share my story with others if I felt that it would help and inspire them. My dedication pushed me to find opportunities to train at all times and locations. Away with the lads on a cycling weekend in North Yorkshire, I still packed my running kit. I remember running through a forest late at night which echoed with the howls of wolves. I was no expert on whether it was or wasn't a pack of human-hungry carnivores but my imagination and pulse rate encouraged me to pick up the pace and sprint back to the safety of our log cabin. On a family holiday to Egypt I would again squeeze in some sessions wherever best. I either trained early in the morning or in the blistering heat of the day when everybody was having a nap.

The training events of aquathlons and duathlons once again took me through winter and into the spring. Crazy moments imprinted on my mind as I would jump out of the swimming pool, put my trainers on and then complete the run section down the hill and around Rother Valley Country Park. I was soaking wet and dressed in lycra as I passed many walkers who were in full winter attire with hats, gloves and coats traipsing through the thin layer of snow. I heard one such couple say to each other, "Oh...it's ok, they're just one of those triathlon type people." I smiled to myself and thought, 'Yes...yes, I am one of those triathlon type people.' The schedule of events for the year was ideal with the British Championships starting it all off in mid-May. This was followed by the European Championships, the World Championship event in London and then the World Championship Final out in Beijing in September. The year was set and I was ready for it.

Winning the British Champs by four and a half minutes early on in the year had given me a good boost for the start of the busy schedule. The event was held at Holme Pierrepont in Nottingham and the cheering crowds in the grandstand had boosted my efforts on the bike and run. My wife had brought down Susannah and Robert to support me and seeing them wave their little Union Jack flags had boosted my smile. By now I'd got a bit of a reputation from other athletes and supporters so that I always smiled when I ran. This was true for many reasons. I loved the support when I was running and hearing my name shouted out. I still didn't take running for granted and thought about all those lost years. I loved to run and running made me happy and when I was happy I ran with a bounce in my step. The spring in my pace always propelled me forward with speed and agility. Smiling and running went well together.

Although the start lists were getting bigger as the sport of paratriathlon grew, I also saw some of my athlete friends absent. On enquiring where they were I was told that they were injured and unable to compete. My heart sank for them as I knew that they had been working hard on the training and that their goals stretched throughout the year ahead. It was a wake-up call for what I needed to do next. The majority of my training was on getting stronger and faster and building up endurance. I hadn't actually spent that much time on injury prevention. Warming up, warming down, stretching. Injury prevention was boring, time consuming and gave you no visible results at all. But right here, right now I was seeing the results of not doing the work. I realised that no matter how good I was at triathlon, none of it would be any good if I couldn't even get to the start line. Injuries were preventable and seeing as I controlled the amount of time and effort that I put into it, I therefore had the responsibility. I needed to take action and start listening to my body more, implementing exercises, routine and habits to support my wellbeing so that I gave myself the chance to perform at my best.

The picture that I had drawn of myself winning the World Championships was stuck up in my bathroom cupboard so that I saw it every day. It ignited the urge to achieve and gave me the impulse to push on and do anything and everything to make that dream a reality. I got a sponsorship deal from some modelling that I did for Ponds Forge SIV (Sheffield International Venues) and so I now had free access to the gym. I would arrive early before my swim set and participate in various strength and condition exercises as well as stretching. A strong core with solid abs was essential for me in all three disciplines and I invested in numerous exercises as well as a 'wobble cushion' to sit on at work. I introduced some yoga into my routine as well as some tai chi to really be in tune with my mind, body and soul. Although time was tight I would force myself to go to the physio even when everything was ok. A preventative physio maintenance check was carried out so that I could carry on doing what I was doing.

Looking over the village of Eckington as I connect with my inner self. Photo courtesy of Jason Newsome

I travelled with the GB team to Northern Spain, from where we crossed over to the top of Portugal on the north west coast for the European Championships. The city was called Pontevedra and had beautiful well-preserved 14th century Gothic buildings. The team hotel that British Triathlon had organised was situated in the heart of the city, making registration and course recce easily accommodating. The European Championships include the Age Group Teams so the city streets were overrun with fellow triathletes and supporters from the surrounding countries. Age group racing ranges from twenty years old to eighty plus where they can compete representing their country according to their group band. Only the top athletes from each category achieve the accolade of competing against their counterparts at world class level.

I had found a stunning park which was shaded by overhanging trees. With my nerves frantically racing even to the point of making me feel sick, I took myself to the park just hours before our race started. With shaking hands I put my earphones in, selected my playlist and put my shades on. I stood there and breathed in deeply and out slowly looking up at the sky, recognising the fast pace of my heart as the adrenaline pumped round my body. As I performed my yoga routine I stretched my arms up into the air, slowly bringing them down and then out to the sides. I breathed slowly in time with the long stretches as I loosened off my shoulders before stretching them out. After a while I brought my leg up, placing my foot onto my other leg's knee joint and held the 'tree' pose. Arms above my head, I was in a full state of consciousness with my body, feeling myself sway and adjust to balance and stand strong against the elements. I rhythmically moved into positions, feeling my body in unison with itself. The spiritualisation and concentration within this moment enabled me to completely blank out any other thing that may have been detrimental to my focus.

Working through the playlist, it eventually reached specific tunes for particular exercises like 'Hannah's Theme' by The Chemical Brothers with its beautiful mellow music and strong, powerful words. This hit the spot perfectly as I performed some self-taught tai chi to give me inner strength, power and confidence. After a good fifteen minutes I would then sit down on the floor in the 'butterfly' pose and remove the earphones. The surrounding sounds would now enhance the moment of reality as I visualised the whole of the race from start to finish. The realism portrayed caused my heart rate to increase as I envisaged every single minute detail and feeling of the race in its true essence: the swim, bike and run sections of the event as well as the technicalities of the transitions. I covered the whole route of the course with the sound of the crowd and even the wind through my hair. My visualisation would always be positive in every way, resulting in me performing at my best and eventually crossing the finish line to grab the gold medal that was waiting for me. I opened my eyes from my meditative state with a beaming smile across my face. 'That was awesome.' My body felt weightless with euphoria as if I was almost in another state of mind. I casually picked up my gear and headed off to the hustle and bustle of the event.

The temperature reached figures of forty-one degrees and we were sweltering as we waited in line in our black wetsuits. I looked up at the sun which enhanced my energy, power and fulfilment. Through the sweat I still had a smug grin which stood out in a sea of nervous faces. "What are you smiling at?" one of the athletes asked. "I've just done the race," I replied. "It was amazing. I want to do it again." He looked at me like I was 'gone out' but he wasn't the only one. My confidence and aura made the other athletes more nervous, thinking that they had missed out on something important. It was great to see my German friend Sebastian again and we chatted. I still had a score to settle as he had been unable to compete in Hyde Park the previous year. I was ready for the rematch and so right here, right now was where it was going to happen. What I couldn't have anticipated at this point was the disaster just five minutes away that would potentially end my challenge before the race even started.

CHAPTER 17

Achievements and Accolades

"Representing Great Britain…Steve Judge." As I walked onto the wooden pontoon I waved to the many crowds that had gathered to watch and support. My misguided left foot tripped on an uneven wooden plank, and I stumbled and smashed the toes of my right foot into the jetty. As my toes are fixed there's no flexibility at all and a sharp electrifying pain surged through me, forcing me to yelp out. I shook it off as I squinted with the pain and carried on down to the water's edge, limping to my start position. My foot was now throbbing and I cooled it off by placing it in the water. It hurt like hell and one of the officials asked me if I was ok. "I'm fine," I lied, as there was no way anybody was going to pull me out of this race, no way. Due to my ignorance and the adrenaline pumping through my body I never imagined that I could have actually broken my toe.

Coming out of the swim there was a ridiculous 200 metre stretch over to the transition area on a gravel road. With my sensitive feet as well as a broken toe the journey was literally like hobbling on broken glass but with gritted teeth and vocal grunts of agony I eventually arrived at the transition site, albeit shaken up with the exhaustion of pain. Off out on the bike and I was in first place in my category. I grabbed my water bottle and drank the warm energy drink on the parts of the course when I wasn't hanging on for dear life with the gusts of wind coming in from the side. Round the undulating looped bike circuit I could see Sebastian chasing me in second place but couldn't work out if he was catching me. I saw my friend Iain and his guide from the visually impaired category at the side of the road. They were having a mechanical issue with the back wheel of their tandem bike and were out of the race. I later found out that the extreme heat of the day had literally melted the glue that held their tyre rim onto the carbon fibre wheel.

Into T2, I slammed my foot into my trainers which sent a shock reminder of the pain from my toe but I couldn't worry about that now as I set off on the 5K sprint. It was the most amazing route through the city streets with supporters lining the entire way, on the pavement, at the barriers or sat outside the cafés. There was a constant cheer of "GO GB…C'mon Great Britain".

The cheers of "Come on Steve" from supporters and friends from the Sheffield Triathlon Club lifted me up the hills of the undulated streets and encouraged me to lift my knees high as I flew down the spiralling lanes, occasionally looking over my shoulder in search of my rivals, but the twists and turns of the ancient streets hampered my view. I was taking on water as the heat was now soaring and ahead of me I saw my teammate Tom from another category collapse at the side of the road. By the time I reached him there was a huddle of officials pouring water over him to aid his rehydration. As I entered the stadium my heart was frantically beating with excitement. I dug down deep to put on a sprint round the corners of the track but there was nothing there…I was spent. I kept at my constant speed as I saw the finish line approach and punched the air in triumph as I looked to the heavens. I'd done it. Through the extreme elements I had achieved my first official international accolade as European Champion. I'd smashed it and won by two and a half minutes to Sebastian Aversch who won the silver medal and Geoffrey Wersy from France who gained the bronze medal.

As I stood there with the other elite athletes waiting for our medal ceremony I was chatting with Alistair and Jonny Brownlee. Alistair had had a mechanical problem on his bike and had had to change his wheel during the race. His brother had slowed the bike pack down for Alistair to then catch up with them, push through and go on to win the gold medal. At no point had Alistair considered giving up. Anything can happen in triathlon. These brothers were so competitive, so tactical and so caring to one another it was incredible. I stood on the podium with the gold medal round my neck. The British national anthem rang out around the stadium while the Union Jack flew high in the sky. A gust of emotion surged through me, giving me an out-of-body experience as I stood there. My smile quivered and my eyes welled up with emotion as I felt so humbled and extremely proud.

When I limped back to transition to pick up my kit I found that my bike shoes had fallen apart due to the sole glue melting in the heat. Also my personalised wetsuit had been taken from my equipment box and although I looked for it, asked officials and followed up with enquiries it was never found or returned. The competition certainly had been eventful in many respects but we weren't done yet. As I hobbled through the security gates of the Spanish airport the alarm rang out. I rolled my eyes in disbelief as my pockets were empty and my belt had been removed. The security guard scanned me with his mobile detector which buzzed frantically at a lower pocket in my shorts that I don't often use. I suddenly had a moment of realisation. I dug my hand in deeply and pulled out my gold medal which I handed over to the officer. He looked at it and then called out to his colleagues as he lifted it high and pointed at me, saying "European champion". Everybody around me cheered and clapped as I acknowledged their appreciation. Yes it had been an eventful trip, but I had the gold medal and I was bringing it home.

Sadly things weren't quite as well appreciated on my return.

My life was busy with many things and it was all about priorities and balance. My job, my wife, the kids, eating and sleeping and of course triathlon. My mindset was very much 'When shall I train tomorrow?' not 'Is there time for me to train tomorrow?' Special dates of the year like birthdays and anniversaries were still highlighted on the calendar but they were not distinguished from training days. It was always a case of thinking how I could do things rather than how I couldn't do things. I would then always work out how I could squeeze in the training within the day so that it didn't impact any of the other requirements that were important to me. This resulted in early mornings or late nights or sacrificing my lunch time. With only twenty-four hours in the day I worked out that spending one or two of those hours on training was ok but what I didn't consider was where my head was at for the rest of the time. I justified to myself more than anyone that my time was split evenly but I never really took into consideration where my focus was and consequently my priorities.

I needed to show my wife that I cared about her and that she was important to me rather than just slotting her into my daily schedule at the allocated time. I needed to let her know more often that she was wanted and that she was loved. Sadly in our arguments this message never came across. I was dedicated to my marriage as well as being committed to my endeavours in triathlon, rather than being obsessed with it, as she would say. I had finally found something that was feeding my need, where my tiger could be uncaged causing the fire in me to burn brightly. The once-in-a-lifetime opportunities enticed me to grab hold of them with both hands and do something with them.

My wife worked three days a week and I worked full time but I was conscious that triathlon was still a hobby and therefore didn't justify me spending lots of money on it. Following my win in Europe and encouragement from others, I started putting the feelers out for sponsorship. "You're bound to get sponsorship now Steve," they would say. "Why not ask the company where you work, that would be a start?"

And they were right. A lot of the other athletes were being helped and supported by their employees so that prospect looked promising. Writing the 'begging letters' was something that I had never done before and I didn't have a clue how to word them or who to address them to. My main pitfall in completing this task was that the time I spent doing it now impacted on the time I could spend on other things...like actual training. 'Do I go out on my bike tonight or do I sit at my desk and beg for some new racing wheels?'

What I really wanted was time and no one could give this to me. It wasn't just during the week but it was also my holiday allocation that was having an impact. With about four weeks' holiday a year I would have to almost split them 50/50 between family holidays and international competition and training but then I came up with a cunning plan. If I could find an 'athlete grant' or some money through sponsorship then maybe I could afford to take unpaid leave or even buy some extra holidays. I prepared my proposal and in my next one-to-one meeting I took a deep breath and asked. They may have had a request to take time off with no pay before but I don't think they'd ever had a request to actually buy holidays. The request needed to be run through HR along with any consideration for sponsorship in any way, shape or form. I was pleased that I had asked and so for me I had no regrets about it. A day or two later the response came back as a 'no'. The company had a strict equality policy and so every employee had to be treated the same and equally. They were unable to make any allowance for sponsorship proposals for an individual and I could not take unpaid leave or even buy extra days off. "No regrets" I said to myself; at least I had asked.

Back home my letters asking for sponsorship had equally negative results and I ended up buying some second-hand cycling shoes off a mate at the triathlon club and a 'last year' model wetsuit that was on sale. I noticed the size on my new wetsuit and it suddenly hit me how much I had 'leaned up' over the last couple of years. Losing about a stone in weight had also become apparent when I had been swimming in the cold open water and I felt how loose my wedding ring had become. 'High elbow, kick legs and keep my fingers tight together so that my ring doesn't fall off.' I'd never taken my wedding band off. The ring itself stands for eternal and long-lasting commitment to one another. It was a symbol of devotion and an agreement between the two of us through our wedding vows. To love and cherish each other for the rest of our days. I took my ring into the jewellers' and for the first time my ring was removed and the band was severed. The ring was altered before it was joined and sealed back together. It was handed back to me where I once again placed it on my finger in its new form.

We had a lovely family holiday in North Wales, taking advantage of the beautiful surroundings on the bikes. Swimming in the sea with my kids was fun as were picnics next to the lakes where we could relax and paddle. I would stay in the valley for some flattish runs and use the natural beauty to get some epic hill training in on the bike. I would cycle up to the fresh tarns for some swimming before doing my yoga and tai chi at the edge. Looking out on the vista was powerful in its spiritual sense with pure inner tranquillity. I was in a good place.

Not leaning on my excuses. Mountains are there to be conquered.

Next up was the World Championship event in Hyde Park. Once again an amazing festival of triathlon where my supportive family came to watch and cheer me on. I even had my mum as my 'transition buddy', standing next to my kit in the heat of the action, which she was extremely proud and excited about. I had a special request for my supporters which was for them to take photos of other athletes as well as me. Finding decent action photos from the event was always a challenge so I thought it would be nice to have some to give to the other athletes. Matching the photos up with the various athletes and passing them on to them turned out to be a bigger job than I had anticipated but it was worth it. I also collected and handed out some of the special commemorative 2012 Olympic fifty pence pieces which had a montage of the three sports that make up triathlon on them, as I thought this would be a nice gift for foreign athletes. Entries were high for the event and once again my category had increased in size with unknown competitors.

The sport of paratriathlon was still fairly new and therefore it was not a registered sport for the London 2012 Paralympics, which was a great shame. However, due to the popularity and growth of the sport there was now an almost certainty that paratriathlon would be included in the Paralympics of 2016.

For me, my focus was on the here and now and the race ahead of me. I had a powerful swim and although I came out of the water in first place, the South African Chris Wagner and James Smith were literally seconds behind me. Through transition and onto the six laps of Hyde Park on my bike. Lap counting was more difficult than I'd initially anticipated, especially when I was in the heat of the moment. When counting the number of laps some athletes used six pieces of tape on their bike or six rubber bands on their arms that they would move or pass over. I had trained and practised an ongoing mantra running inside my head: 'I've done four laps I'm now on my fifth; I've done four laps I'm now on my fifth. I've done five laps I'm now on my sixth; I've done five laps I'm now on my sixth.' This worked for me and so I stuck with it.

Off the bike…after exactly six laps and I sprinted off on the run. My broad shoulders powered me round the course with my head held high. 'Keep focused Steve and this race is ours.' But then shock and confusion struck. I couldn't believe it. As I looked straight ahead a flush of nerves hit me in the stomach. My thoughts of winning were dashed. I was about half way round the course and my eyes focused on the athlete up ahead that I could see. I shook my head. 'Focus, focus!' I looked again…it was! Ahead of me was the South African Chris Wagner. I was baffled and perplexed. But how…? I struggled to pull my thoughts together on top of the adrenaline rush. He hadn't overtaken me on the bike so maybe he only did five laps. Maybe no one knows that he only did five laps or maybe he overtook me through transition? I couldn't make any sense of it and the thoughts were rushing through my head until I managed to quash them. "It doesn't matter!" I said to myself. "What matters is here and now." And I knew exactly what to do. I had practised this many times in my training and rehearsed it in my visualisation.

The playlist in my head selected the tune of 'Thunderstruck' by AC/DC. As the beating chorus reached its pinnacle I gradually crept up on Chris in stealth mode, ensuring that my feet weren't making too much noise. My lungs pumped oxygen around my body as I rested behind him and caught my breath. Then like a clap of thunder I dug in deep and accelerated at full throttle, overtaking him and pushing onwards to get some distance. I heard his pace quicken but his grunts also became louder and I knew he couldn't keep up. I was in control and he had just been…'Thunderstruck'.

I left him in my wake just as in my visualisation and now with one kilometre to go I was ready to expend all reserved energy. Sprinting down the final finishing straight I once again grabbed the Union Jack from my brother Bruce. The crowd cheered and my family waved as I punched the air in triumph and crossed the finish line in glory.

It transpired that Chris had mistakenly only counted five laps of the course and was consequently disqualified. This resulted in Sebastian winning second place four minutes after me and James in third place. I'd always said "anything can happen in triathlon". For me, it was about controlling as many of those variables as possible and preparing myself for the other ones. It was an awesome result and a fantastic confirmation for the next race on the calendar. Arguably this was the biggest race of my life. China, Beijing, representing Great Britain against the rest of the globe in the World Championship Final. New experiences, new challenges and I had everything to play for and a lot to prove.

Chatting, drinking and even dancing until the early hours of the morning...perfect! Celebrating Bruce's 40th birthday in the Derbyshire Dales with champagne round a fire.

CHAPTER 18

To Conquer a Dream

I travelled down to Loughborough for a team training weekend while my wife took the kids to the Lake District with her dad. It was an extremely useful weekend, honing in on our disciplines and technicalities as well as preparing us for the World Champs in China. It was constantly stressed to us how important cleanliness was in a foreign country and we were instructed to carry hand sanitiser and be aware and mindful at all times. Diet and nutrition were highlighted and regular tests would be carried out on us to monitor our hydration levels in the humid environment. Jonathon Riall was thinking about every single thing possible that would help us to be at our best and stay at our best so we could perform at our best. With Jonathon and his British Triathlon Federation (BTF) team we were going into the event with the preparation and confidence of true elite athletes.

Due to my time constraints with work I caught a later flight than the rest of the squad. Arriving in Beijing on the Wednesday, I joined the rest of the GB team at our hotel. I dropped my bags off and went straight out with the squad for registration and race briefing. There were disabled athletes from all over the world but I was on the lookout for my competitors. I had done as much research on them as I could possibly do but I still wanted to meet them in the flesh. James introduced me to the USA athlete David Kyle who was a main competitor for our category title following past race performances. I introduced myself and we chatted about training and race preparation but neither of us gave anything away. At the end I said, "Well, nice to have met you David, and good luck for the race." David replied, "Yeah…likewise…erm, sorry, what was your name?" "Steve, Steve Judge," I replied as we shook hands. I was perplexed but I suppose not every athlete prepares in the same way. I had spent the last couple of weeks using the internet to carry out research on all of the athletes that were registered in my category. I knew their race results, their splits, and their strongest disciplines. I knew where I had to be in relation to them at each part in the race. From their photos I had included them in my visualisation of the event mixed with footage of the course itself. I knew everything about them, their strengths and their weaknesses and how I was going to beat them.

Back at my hotel room I started assembling my bike from its travel bag. I had been very apprehensive about dismantling my bike and transporting it half way round the world but it had arrived safely and with no damage. Assembling it should have been the easy part, or so I thought. As an engineer I was very methodical about the process. As I was screwing in the rear derailleur I was very careful not to 'cross thread' the bolt and although it was stiff I kept winding it back and forth and proceeded with caution as I put more force and effort into it. Something didn't seem right and I stopped. I checked everything and then I saw the problem. Shit! … Shit shit shit! The bolt was fine but as I'd been concentrating on screwing it in I had been slowly bending part of the metal frame. With my heart racing I frantically looked through the limited tools I had brought with me and worked out how I could sort it out. My hands were shaking as

I thought about the overall consequences of my actions in relation to the race.

I managed to remove part of the gearing system to expose the damaged part and sat on the floor in my room constantly looking up to the ceiling to compose myself with long breaths before I tried again. I was desperately trying to straighten part of the derailleur system that held a very tight spring. Palpitations were now pulsing through me. I knew my efforts were futile and eventually the tears ran down my face. "You IDIOT!" I screamed, "you flipping idiot", as I slammed the floor with my fist. I couldn't do it with the tools I had and I needed another pair of hands.

I don't know what upset me the most, the fact that my chances of competing in the World Championship were now in jeopardy or the fact that I was going to have to ask for help. Probably all of the above but I wiped my eyes, took a deep breath, grabbed my bike frame and set out for help. I found Steven Paley who was a coach working on one of the wheelchairs, and with some extra tools and a much needed extra pair of hands we managed to get the whole thing sorted. The relief for me was overwhelming and I thanked him profusely for his assistance. I've always liked Steves. I went back to my room and collapsed on the bed with exhaustion from the turmoil and thanked my lucky stars for the resolution. Little did I know that that wasn't going to be the only 'mechanical' issue that I would encounter and that the next one would be during the actual race.

The course recce went smoothly. I checked out the swim and where to 'sight' with the buoys and then went out on the bike course which was a two lap circuit of the reservoir. The course tied in with the video that I had been watching that was posted on the internet. I worked out where to take on water and what gearing to use; this information would help me with my visualisation and on the race day itself. Friday was race day and I took myself off to the beautiful Chinese gardens of the hotel to carry out my pre-race routine. My carefully selected playlist including the uplifting tune of 'Only If' by Enya. The words reiterated to me that

I can find the positive in any negative and that I can turn adversities into opportunities. Completely relaxed, focused, pumped and happy, I opened my eyes and was ready to compete.

As a team we arrived, set up our transition areas, got ready and then lined up in front of the grandstand while they called out our names. "Representing Great Britain…Steve Judge."

This was it, this was my time and this was everything that I had been working towards. The honour, excitement and prestige of representing my country in the World Championships. I stood there, tall and proud with absolutely no regrets and then lowered myself into the water ready for the start. The horn sounded and a massive horde of swimmers set off, all aiming for the one target buoy ahead of us. Arms and legs and feet all thrashing furiously. My swim was strong and I managed to get into a steady and durable rhythm. Out of the swim and I was leading in my category against the rest of the world. Efficiently through the transition, I jumped on my bike and took the steep gradient down away from the reservoir before I hit the exterior ring road. As I reached the bottom of the slope I turned my handlebars but disaster struck as my wheel didn't turn! "What the…?"

I was heading for the barrier and had to lean into the corner to force my bike round so as not to crash. As I straightened up I assessed the situation and, looking down at my front wheel, saw that it was straight but my handlebars were at an angle. 'Shit!… That's not good,' I thought. My brain quickly calculated what to do as my legs continued to power me forward. 'Can I cycle like this for the next twenty kilometres?' A quick thought process which came up with the answer, 'No way, too dangerous, too slow and might get worse'. Before I knew what was happening my instincts had kicked in and my anger screeched my bike to a stop.

Hopefully the Chinese crowd in front of me didn't understood the vile words that were coming out of my mouth but they would have got the gist that I was not pleased with the situation. Now, for some reason unbeknown to me even to this day, I had left my toolkit under the seat of my bike. This is unheard of, ridiculous and a crazy thing to do because when I'm in a race I don't have time to tinker about with mechanics but lo and behold, there it was. As I repeatedly muttered expletives the Chinese crowd looked on in bewilderment while I unzipped my saddle bag and took out the Allen keys. Selecting the tool I got to the front of the bike as cyclists were whizzing by me at breakneck speed. I clasped the wheel between my legs and twisted the handlebars straight and with a quick twist of my wrist it was tight, job done. I was just about to throw the tool into the bush and get on with the race and then I suddenly thought to myself 'I might need this later' and quick as I could I popped it into my saddle bag, zipped up, jumped on my bike and pushed off.

The anger and frustration alone powered me up the next hill, leaving my lungs raw although that could also have been from all the shouting that I'd done! I settled into my race pace but I had no idea what position I was in with regards my category. With my heart beating fast and at times just hanging on for dear life round the corners and slopes, I found it hard to focus on the other athletes and work out what category they were in. I was desperately trying to work out how many arms and legs the athlete in front of me had so as to establish if I should chase them or leave them. My speed was good and knowing the course inside out gave me reassurance. I took on plenty of fluids so when I arrived at T2 I was feeling good, hydrated and ready for the final assault.

I swept into the transition and straight to my area where all my kit was laid out. Bike racked, helmet off, I sat on the ground, left shoe off, trainer on, right shoe off, trainer on. I then went to grab my 'foot up' strap for my left 'drop foot'…and…it wasn't there!!! What the hell!!! Literally hours of me practising in my garden day in day out, making sure that I carried out the most slick and efficient transition and just when it counts most my equipment isn't even there. "Where's my fu@#ing 'foot up'?" I screamed as I scrabbled about rooting around in my box of equipment. I was later told two things:

1. The officials had told my transition buddy to keep the transition area tidy and so in her wisdom she had placed my 'foot up' strap into the equipment box.

2. The GB coaches and helpers told me that that was the first time they had ever heard me swear and they were quite shocked!

My conclusion from the situation was to never use a transition buddy ever again.

I found my piece of kit, strapped it on, clipped it to the trainer and then dashed off with the anger blowing steam out of my head like a locomotive. The positive I took from T2 was that I was still in first place. Despite the problems that I'd had to deal with I was going into the 5K run leading my category. I knew that on the run our times were all pretty equal and set off on the lapped circuit with inner confidence. With the repetitive linear loops I could see my competitors. James Smith, Geoffrey Wersy from France and David Kyle were all chasing me down but I was flying. My strides were long as I synced them in unison with my arms. My chin was up as my tiger galloped along the next to me, the fire glowing from deep within.

After four and a half Ks I came around the final corner and the crowd was going crazy. "Go GB!!!" the crowd screamed. "Come on Great Britain!" "Come on Steeeve." I allowed myself to smile to lift me up, but then got back to taking on oxygen to fuel my body and then looking up ahead of me was my goal. What I had been specifically working towards for the past twelve months. The finish line was 200 metres away and as my sturdy legs carried me closer and closer to the end of this ordeal my stomach tightened up with nerves. Adrenaline and autopilot kicked in as I approached the line and punched the air in triumph. I had done it! I crossed the line with both fists raised. I turned to the grandstand and repeatedly punched the air with clenched fists as a salute to the respect and support they had given me. I had done it. I was champion of the world by a clear two and a half minutes in front of James and followed up by Geoffrey.

I later found out that as my race had been livestreamed my supporters back in the UK had been joined in unity. My brother, sister and mum as well as my wife and even someone from work had logged on to watch my progress and post messages of support and congratulations. Finding this out was just as emotional as seeing the Union Jack being hoisted in my honour and once again hearing my national anthem played. My smile beaming from ear to ear, wearing my GB kit and the gold medal round my neck. I'd reached the pinnacle of my endeavours and proven now to the world what was possible. I'd had my share of troubles along

"Get in!" That feeling of absolute euphoria as I achieve my goal that I strived for: Tri 3 Champion of the World, Beijing, China, World Championships 2011. Photo courtesy of British Triathlon Federation

the way but now that didn't matter. Sure I would learn from my stupid mistakes but at the moment it was time to celebrate. We went back to the hotel where I feasted on two main meals and some beers to wash it down.

The next day was Saturday and before I left for home I had one more goal that I needed to complete. Dropped off at the lower car park, I started my torturous trek up the Great Wall of China. With my injuries screaming out in pain I used the banisters and the rope to aid myself up the drastic incline of the structure. After a good hour of climbing I reached the summit and took in the epic scenes that surrounded me. Reaching up I touched my Go-en that was secure round my neck and reflected on my rocky journey that had brought me there. I was a long way from the China Wall in the outback of Australia but I had certainly heeded Taka's advice when he had given me my gift. I had certainly been aware of my vision and had seized opportunities.

Back at the hotel I promptly packed my bags and grabbed a shuttle bus to the airport. Once again I left the rest of the GB team and travelled on my own as I had to be back in Sheffield ready for work on the Monday morning. I travelled for twenty hours straight to get home on Sunday afternoon in time to share my stories of adventure with the kids before I tucked them up in bed. At work I shared my success with those that wanted to know but otherwise it was very much just another day at the office.

It had been a very busy year and now I enjoyed catching up with family and friends while still keeping my fitness ticking over, which included the sporting event at Sherwood Pines with the family. I completed the gruelling duathlon event and my wife took part in the 5K women's race. My son did the 3K run and my brother did the 10K cross-country race…and won. It was a fantastic day of solidarity, fun and achievement. I thought that I had done well over the last twelve months with the balancing of my schedule between all of the things that were important to me but I was wrong.

Sheffield Triathlon Club were themselves celebrating 25 years and I was completely surprised to win the 'Outstanding Athlete of the Year' award. It was a true honour to receive this from such a great club that I have so much admiration for. Once again from the votes cast by fellow triathletes I was super-proud to win Male Paratriathlete of the Year Award at the prestigious British Triathlon Awards night.

I was privileged to be interviewed by various newspapers and triathlon magazines and loved the accolade that I had achieved.

In nearly all the interviews the ultimate question was; "And so Steve, what's next? What's your next goal?" I would tell them that I was on the 'road to Rio' and I wanted to be a Paralympian Champion but actually this was far from the truth. I was completely driven to have the sport of paratriathlon confirmed in the 2016 Paralympics but not so much for me to be included in the games. I'd loved the fitness, competition and personal achievement of being an elite athlete but I'd also found out how difficult it was. The prospect of continuing at this level for the next five years seemed almost daunting.

My wife supported me with her attendance at events and the various awards nights and yet depicted herself to others as a 'triathlon widow'. At the time I remember being agitated and annoyed at the negative connotation of the phrase. Now when I look back I recognise that it was really important to her that I spend time with her and so for her my absence may well have felt like a loss and grieving. I assumed she was like me: when left with time on my own, I simply find something to do. I lacked awareness of how differently we experienced the same thing.

My wife and my family cared about me and I didn't want to hurt them through my actions. They had seen me putting myself through extreme pain throughout my rehabilitation to achieve my goals and now they were witnessing it again. The time, commitment and dedication that I put myself through was exhausting and all consequences had to be considered. The pain that I suffered and endured as a result of some of my training sessions brought reality to my foresight. For all of these reasons I would not commit myself to the goal of the Paralympics, however I still saw opportunities that I wanted to seize. I was 38 years old now and I was taking it year by year. The goal that I was truly passionate about was becoming World Champion in 2012, this time in New Zealand.

I had come so far on my journey and it was important that I thanked the people who had helped me along the way. As I drove out to the Northern General Hospital on the outskirts of Sheffield it brought back many memories. I sat outside Simon Royston's office for nearly two and a half hours waiting for him to return from his hospital rounds so that I could grab ten minutes to chat to him. Finally I was able to thank him properly and express clearly what he had enabled me to achieve in my life. His nonchalant attitude didn't give much away but he did divulge that he had seen something within me in those early weeks in hospital.

"A fighter," he said. "We could see that you were someone that wasn't going to give up, no matter what we threw at you."

My attitude and commitment to my rehabilitation goals is what gave him, his team and the other practitioners the confidence to push me beyond expected boundaries. He said that without my positive outlook and dedication to the situation in hand the outcome could have been very different. Not only might I never have walked again but there was a compelling possibility early on that I might not have even survived. I joked with him that it was in my blood to have that outlook as I reminded him of my blood type: B+ (B *positive*). We shook hands and agreed that it was 'team work'.

I was so proud to have finally shared my accomplishments with Simon but for me I wasn't done yet on my journey. I was far from finished on the goals that lay out in front of me. I'd had a good win in Beijing but the messages from my rehabilitation phase reminded me that this wasn't acceptable: 'Complacency is an excuse for giving in'. I knew that there was still room for improvement with regards my kit and from me as an athlete. I had more to give and more to prove. I knew I could excel even more to be the best that I could be. For me, I was just getting started.

My focus once again was very much on me and what I endeavoured to achieve. I was seeing opportunities and grabbing them but in my blindness I lost sight of what I already had and of what I might lose. Among all of the goals and sub-goals that I set myself to accomplish, at no point had I considered the imperative goal that I had shunned but was now awakened to. This was to be the hardest and emotionally the most challenging goal. This was the goal of saving my marriage.

CHAPTER 19

A Tough Year

With the curtains drawn and having had the conversation that we needed help, I typed the words 'Marriage Counsellor' into the internet search engine. I felt that I had crossed over the line of taboo and just typing in those words meant that I was admitting how bad our situation was. I felt that it was maybe a sign of weakness or failure and had the niggling thought that surely only Americans had counsellors or therapists? And yet our arguments had escalated and our attempts at sorting things out ourselves were futile; we needed a referee.

I fully appreciate there are always two sides to every story and I know the power of the mind and equally how our imagination and memory can distort reality. So the following descriptions of events are from diary notes that I kept through this period as well as how it felt to me and how I recall the experience. And it might well be that my wife's version of events is very different and that's fine.

Driving to our sessions on the cold dark evenings caused me to shiver, or maybe that was the fear of the approaching conflict. My wife would enter the building first as I limped behind. The hour-long sessions were never long enough as our discussions always ran over. For me as the bell rang for 'time out' I was left emotionally exhausted. I would book the session for the next week and then catch my wife up before we drove home with only the sound of the windscreen wipers breaking the silence.

I just wanted to be happy again and although I was repeatedly informed that happiness is a 'byproduct', this need is what drove me forward.

Our overall goal was to keep the marriage together, for us and for the kids. I was left feeling like it was just me that had to change, but deep down I knew it was about both of us needing to learn to communicate in a new way. The difficulty was that we were set tasks that required both of us to action and for the first time I could not control the results by my actions alone.

The accident had been ten years ago and it had put a massive strain on our relationship but also the changes that come from starting a family were impacting how we worked together as a couple. We now had new responsibilities, interrupted sleep, and there was the fact that my wife had also changed roles at work and it was especially stressful. We were all experiencing change and we hadn't found a way to navigate this new territory together. I was aware of what I considered to be my responsibilities and the things I needed to do and be. To support my wife and family I would schedule them very carefully into my plan. I also saw the importance of having my own space and allocating time for me to work towards my objectives within the sport of triathlon. The only support I needed was freedom to get on with it. I didn't need anything physically done for me. But now I could see how things had become so bad and so I wanted us to work on joint goals together as well as having our own separate goals throughout the year.

As my wife was working part time she started doing a range of activities for herself including a creative writing course and becoming a cycling group leader. On various Sundays throughout the year she was out on her bike and I supported her by way of dropping her off and picking her up when she completed some long cycle challenges. She also went away on some more fitness bootcamps and she took part in some charity walks.

But we still didn't see eye to eye on our 'down time'. I didn't have the desire or the time to relax and watch television every night. She described it as time to wind down and I didn't want or need that time but what I overlooked was the fact that it was more than that. By not sitting watching TV I was actually missing out on time together that was important to our relationship.

I wanted us to be open and have shared goals and achieve together. I didn't want any jealousy or disinterest to come between us. I wanted to share results, victory and achievements. I wanted us to give each other support, time and help...

Thoughts, Feelings and Reflections
2012: Our Journey Together

If I growl like a tiger there's a pussy cat inside me
If I look like a stranger this friend won't agree
If your life is a tempest the sun will shine through
If you believe this mad athlete is fighting for you

Our hearts can be mended this we all know
The long stormy journey may be uncomfortable and slow
So tune up your bike, get ready to ride
Into the black water, swim through that strong tide

When we start to look back at the progress we've made
The miles put behind us will simmer and fade
As the wound is closed the bond must be strong
The bone must not weaken for both our lives long

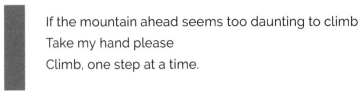

If the mountain ahead seems too daunting to climb
Take my hand please
Climb, one step at a time.

Searching for sponsorship continued to be a hard graft but it was what I needed to support me in my quest. 2012 was the year that the Olympics and Paralympics were being held in the city of London. There was a lot of hype about sport and everything associated with it throughout the country. At a works function I'd found myself talking to the owner of the company where I worked. He was a keen sportsman and was astounded and hugely intrigued at my journey and what I had achieved. He had no idea that an employee of his had such accolades and as a shrewd businessman encouraged me to put some kind of sponsorship request together. I struck while the iron was hot and by the Monday morning I had emailed over some information and proposals. I stipulated how I could help the company through sponsorship by use of branded logos and marketing and equally how the business could help me towards my goals in representing Great Britain. I was confident and eagerly awaited the response, only to get the same reply as the last time. The company had an equality policy and no individual could be treated any different from any others.

I had been more optimistic this time but once again I shrugged my shoulders and shook my head with no regrets. I had grabbed the opportunity and done my best but it just wasn't to be. I felt that there was a lack of acknowledgement from certain areas. I'd wanted people to learn and understand. It was about feeling more than just a number. It was about being appreciated for who I was as well as what I do. I carried on with my secret training with my curious odour of chlorine in the mornings and doing my 'Clark Kent' performance at lunch time within my changing cubicle, at other times arriving early to work in my skintight lycra and covertly hiding my bike behind the A4 boxes of paper in the stationery cupboard.

I'd reached the position as an athlete where I needed to upgrade my bike. I needed it to increase my speed and efficiency but also, I will openly admit, I needed it to reduce my embarrassment. Turning up at events where everyone else had bikes that looked like they had been designed by NASA just put my bike to shame. Pushing with the sponsorship once again, I eventually managed to get a £600 grant from Charities Aid Foundation (CAF) which went towards my new bike from Planet X who gave me a 30% discount on a Stealth carbon fibre time trial bike. It was as light as a feather with a high technical spec and looked like a beast. It was perfect.

My athlete friend Paul Thomas said that with the two handlebars sticking out the front of the bike it looked like a bull. I named my bike 'Taurus' which is also my star sign. I'd never named my bike before but apparently it's an acceptable thing. Naming the bike seemed the right thing to do because I needed to get close to it, treat it with respect and look after it. I needed to be 'at one' with it. As I perched myself on top of the high seat and wrapped my body round the frame, hugging the front aero bars, I would say "We are Minotaur", bonded as the head of a bull and the body of a man. This may sound a little bit cringeworthy and almost a tad embarrassing but I was in a different world with all of this. Doing this was connecting me with my spiritual side and if that's what I needed to do, if that's what would help me towards my goal, then I was willing to give it a shot.

Our relationship was not always so connected. The first time I took Taurus out I learned of his power. After twenty minutes on our maiden voyage we started on a decline and the speed picked up. In the 'tuck' position with my arms outstretched for aerodynamics there were no brakes! "What the..?" NO BRAKES! Speed was picking up. I looked down at the super-thin wheels bouncing on the rough surface. I watched the road ahead speed towards me with its potholes. Teeth clenched, I was hanging on for dear life. As wind gusted in from the right it swayed us into the kerb. The huge aero rimmed wheels were acting like a sail on a boat. I counterbalanced the movement with my heart in my mouth. My hands gripped the beast's horns. I was in too much fear to let go and move my hand over to where the brakes were. With momentum thrusting me down the hill I needed to take action and so I took a deep breath. My hands let go and moved over to where the brakes were and I squeezed them, pulling back on Taurus, and managed to stabilise us. As I controlled the speed we slowed down although my heart was still racing off the chart. "Shit, shit, shit…what the hell?" I said to myself. Still fighting against the sidewind, we got down into the valley and I caught my breath. It had scared the living daylights out of me and I was shaking all over. "What have I bought? Wh…what is this thing?"

I was exhausted, sweating from fear and distraught about my purchase. As we continued slowly on our journey home my brain whizzed through scenarios. What to do? What to do? It wasn't like a wild stallion that could be tamed by me; it was more like a buckaroo that I had to learn how to ride. I was going to have to adapt to the new bike. I needed to get used to it, know it, bond with it and use it. I had the European Championships coming up in two weeks and so I made a pact to myself to go on the bike every day leading up to the event, even if it was just for five minutes. The bike had so much potential and I needed to work out how to use it. It certainly was a beast and clearly had speed due to its efficiency and on top of that…it looked absolutely awesome, job done.

For once sponsorship came to me in the form of Lynwen and Rachel who had been watching my progress in the sport and were keen for me to try their high protein smoothie called 'NouriSH me now'. Throughout my regime I have always kept things very basic and very natural. The secret of my diet as a World Champion has always come down to a lot of common sense with a balanced diet. Potatoes, pasta, rice – carbohydrates for energy. Vegetables and fruit for vitamins. Meat, eggs and fish – protein for muscles. All washed down with litres of water. I was unsure about some of the sports drinks or supplements that were on offer due to possible hidden ingredients as well as cost. After some quick research on the internet I used to make my own every morning with water, a dash of cordial and then I ground some salt into it. The taste was just as bad as the real stuff but it did the job and at a fraction of the expense. I do remember one morning in a sleepy phase I ground the 'salt' into the drink and then realised that I was holding the pepper grinder! "Bother!" I smiled to myself, shrugged my shoulders, applied the salt and just hoped that I wouldn't be sneezing during my swim set that morning.

The active nutrition drink that the ladies produced themselves was very natural in all ways and I approved. The taste was delicious and its contents were natural, healthy and beneficial for muscle repair and performance. The drinks quickly replaced my milkshake and hard-boiled eggs that I used to have after swimming which also meant that I didn't fart so much in the office and that was good for everyone. 'NouriSH me now' became one of my sponsors and supplied me with all the drinks that I needed for my busy training schedule but more than that. Lynwen and Rachel supported me as a person throughout the rest of the season and beyond which meant a lot to me.

My dedication to training continued and one lunch time I even ended up going for a run with two left footed trainers. I knew that it was my only chance of a run that day and my own stupidity of packing the wrong trainers was not going to stop me. That night I added an old pair of trainers to my 'excuse busters' pack in the back of my car…just in case this ever happened again.

My work involved me travelling around the UK visiting construction sites which meant an early start. When I did get home from work I wanted to be with the family and I found it ever so tough to drag myself out of the house again. Sometimes to eradicate this and be more efficient, I would pack my running gear into my car at the beginning of the day. As I pulled off the motorway after a long day I would stop off at the park not far from home, change in the car park and go for a quick run. Then I knew that when I was home, I was 'home' and I'd have time to play with the kids and put them to bed.

There were other times when it was necessary for me to work away and stay overnight in a hotel. I would always search out run routes from the hotel or where the nearest swimming pool was and check out the lane swimming times. Sometimes I would even take my bike with me and set up the static turbo trainer in the hotel room. I'm sure the other hotel residents were dumbfounded at what on earth the droning, whirring sound coming from my room was.

I was always conscious about getting my training in and not leaning on any excuses that presented themselves to me. I would see tough scenarios as a challenge and rise to them. 'So how on earth CAN I do this?' Last resort training sessions usually meant planning in a super early morning run along the illuminated pathways, yawning as I urged my body to wake up in the cold morning air. Then I'd be happy in the knowledge that I had done something to work towards my goal and wouldn't be guilt ridden.

Saturday mornings I always had an early training session with cycling, swimming and running but it was the Friday nights where I had a battle going on inside my head. While watching Robert at his swimming lesson from the balcony I would do my stretches and 'dry land' warm-up exercises ready for my 'Masters' swim group which started at nine o'clock. It was a rush taking him home, helping him get ready for bed and tucking him up with a goodnight kiss before grabbing my bag and heading back to the same pool for my swim session. There were times when I was shattered after a long week and I would fight the voices in my head. The line between right and reason became very blurred at times. 'You get what you give!' was the instruction from one of the voices inside my head and I knew that once I got started the adrenaline would pump through my body and help me survive the punishing hour set. 'Listen to your body' was the calming voice of reason that I had to learn to tune into and interpret. I was fatigued and needed to rest or else there would be consequences. The words from the Linkin Park song 'Papercut' clearly reiterated my feelings. With the heated debate from the voices inside my head, I had to decide which one I was going to listen and adhere to but ultimately which one would control me so that I had no regrets.

Training became an escapism for me where I could go into my own little world. I used the workouts to drag myself away from the unhappiness in my life and push myself to achieve. Here, I couldn't be hurt; I was in the zone and I was protected by it. My visualisation technique was so strong that I could take myself out from where I was and into the mindset of where I wanted to be.

For me it was my 'time out'. Sitting on the rowing machine in the darkness as the torchlight shone on the screen of figures clocking my progress, I would stare into the dimly lit mirror in front of me and see a man dedicated and committed on a mission to achieve. There was fire in my eyes as I beasted my body through the barriers of pain. I had an extremely high pulse rate of 191 beats per minute. An equally high score of 19 on the 'Borg Scale' which measures perceived exertion meant I was just one point off nearly dead. I was really digging in deep, just short of passing out. I wanted this…no…I needed this.

I continuously pushed myself beyond my threshold. I used the endorphin release as a drug to rid myself of the temptation of turning to other vices. I could have turned to food or alcohol or slammed doors when I was angry but instead I used my testosterone in my training. I needed this in my life, I needed triathlon in my life and without it I'm not sure how I would have coped or survived. Walking back into the house after my 'fix', refreshed and buzzing with my chin up, I was ready for the next 'round'. Prepared for whatever life was going to throw at me next.

Training Notes February 2012: Believe

I have to believe in myself. Training with other athletes I'm mid range. In swimming, cycling and running. In fitness classes there will always be certain exercises that I can't do but I have to keep going and believe in myself. Always be the best that I can be, within myself, that's when I excel and in Paratriathlon is when I can win.

"Aye up, you're Steve Judge aren't you?" said a guy at the side of the pool. It was Sunday and I was there with the Sheffield Triathlon Club queuing up to take part in a club aquathlon (swim, run).

"Yes I am," I said, "and you?" "Oh, I'm Phil, Phil Cowley." Phil knew me from other events that I had done as well as some training sessions that we both went to. He wasn't doing the aquathlon that day because he had come straight from the local cross-country champs that I also liked to do.

The inter club cross-country championships were an annual competition between the five local running clubs of Retford, Clowne, Killamarsh, Worksop and Phil's team Handsworth. I had recently started doing these again for my team of Killamarsh Kestrels. I have always found that running is a very solo sport but with this event it was very much for your team. Basically the more members of your team that come in before the members of the other teams, the more points you get. This means it's an advantage to encourage your team members along and for you to both beat the person in front.

The competition is tough for everyone because it's cross country, it's winter and it starts just after Christmas when you've gorged yourself with enough food and drink to sink a battleship. For me it was extra tough. The uneven ground is a nightmare with my rigid ankles. On the flat I can hold my own with able bodied runners but the frustration comes when I hit a hill, and there are many of them. I just can't manage to keep up. I'm literally powering myself up with just my left leg and that's not that good either. The amount of effort and energy it takes me to get to the top of the hill is massive and I have to dig deep. At the top I keep my chin up and do my best to catch up the other runners and then round the next corner...there's another bloody hill. It becomes draining and demoralising but still I continue as runners overtake me and move forward out of my sight. This happens on every race but every year I enter because I love it. Not the hills, I hate the hills, but I love the event and the teamwork and the fact that it's not based on time. It's based on every single person being the best that they can be.

When I cross the line covered in mud and scratches with my lungs on fire I know that without a doubt, I have been the best that I could have been and that's what counts. It made me realise that being a good runner wasn't all about my legs. It was about experience and tactics, overall fitness, lung capacity and heart. It taught me about discipline, focus and having the mindset to push on and keep going even when my brain shouts out "Stop!" and my temper wants me to quit. I used to be one of the runners that got the high points and now I'm lucky if I just get one or two. After the event the pain hits me in a big way, mainly

Those hills! Those damn hills! Representing Killamarsh Kestrels in the inter club cross-country event. Photo courtesy of Peter Down.

on my right ankle, and I'll be limping severely for a couple of days. The frustration of losing sight of runners on those damn hills haunts me for days. The competition is tough for me, in many ways, but I'll do it while I can. There was an eight-year period when I physically couldn't do it but now I can...so I do, and I love it. 'Go Kestrels!'

Anyway, talking to Phil at the side of the pool I explained that I hadn't done the cross-country event that morning because I'd had to make a decision and to do a swim and a run event made more triathlon training sense than just a run. Nothing to do with wet and muddy ferocious hills compared to a flat run route round Rother Valley Park!

We got chatting and he told me that he was an age grouper for the 25 to 29s. He was training hard because his goal was to compete in the European Championships in Eilat, Israel the same weekend I would be there. The more we chatted the more we connected and also realised that our training regime was very similar. All things considered I had just found myself a training partner and more than that a good friend and someone that I could relate to.

My dedication and commitment to my goals within the sport of paratriathlon were strong but I became oblivious to the full effect that it was having on my wife. My justification was that my time was being split equally and fairly but whilst it might have felt fair in my head I wasn't giving my wife the kind of thought or attention she needed, and this became apparent when I received a text from her while I was at work one day that said *"I phoned your coach yesterday and stopped your training"*.

My stomach felt hollow as though I had just been punched as I read the words on the phone over and over again. Having a coach was important for my support and further development as an athlete. Even this was now being challenged as my wife had become so desperate for me to quit triathlon. This text was followed up with a very much one-sided phone call where she told me why she had done it and how angry she was. I didn't really get a chance to say anything before she abruptly ended the call.

I visited my coach on the way home from work where he relayed the conversation he'd had with her the day before. She was deeply concerned that my training was taking precedence over family and work. She was troubled that my ongoing commitment with my training schedule would put an unprecedented strain on our relationship. She had consequently not only phoned my coach but also my boss to reiterate her deep concerns. My head was spinning in a whirl of nothingness as I tried to register what had happened.

I 'got it' and I understood my coach's predicament. I really didn't know what to do or say. I felt guilty that he had been dragged into our dispute. I wasn't angry or upset, I was just dumbfounded and derailed. He was fully aware of the pressures of training on relationships but he also mentioned that in all his coaching years he had never received a phone call like he had on that day.

I can't recall how the conversation went on my return home but I do know we did carry on going to our Relate sessions and I carried on with my training. My coach accepted that there was a clear implication that he was at least partially responsible for this domestic disharmony. Having said that, he had designed and agreed the training programme with me and we had taken into consideration family and work commitments. I, however, had never relayed to him any conflict. I just kept it all to myself. He felt he had a duty of care both physically and emotionally for the well being of his athletes. Now, with this new information, he explained that the ball was in my court for me to discuss with my wife before any future coaching could take place. I wasn't using the coach very often anyway and this attempt to pull the rug from underneath me had the opposite effect. I just focused more on what I could do on my own and did more of that. I did keep in touch with him via email for specific training plans for big events over the next couple of years.

I was hearing that I was wrong to follow my vision. I just knew deep inside that I had to do this and despite not being able to communicate just how important it was to me, I was able to use music to keep me strong. So far my tunes had always been there to hype me up, push me or even relax me but now I hung onto every lyric of the song 'Titanium' by David Guetta & Sia. Even though I was being knocked down, I was standing up...tall and robust. I would sing along to the tune; I was titanium and I would not be hurt.

The European Championships were the first in the schedule of major events for the year in the beach city of Eilat. Security for Israel was tight and after I had checked my bags in I took my bike over to the large luggage area to check it in. I had borrowed a bike box from a friend as I couldn't afford one myself. As the security clerk asked to open the case my heart sank. I'd spent a long time and lots of sheets of bubble wrap ensuring that my bike was tucked up nice and cosy and secure for the long trip. Opening the case, they took a swab of the inside, checking for some sort of bomb residue. They put the swab in a little machine that carried out a quick analysis. Suddenly the buzzer sounded and the light flashed red. The security operator turned to me and said, "It's tested positive. You can't take this luggage onto the plane!"

"Uuh…what?" All sorts of things rushed through my head.

My bike case has explosive residue inside it?

I can't take my bike to Eilat?

Whoa…I can't compete!!!

Hold on…my friend has carried a bomb in this case?

I quickly asked as politely as possible, in a desperate manner, if she could please take another swab. She took a look at me and perhaps it was the sincerity in my eyes along with the fact (I hope) that I looked like a pleading athlete in my GB tracksuit rather than an international terrorist. Anyway she conceded and took another two swabs. I waited with bated breath for the result from the little machines as to whether or not I could go and compete in the European Championships. The swabs got individually whizzed round and then the lights went…green. "All clear," she said. "Thank you," I replied, almost out of breath and trying desperately not to roll my eyes at the ridiculous farce that had just taken place. However, I needed to ask my friend some serious questions about what he was using his luggage for.

Arriving in Israel and going through another strict security procedure, we eventually arrived at the team hotel. Familiarisation and course recce was always at the top of the agenda so that I could insert the aspects into a more accurate and 'real' visualisation. The bike course was super windy and I was apprehensive about using Taurus. We'd only been together a couple of weeks and we were still getting to know each other. We repeatedly went up and down the lapped circuit getting a feel for the corners, selecting the gears and working out how to react as the crosswinds hit us from the sides. I was as ready as I'd ever be. Supporting Phil in his race was fantastic and it was so exciting to see my mate compete against other age groupers from the rest of Europe. I cheered for him as all those hours of training came together and he smashed the course especially on the run, claiming an awesome result from all his efforts.

At one o'clock it was my turn in the blistering midday heat. Relaxed and focused I entered the transition area to set up. My friend Sebastian informed me that there was a new competitor in our category from Italy. 'Oh' I thought, 'he must have registered late' because I wasn't aware of him and consequently had done no research on him. I checked out his bike that was racked and although I'm extremely ignorant on styles, brands and technicalities I could see that it was a good one. More than that, I could see that it had been well used, so he looked like an experienced and seasoned triathlete. 'It's fine,' I thought, 'it is what it is, stay focused.'

Down on the beach as we were lining up ready to have our names announced I got to meet the Italian Michele Ferrarin, a tall slender man with broad shoulders. But what stood out for me was his Ironman tattoo. I had total respect for any triathlete who has punished themselves through a 2.4 mile swim, 120 mile bike and a 26.2 mile run, but the event is no comparison to the sprint distances that we cover in paratriathlon events and that's what I held onto. 'Yes, he may be good at long distance but how good is he at short fast ones? Focus…run your own race…It's fine, we got this! Yeah? Yeah…we got this.' I nodded to myself.

"Representing Great Britain…Steve Judge," the tannoy announced.

Out of the swim and into transition and I saw that the Italian's bike had gone. I jumped on the back of Taurus and I was chasing in second place. As 'Minotaur' we got into a steady rhythm on the straights and braced when we hit the wind turbulence, selecting gears and pumping my legs hard. We braked only when completely necessary through the corners of the city as I heard Phil screaming out my name.

"C'mon Steeeve!" When I could I would look up and sneak a peek at the riders up ahead. With the bike course on a four lap circuit I thought I might be able to see my competition on the opposite road on one of the loops but I was concentrating too much on the job in hand.

Off the bike and into T2 and his bike was there racked. I racked my bike, trainers on, and sprinted off at breakneck speed hunting down my prey. It was hot, very hot and as I ran away from the city centre and towards the desertlike environment the lack of support was screaming in its silence.

The horned beast Taurus...together we are Minotaur. Eilat, Israel, European Paratriathlon Championships 2012.

"Come on Steve, where's that smile?" Jonathon Riall shouted out as he had made his way out to the barrenness of the desert to cheer on the GB team. I smiled at his comment; that was what I needed. The feeling lifted me and I pushed on with the heat beating down on my back.

Always smiling! Eilat, Israel, European Paratriathlon Championships 2012.

Back into the city and finally coming round the last corner and in front of the grandstand where someone held out a Union Jack which I grabbed. I waved to the crowd and even high fived supporters before crossing the finish line with arms aloft.

The fast pace and blistering heat had made the event formidable but my only thought was 'Where did I come?' I quickly found out that I was second and I'd won the silver medal. I was ok with that. I was completely spent and couldn't have gone any faster. "What were the timings?" I asked. "How much did he win by?" "By about four minutes," came the reply. "FOUR minutes…wow! That's incredible!"

Beaten…by the Italian…but still smiling. Eilat, Israel, ETU European Championships 2012. From left to right: me, Michele Ferrarin, Geoffrey Wersy.

The Italian was some real mean machine tearing up the course at that speed and I was intrigued looking at the 'splits'. Two and a half minutes after me Geoffrey Wersy from France came in and then Sebastian another three minutes later. The information was relayed to them and they were even more gobsmacked. Sebastian in fourth place had been beaten by the Italian by a full ten minutes. He struggled to accept this and was rattled. Even Geoffrey who had been beaten by six minutes was perplexed. They both asked for a steward's enquiry as they questioned whether or not the Italian had done the full four laps of the bike. The timing chip monitoring confirmation was carried out very efficiently by the race organisers and it was proved that Michele Ferrarin was the new European Champion in a time of 1:07:29 minutes. Four minutes! FOUR minutes was massive. I couldn't have pushed myself any more on the run to make up FOUR minutes! What about the swim or the bike? I needed to look at the splits and work out how the race had unfolded. We went out for a few post-race drinks and shared a couple of beers with Sebastian and my new racing nemesis Michele. A thorough analysis of what had just happened would wait for the morning.

Friendly rivalry. My nemesis Michele Ferrarin.

The next day I was up at 6am and on the long journey back home. The pain in my ankle was excruciating and I couldn't disguise my limp down the long corridors of the airport terminals. Every step and every jab of pain was draining me to the point of exhaustion. Back home I sat slumped over the results of the race and the first thing that stood out to me was his swim. Wow...his swim was immense! I'd found out that he was a Paralympian swimmer and his results showed that. Basically he swam like a fish. He was three minutes faster than me on the swim and three minutes faster than me on the bike. I was catching him up on the run but clearly not enough. The pain screamed from my ankle and I closed my eyes as my face wrinkled up. Shoulders slumped and body fatigued, I was beaten.

My thoughts jumped to my goal for this year which was to be World Champion again. That was in six months' time in New Zealand. I couldn't do it. I couldn't get four minutes faster in six months. I'd given one of my best performances and not even got close to winning. I hate giving in and I hate going back on something that I said I was going to do. All my visualisations were a waste of time if I couldn't physically make it happen. What's the point? I'm just hyping myself up for another defeat! It was too unrealistic for me to pin all of my time, hopes and efforts on an unachievable goal.

I sat in silence, my head spinning with thoughts and scenarios. OK…I wouldn't give in as such as I would still compete in the World Champs final but I seriously had to think of my goal. What was I realistically aiming for? With these figures that were in front of me the best that I could possibly hope for was a silver medal, maybe even a bronze depending on what other para-athletes were out there. My time as World Champion had come and gone as quickly as that. This was tough, admitting defeat before I'd even got there.

I started thinking of other times when I had felt this low and so utterly defeated. The pain that I was feeling at that moment took me back to my leg straightening episode. I remembered being sat on my living room floor in tears as the results shouted out 'FAILED!' I'd felt so utterly distraught and beaten. "I did it though, Steve!" I whispered as I lifted my leg up, pulling it straight. 'Ugh…that bloody double cage.' I shook my head as the painful memories flashed back. 'Yeah…but we did it.' 'But I NEEDED a straight leg, there wasn't a choice. It had to be done!' 'Then you've got to NEED this…not want it!' I sat in silence as I listened to the voices in my head. 'It's yours. That gold medal is yours. YOU deserve it.

Think how far you've come. Think about what you've achieved. Think about where you are. Don't let anybody take it away from you. Don't start leaning on excuses. This is a challenge, this is YOUR challenge.' My heart was beating fast now as the words circled around in my head. 'This is not failure, these results in front of you, it's feedback. You're catching him on the run. You can get faster on your bike. The swim!... Well...we'll let him have the swim but just don't get any slower. Let's NOT change the goal, let's change the plan.'

I made a lot of sense to myself and I was hyped, I was energised. I didn't have a clue how I was going to do it...but I knew that I was. I needed to visualise it, see it and conceive it. Only then could I believe it in my mind and only then would I be able to achieve it. I closed my eyes and said to myself: "I have six months to get four minutes faster."

CHAPTER 20

Turn Your Excuses into Challenges

My friend Phil had organised for me to speak at a special 'Meet the athletes' panel event being held at Sheffield Hallam University. Along with other athletes I talked about my positive outlook of going for gold in the World Championships but still skirted round the question of Rio. After the event the videographer, Leon Seth, approached me and we chatted. Leon was very interested both in my story and in me as a person. He asked if I would be interested in him filming a mini documentary about my journey later on in the year. I saw this as a great opportunity to inspire people. I'd learnt from telling my story to others that it not only inspired people but also motivated them to follow their own dreams and visions. For me it was about how to get my story 'out there' and a mini documentary would be awesome to share over the internet. I also connected with someone from BBC Sheffield radio who invited me onto a daytime show to share my story. The session went extremely well and I ended up being a semi-regular guest on one of their morning shows over the next five years. A little out of my comfort zone, I still grabbed the opportunity, realising the potential good that this would bring.

Back to training and one of the big areas that I needed to improve on was the bike. A small percentage of improvement from me could equal a big chunk of time on the event. I submerged myself into a whole different world so as to improve. I found out where the nearest time trial was which was run by the local cycling club, registered and turned up. I grabbed a number, waited in line and then sixty seconds after the last person went they would say "Ready...go" and I pedalled for all my life was worth. Up the five mile stretch of road with minimum hazards and zero junctions. At the top I whizzed round the roundabout and then pushed with all my might through the ten mile line to clock my result.

With the slight undulation of the road, gears were still necessary on the brutal challenge. It was a great training event for using benchmarking on my improvement and monitoring my performance on the results. I found it incredible that even though my head was down, legs pumping like fury, someone dressed like a lycra-clad slimline astronaut whirred past me and then off into the distance. I'd shrug it off and tell myself that their bike was clearly a higher spec than mine or maybe that awesome helmet was aiding their aerodynamic performance. Deep down I knew it was the engine. The time and commitment that they had put into their sport was what was helping them churn up the road. There's no substitute for that and I was in total admiration of their performance. My times and endurance were improving but more important my connection with Taurus. Together we excelled, together we were Minotaur.

Next up was the British Paratriathlon Championships being held at Holme Pierrepont in Nottingham. I was on top form as I smashed the course. A slick swim, I blitzed the bike and was flying on the run to win in my category by a good seven minutes. Afterwards, as I attempted to congratulate other athletes on their performances it became clear to me that what was a competitive rivalry to some had now sadly become more of a personal one to others.

Our family holiday in Portugal was awesome, spending time with my wife and playing with the kids while soaking up the sun. We celebrated the Queen's Jubilee with extended family fun and games. While it was relaxing and chilling I still put in some decent training in the sea, on a hired bike and running around the resort. The goodness from the sun's rays had energised me internally releasing my melatonin and securing an inner glow. I was feeling good, pumped and at my peak. I loved the feeling of being a 'triathlon machine'. Anytime, anywhere I could do a triathlon. It was like having a new skill in my back pocket…that ability to dive into water, jump on a bike and then go for a run. An amazing skill although I'm not too sure how these skills could be used in everyday life? However the self-belief can be applied to anything.

It was an awesome feeling of inner power and euphoria. The down side of all of this was that the World Champs this year were late in the season in October. That was a full sixteen weeks away from now. It was going to be tough keeping up my physical state as well as my emotional state. It was like filling a void by finding events that I could use as stepping stones to get me through it. In the Yorkshire Triathlon up in Leeds I honed in on all of my preparation and mindset to deliver an elite performance in a field of 100 able bodied triathletes. I ripped

Chilling out with Robert on our family holiday as we venture into the clear blue sea of the west coast of Portugal.

up the course with such concentrated vigour that I came fifth overall. This was one of my proudest results to date and with a feeling of 'job done' I drove back home, still in time for an early Sunday lunch with the family. Fourteen weeks to go.

Like a triathlon machine. The Yorkshire Triathlon 2012.

Training Notes July 2012: See it

Achievers see what they want to happen, defeaters see what they fear.

We had another superb holiday in North Wales with the family where we had the excitement of crowding round the television to watch the opening ceremony of the London 2012 Olympics. Later in the year as a family we had tickets to go down to the Paralympics where we saw a range of amazing events and competitions. The buzz of the games and the friendly atmosphere was positively enthralling. We watched the GB athletes compete in arguably their ultimate pinnacle of sporting endeavours. Their elitism and professionalism in representing their country brought excitement and pride. The spectacular show and performance didn't sway me in my focus as my mind was clearly set on 'One Vision'. New Zealand was in thirteen weeks.

In August my wife and I celebrated our ten-year wedding anniversary; we made it. There had been many ups and downs over the seventeen years that we'd been together, especially in the last ten years. Dealing with the adversity of the accident was hard and having two kids brings its own challenges into the relationship. As a hands-on dad I was proactive and we had worked together with compromise and understanding. We had got through it and shared the responsibility.

But the challenges we were dealing with now seemed more emotional, something deeper inside, and it was harder to pinpoint exactly what was causing the rift between us. There was something that was tearing us apart and although we were holding it together it was only on the outside. Under the surface there was emptiness and a darkness we were struggling to illuminate. And with the constant arguments and misunderstandings it got darker and darker. Round by round I would pick myself up and carry on. What used to be a passionate and burning fire turned into a glow which had now diminished into a fragile candle blowing in the wind.

In the midst of all the blackness I believed I was trying everything I could to keep it alight but I just couldn't do the one thing she needed me to do and that was to give up my dream and quit my training, although on this occasion the decision was mine not to train over the weekend even though the World Championships in New Zealand were just eleven weeks away. Instead we took a trip to the French resort of Nice where we had a relaxing time together and saw the sights of the beautiful historic city. We had a lovely weekend and it was times like this that made me think we were okay.

Training Notes August 2012: Time Management

My life seems to be a matter of Time Management. Prioritising, organising, coordinating and execution. Getting it right plays a crucial part to the success of all aspects of my life.

Leon ran through the synopsis of what he wanted to capture in the film that he was producing and very much wanted to present the emotional side of the accident. For this he wanted my version of events mirrored with my wife's rendition. An important part of the film was the relationship between my wife and me. How we had met, our engagement, marriage and her support through the accident. This was to be mixed in with my determination to seek goals and work towards them through my rehabilitation and onwards on the road to Rio. I kept quiet about the 'road to Rio' bit; well you never know! This was a chance to be open and express the hurt, pain and torment that both of us suffered as I pushed myself through my rehabilitation goals and then onwards. My wife refused to have anything to do with the project and instead took the kids to the Lake District with her dad. I subsequently asked my mum who was more than happy to be included and travelled up from Hertfordshire for the day.

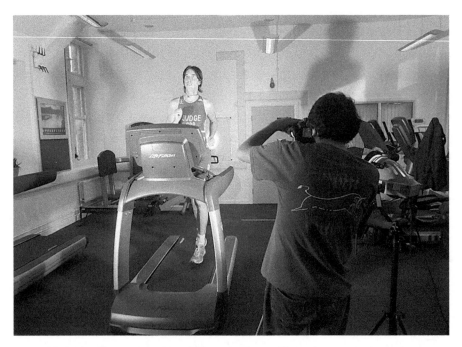

My instructions were clear: "Keep running until you have sweat running down your face." Leon Seth filming the mini documentary.

Despite brash comments of self-absorption and egotism it was actually very intense and emotional as I dug down deep to be as authentic and honest as possible. I broke down at one point as my love for my brother and sister was defined through my tears. Over the rest of the week more film footage of me training and the church where we got married was captured before I travelled up north to catch up with the family. Playing with the kids, jumping and swimming around in the lakes was amazing but we also had a particular goal that we all wanted to achieve which was to climb our first mountain together. For the kids it was their first ever mountain in their lives and by comparison it was my first since my life had been saved. The track was certainly rocky and hard work but together we made it and we all reached our shared goal. After a great couple of days I had to leave the family as I had to go back to work. My wife continued the holiday before travelling further up north to complete her Coast to Coast cycle challenge with her group of friends. Nine weeks to go until the World Champs.

A cheeky swim in Derwent Water in the Lake District with Robert before rowing back to shore with help from Susannah.

The following weekend I took Robert and Susannah camping. We laughed so much that it became contagious and my throat began to hurt but I was afraid for it to stop. The feeling of delight and endorphin release that came with it got me thinking of when the last time was that I had felt like this…but I couldn't recall. It had been a tough year up to now but I had no idea that things were about to get even worse.

The weather turned cold. My wife went back to her part-time work which she detested. I knew she was unhappy in her role. She hadn't seemed happy since she stepped down to give her more time at home with the children. I would try to help and support by making suggestions and offering solutions but what I now know is that this was the wrong way to help. I've learnt that people need to find their own goal and no one can tell them what that is or what they should do. Sometimes it's just about listening and support, it's as simple as that.

So, my training continued although the temperature of the lake became so cold that I had to wear rubber bands round my fingers to stop them spreading open. The days were beginning to get shorter as the blackness started to envelop the time available. It was tough, to keep pushing myself. It was draining to keep to the fixed routines, the early mornings and the dedication with all things elite. I was beginning to get fatigued both physically and mentally. How much longer did I have to stay on this treadmill while juggling so many aspects of my life? I was strong and I was fixated on my goal and I dug down deep to pull myself through.

I would recall my vision of what I wanted to achieve. I reignited over and over again my gratification with this opportunity that I had been given with the consequences that I had endured. I'd come such a long way now that I wasn't prepared to stop. I needed to believe in myself and believe that I could do it but I was in a fragile state. I was walking on a thin tightrope forwards on my journey towards my goal. The winds of work, relationships and training were swirling around me, threatening to knock me off balance. Through fixed concentration and becoming at one with my body I knew what my destiny was and my true direction, onwards to my goal.

I was going to keep going and I was going to stay on line and I was going to succeed. I truly believed that there would come a time in the future when I would step off, but for now I needed to fight, I needed to stay focused on what I believed in. I'd grabbed this opportunity with both hands and I was not letting go. No way. Not until I reached the end. For so long I had been held back, first the accident, then I had to have more surgery, on my left leg, on my right leg, on my toes. But now I was free and I wanted to go for it and I wanted to do so for as long as I could. I have always been someone that would keep going until the end.

But it had to be my choice; nobody could tell me what to do. 'Only I can do what I've got to do.' With a passionate belief I fell deep into the words from Duracell's B.O.B. and O.A.R. song 'Champions'. No matter what others said I knew that this was my time, my moment and something that I could control from inside of me.

The life that I had thought I was going to have had been taken away from me by the accident. I wasn't in control when the goals were given to me in the form of standing and walking again. I had used my dedication and commitment to achieve these goals but now things were different. Going for gold was my choice, my decision and in my control. After so much that was out of my control, now I had a choice and this was very important to me. Again, I would use my dedication and commitment to achieve in this quest and that too was important to me. But the main thing was that I had chosen a goal that I wanted. Something that made me excited as well as nervous but also something that when I thought about it made me smile. The accident was not a choice, competing in paratriathlon was my choice.

Training Notes August 2012: Your Choice

I sacrifice so much, I don't see my friends, I don't go out and watch sport or watch television. I don't go out drinking or go out 'clubbing'. I like to keep fit, I like to be healthy and train towards my goal. My life was taken away from me and I have worked hard to get it back. This life style makes me happy and is what I need and that is my choice.

A very 'late in the season' triathlon at Rother Valley was the ideal final stepping stone that I needed to keep my competitive edge up and running. The field of 500 able bodied athletes included members from Sheffield Triathlon Club including my training buddy Phil. I delivered a sterling performance and one that would give me enough confidence for the remaining five weeks before I set off to the other side of the world to represent Great Britain and defend the world title.

With two weeks to go I'd had enough. I wanted a break from the treadmill of training. It was so hard and my motivation was struggling. Just a couple more hard sessions and then I could taper off a bit. Until then I had to dig deep through the dark times. I had to find the glow, stoke the fire and reignite the desire. I had to focus and energise the beating heart. Just a few more sessions and then the fun would start because then I would get to race.

Training Notes October 2012: Keep Going

> *I can do this, Believe! Focus! Plan the fun but only after the need has been fed. The need to succeed and the need to get up and train. The need and determination to finish this journey off with no regrets.*
> *I've got this.*

As with any big event in my life the last couple of days are when the tension really ramps up. For me I had a thousand thoughts rushing through my head. Any injury niggles that I had, last minute training sessions, my kit, my itinerary, my tickets. Everything that I'd been building up to was finally here. The logistics of flying to the other side of the world worried me, the pressure of representing my country and the expectations of the results that I had set out to achieve. Nervousness overpowers me and transforms me. Focused, stubborn, I become a sombre shadow of myself who grunts and growls at annoyances like a grouchy bear. Aware of my emotions and seemingly unable to control them, I would advise others that if they couldn't help or support me then probably best if they just stepped to one side and left me well alone. Sadly, not everybody heeded this advice. Driving to the airport my head was buzzing with many thoughts. "Have I got my bike, my helmet, my trainers, my passport?"

As I scanned through my checklist for the umpteenth time for clarification I took a deep breath. I was finally moving physically towards my destiny. Away from the tough training regimes and the cold and dark mornings. Away from the fragile balance of time. Intimidation that attempted to drag me down into the darkest pit of turmoil with comments like "You're getting slower!" and "I hope you lose!" These had left me empty, deflated and defeated. I'd had to pick myself up after a verbal attack, and set off on my bike with the wind chilling my dried tears as I attempted to cycle away from the tempest that harrowed me.

Now, in my car, I was moving away from the pain and from not being understood. I had hugged my kids and squeezed them tight before I left for what seemed like an exile. The door was closed on me and so I went onwards on my solo journey.

CHAPTER 21

And the World Thought I Had It All

Late October and I arrived in Auckland, New Zealand. I dumped my bags in my room and headed down to the docks for registration and the swim recce. All the other athletes had already arrived but due to my limited days off work this was the earliest I could get there. On my arrival the head coach took a look at me and commented "Are you ok? You look a little rough." My appearance was an understatement of how I actually felt. It had been a hell of a long journey for me but I'd made it. Now it was time to focus and concentrate on the matter in hand. I was out here on business and I was itching to get on with it.

The very next day we were competing in the 'swim, run' Para-Aquathlon World Championship Final. Michele Ferrarin was not in the final and so the swim and run event for me was to be treated as a warm-up for the main event in two days' time. The brisk temperature of the water shocked any remaining signs of jet lag away and I came out of the water in first place and set off efficiently on the run. Guilty of 'showboating' and soaking in the atmosphere of the cheering crowds, I felt relaxed and confident. After 2K I casually looked over my shoulder and was shocked to catch a glimpse of James. I rattled my cage, waking up my tiger and promptly unleashed him. As I picked up the pace I sprinted the last two kilometres to cross the finish line as World Champion. It was a wake-up call for me but I also smiled as it reaffirmed the power that I had under the bonnet as and when I needed it. My roommate Matthew Emmerson also won in his category, bringing his gold medal back to the room to sit next to mine.

The days leading up to the race were difficult and almost boring. A week before the event I can't get any fitter or faster and so it's just a case of making sure I'm ticking things over. A little swim and bike here, a little jog there and lots of time sat in the hotel 'chilling'. I went out on the bike to check out the course as well as the wind factor which was not good. At one point the wind turbulence was so strong in the city that I had to get off my bike and hold onto it as it was flying at ninety degrees to my body like a kite. My bike shoes had no grip on them so I was being dragged by the wind along the road like I was wearing skates. An almost comical vision but instead I was petrified, realising that I had to make some serious decisions for race day with regards my choice of wheels. As I went through the final preparations before the biggest race of my life and a rematch against the Italian, some of the other athletes were creating fresh tactics for the race ahead. One of these even involved raising a query on the re-categorisation of the Italian. I didn't get involved; I had my plan and I'd visualised it to the nth degree. I needed my 'eyes on the prize'. Blitz the swim, push hard on the bike so that I could at least see Michele. Catch him on the run, take him and win, job done. I was just itching to race.

Even though I was on the other side of the world I still received encouraging messages from Bruce and ones of support from Dawn. Lovely text messages from my mum telling me that they were thinking about me. My friends, Phil and my sponsors from 'NouriSH me now' continued with messages of good luck. It was a shame that when I phoned home it always seemed to be inconvenient to talk to my kids but maybe that was due to the time difference.

Training Notes October 2012: Fear and Nerves

Fear and nerves are feelings that we have, they are not actual physical things.
The only thing we are nervous of is being nervous and the only thing we fear is fear itself.

With two hours until the race started, I went to the park that I had sought out a couple of days earlier. It had a large circle of shrubs and flowers surrounded with some tall trees if shade was needed. It wasn't too busy and there were definitely no other athletes to be seen as I needed to be cut off from the goings-on in the other part of the city. I went through my usual routine of yoga and tai chi to relax myself, focus my thoughts and visualise the race from start to finish in immaculate detail. As I finished the scenario I saw myself crossing the finish line and reaching out to grab the gold medal in celebration. At this point what usually happens is that I open my eyes with a big smile on my face…but…there was a problem… the Italian. Because of him there was no certainty in the race. Because of him the gold medal might not be there to grab. Because of him my visualisation had not worked and I opened my eyes feeling nervous. This was not good. I looked at my watch. Twenty minutes had passed. It was ok, I still had time. I took a deep breath and relaxed. I closed my eyes and focused on my breathing. I knew what made me happy and that was performing with speed and agility. I loved the sense of being what I called a 'triathlon machine' where I felt able to release my tiger to its full extent. That made me feel good and that's what I needed to do.

I started all the way at the beginning again. Getting my wetsuit on, hat and goggles fixed. Just like before, the perfect swim, gliding through water and efficiently moving through transition without a hitch. Whizzing round on the bike, racking it and then finishing on the run. As I came down the final stretch towards the finish line I was at full speed, my lungs gasping for air. Crossing the line, I felt absolute exhaustion. Nothing left in the tank, even feeling a little bit sick, which as an athlete I've learned is quite an acceptable thing to do, to push yourself until you're physically sick. It's almost a badge of honour. My visualisation finished this time, not with a gold medal but with the satisfaction that I had been the best that I could be. I opened my eyes smiling. I felt awesome; it had been a good race. For me now, deep down the result didn't matter. For me it was about going out there and having no regrets. I packed my things up and set off to the start line with a spring in my step and a crafty smile. "Let's do this," I whispered to myself.

There were 109 athletes from 21 countries all setting up their equipment within the transition area. I placed my headphones into my ears and put on my sunglasses to cut myself off from the hustle and bustle. No eye contact so I could stay focused on what I needed to do. You're actually not allowed to listen to music in the transition area so my headphone lead was not plugged into any music device but it prevented people coming up to me and talking to me. I needed to be with myself. I needed to retain my composure and keep myself in the zone. There were ten athletes in my category. My main threat was Michele Ferrarin but there was also David Kyle, Geoffrey Wersy and James Smith. On top of that there were some other athletes that I had never competed against and some that I'd failed to find race results on. These guys weren't even a consideration anymore. There was nothing I could do about them now and wasting any kind of thought process on them was out of the question. I focused on what I knew and concentrated on what I could control.

The temperature of the water had been a concern and it was finally announced that due to how cold it was the swim distance would be reduced. 'It is what it is,' I told myself. 'Let's not waste too much time on overthinking the situation.' A shorter swim gave me an advantage against Michele but it also took my advantage away from James, David and Geoffrey. It wasn't just going to be about me chasing, it was now going to be about me being hunted!

"Representing Great Britain…Steve Judge."

Floating in the water, we all hung onto the pontoon with our heads turned and facing out to sea. The water was choppy but I didn't care about the coldness as my body was electrified with anticipation. "On your marks…" The horn blasted and all the athletes set off in a flurry of hands and feet grasping for the water in front of them. The Italian propelled himself forward like a fish. The rough water was tough to contend with and coming out of the swim in second place I was eager to get on with the next bit of the race. I had a seamless transition in front of the roaring crowd as I grabbed Taurus and jumped on him in hot pursuit.

I had heard cheers from the French team and knew that Geoffrey was less than a minute behind me and saw that James and David were equally ten seconds after that. Already I was being hunted down. It was a good solid bike and the strong crosswind confirmed my choice of wheels. On the three lap circuit I managed to get a glimpse of my competitors but it was insignificant. I was doing my own race and squeezing out every ounce of effort, skill and technique that I had to propel me forward, slipping through the gears and keeping a high cadence. As 'Minotaur' we were bonded in unison. There was no sign of Michele in front of me as I finished the bike section, racked it, trainers on and off I sprinted to seal the fate of this race. I had no idea where the chasing pack was but my focus was ahead of me. In tune with my visualisation, I'd been here many times before and there was an inner voice whispering 'You've got this…go for it'.

The crowds were going crazy shouting "Go GBBB!!!" I had my race face on, staring straight ahead and looking for the blue outfit of the Italian. "Come on Great Britain!!!" I could see David, James and Geoffrey chasing me down on the opposite side of the four lap circuit. "Come on Steeeve!" I allowed myself to smile and affirm where I was and what I was doing and to bring a spring into my step. "Concentrate on the race… stop smiling!" puzzled onlookers shouted which consequently made me smile even more. At last I saw him up ahead and I was catching him fast. A hollowness appeared in my stomach as my visualisation came to fruition. Lifting my legs up slightly to give me a burst of speed, I sprinted past Michele and onwards. I didn't look back. I'd unleashed my tiger and to be honest he was pulling me along and I couldn't keep up. I was too far out to retain this speed and unsure how I was going to keep it up but nevertheless I held on tight as I gasped for air.

'Stick to the plan: "spent" on the line, no regrets. Leave nothing in the tank, absolutely nothing. Don't look back, look forward. Go, go, go…PUSH IT!' My lungs were raw as I swung my arms to power my legs faster and faster. 'This is yours! This is your chance, your race…COME ON!… PUSH IT! Don't look back, go for it.' Round the final corner and I saw it. The crowd was going wild! My goal, ahead of me. "Come on Steeeve." I had nothing left but somehow I was still sprinting down the finishing straight. Running on empty as the momentum carried me across the line. I grabbed the finishing tape and held it aloft to the heavens as I screamed with euphoria. "I did it…I DID IT!"

I stumbled aimlessly as a bottle of water was thrust into my hands. I was done. As I bent over and rested my hands on my knees, a wave of heat rushed through my body and the emotion hit me. My mouth started spluttering and my eyes welled up. 'I've done it, I've done it…I'm exhausted.' My body went limp. I lifted my chin up and my body followed as I stood up straight. I put my hands behind my head as I looked to the heavens and the tears rolled down my cheeks. I squeezed my eyes tight…even tighter and gritted my teeth. To the world I might have looked like I had it all and they may have presumed that the tears were simply due to the physical exhaustion of the event, whereas in reality everything

"I did it!" Exhilaration, exhaustion and completely spent on the line to claim the title World Champion for the second year running. Auckland, New Zealand, November 2012. Photo courtesy of British Triathlon Federation

was coming out. Everything I had held onto and not told anyone was pouring out because I had nothing left to hold it in with. It had been such a tough year and I was done in. My shoulders were hunched and I folded my arms as my body started to shake. I just wanted my mum. I wanted to hug her. I wanted to hug my kids. I wanted to speak to them, tell them that I was ok and tell them that their dad did it.

The other competitors were going into the athletes' lounge area for recuperation and rehydration. I breathed in through my sniffly nose as I staggered off towards the transition area. I rummaged through my bag and found my phone. The rain blended in with my tears as I wiped them off my face and dialled the number. I knew it would be about 5am in the morning in Britain but my mum had always said "Any time! Call me anytime you need me", and this was one of those times. "I did it Mum...I did it!" The conversation was kept brief but hearing my mum's excitement and happiness put a smile on my face. I didn't go into too much detail but it was enough. I had shared and I had received my mum's acknowledgement and my heart glowed as I stood there with the rain coming down. My dad would be gazing down on me as I looked upwards with the rain falling on my face and I felt his tears of pride and joy. A quick check of my messages and I saw a "Well done mate, Great result" from Phil. I later found out that he had stayed up until the very early hours of the morning to watch the live feed of the event. He even recorded the screen footage and as I crossed the line as champion of the world he gave out a "YESSSsss" with sheer uncontrollable delight and pride.

I grabbed a top as I was starting to feel the chill and went to join the celebrations. I felt a release of my emotions and was now happy to bask in my glory. I'd won for the second year in a row. Looking at the results, I was a good minute in front of David Kyle and two and a half in front of Geoffrey Wersy. I'd beaten Michele by a solid four minutes. My roommate Matt had also won in his category and we joked that our room with its four World Championship winners' medals quite literally stank of gold. The next day I limped around the city in excruciating pain as I collected souvenirs for family, friends and people who had helped me on my journey. Some athletes' partners or family had come over to see them race and then were staying on, using the opportunity to extend the trip into a sightseeing tour of the two islands of New Zealand. I chatted to various athletes and had 'selfies' with others.

After a long and exhausting 24 hours of travelling I landed in the UK and drove all the way back to my village of Eckington. The coldness had increased, giving me a harsh and frosty welcome home. Soon after the unloading was done the bell rang for 'time out' and I grabbed the opportunity to go and pick up Susannah from school. The doors were flung open and Susannah was so surprised to see me as she ran up to me with her arms outstretched. I knelt down to embrace and squeeze her tight as I smiled from ear to ear. The love that I felt through the contact with her was like a lightning bolt of energy connecting us. I closed my eyes in ecstasy as my arms were wrapped round my loving daughter.

Contrary to what I had been told, Susannah looked me in the eye and said, "I've missed you Daddy." I hugged her again and whispered in her ear, "I'm home now." And I felt complete.

Back at work the following day, I did receive some acknowledgement from my colleagues on my achievement but nothing from anybody else. Not a "How are you?" or even a "How was the weather?" Just nothing!

I attended the Sheffield Triathlon Club awards night with my wife and once again was astounded to receive the trophy for Outstanding Triathlete. I had so much to thank the club for with their full and comprehensive training sessions and ongoing encouragement. As we left one of the veteran triathletes called Dave and his wife approached us and told the story of how I had independently gone to visit him in hospital back in 2004. It had been following a club email which said that he was suffering from a collapsed lung. I had felt compelled to go and visit him. He joked that after an hour of me chatting to the two of them with positive words of encouragement his wife turned to him and said: "Well that was nice wasn't it, who is he?" and Dave had replied "I have no idea darling".

During the evening I circulated and chatted to fellow athletes and thanked them individually. I was guilty of leaving my wife on her own while I did this, and now in the taxi home I faced the consequences. Through the twists and turns of the journey home into the depths of the night my smile was wiped clean off my face and replaced with tears. My trophy was placed in a drawer and we never went to another awards night together again.

A rare photo of neither of us wearing lycra for once. Training partner and friend Phil Cowley.

My win in New Zealand gained the interest of the biggest global triathlon magazine. The interview was preceded by a professional photo shoot of me training around my local area. I explained to the interviewer how being part of such a unique and forward thinking GB team was incredible. How the athletes worked hard on their own goals and in conjunction with Jonathon Riall and all of the other practitioners. Britain had now topped the medal table in every major competition since 2010 and we had left New Zealand having stretched out our advantage over the rest of the world by winning five gold medals. I was proud to say that I was at the forefront of laying down a legacy. I stated how it had been an exceptionally difficult year for me and if truth be told I was shattered. Training six days a week was physically demanding. The pain that I had to endure and work around was draining and never got any easier and never would.

I disclosed to the interviewer that juggling work, life and a relationship with triathlon was increasingly hard and I couldn't see any imminent reconciliation. I referred to the equality policy that my company was committed to and also how I used my time effectively and efficiently. I joked about the lack of facilities and how I used a bucket and a sponge after my lunchtime run. Although it wasn't ideal I wasn't prepared to lean on this situation as an excuse. I was fatigued by triathlon and I was exhausted physically as well as mentally. My training regime was tough and through lack of support I found it increasingly difficult to pursue my dreams but not impossible. With all of the problems that I had, I would continually focus more on my goal and the opportunities drawing me in, whispering to me, calling me to seize the moment, grab it with both hands, a chance in a lifetime.

Training Notes November 2012: Courage

Courage is: knowing that there are tough times ahead but still pushing forward.

I'd won by a full minute in New Zealand and physically I was at the top of my game with nine and a half months away until the World Championships grand final in 2013. Not only that, but the event was being held in London. For me that was a no brainer. There was no way that I could NOT set this event as a goal. I couldn't sit at home in peak performance as a reigning World Champion while athletes from around the world would travel to my country to attempt to take the crown. It felt like the song 'Hall of Fame' by The Script had been specifically written for me: the clear and precise lyrics about becoming a hero not just for myself but for my country.

My wife and I discussed the situation to see if we could come to a resolution. I knew how hard it had been for her up to now and realised that another nine months could put an even bigger strain on our marriage. Deep down I hoped that she would support me in my quest or at least allow me to fulfil my desire. I wanted her to understand why this opportunity meant so much to me and why I felt I needed to complete it. But what once was an opportunity was now changing into a responsibility and more of a necessity.

Think stubbornness, think patriotic integrity or think greed. Whatever way I looked at it I felt I had to do it. I had to go for the championship. I needed to do it. Wouldn't it be great to finish on a high? Here in my own country. In front of a GB-strong crowd. In front of my wife, kids, my mum, brother, sister, family and friends. With the vision flashing into my mind I was unable to shake it out. One last time! We agreed that this would be my last ever World Championship and that I would retire from international competition after the event in September. My wife also made clear and reaffirmed to me her decision that she wanted absolutely nothing to do with triathlon in any sense of the word.

I knew that it wasn't always about being physically up for the quest as a huge part of it was mental. My mindset was strong and positive and the visualisation I used kept my focus healthy. What became difficult was when things weren't going so well. The strain on my mental health was increasing mainly due to not having a release. Training gave me a physical release, a sense of purpose and achievement but it didn't give me the emotional release.

I now didn't feel that I could talk to anybody about how tough it was. I felt isolated and alone at home and work. I didn't feel it was appropriate to talk about at work and I certainly didn't want to talk about my difficulties. I wanted to be able to share the triumphs and the wins and besides, time was tight. Training would always take priority over such conversations.

I accepted this was my situation, having no release and no one to talk to about the problems, but it was difficult. I had friends and family who would have understood if I shared but I didn't. I didn't want to trouble them with such small matters and so I would bottle them up. I felt very much that I was on this journey on my own. And being as independent as I am, I thought I would be ok not asking for help! 'Independent and self sufficient.' I'd done well on my own up to now and so I was under the impression that I could continue in this line.

What I didn't realise was how much it affected me if I didn't communicate my concerns, my thoughts or my worries. By keeping things inside and pushing them down and locking them up they felt safe but they festered. No matter how strong or robust I was physically, without true mindfulness I could be broken. If you took away my emotional health then I was only as good as a sack of potatoes.

Now, as I look back at this situation it makes me really appreciate the value of being able to download and talk about what's not working, something that in the past I might have found difficult to listen to. I would perhaps have labelled someone as negative and wanted to shift them from talking about the problem to taking action and doing something.

I also find myself remembering how much my wife wanted me to give up triathlon and it makes me think that this could have just been her way of wanting me to be at home, spending time listening to her needs without always trying to fix everything.

Going for the goal that I had chosen would push me to a new level where I would discover not only the importance of the athlete's mindset, but also the necessity for the mental health of one. I'd discover the consequences that followed when I got it wrong. The despair and breakdown would result in me seeking professional and medical help.

Thoughts, Feelings and Reflections
December 2012: The Day is Over

The day is over and it's time to rest
You know that you have been your best
If your goal is not yet complete
Learn to adapt there is no defeat

Think of the good things and show a smile
Your goal getting closer all the while
Believe and conceive but remember to pause
Rest, recharge and give applause

Tomorrow's a blank canvas, clear and new
And only YOU can do what you gotta do
But for now the day is over and it's time to rest
Sleep in the knowledge that you've been your best

CHAPTER 22

Pushing
the Senses

As the new year began I had my goals lined up in front of me. British Champion, European Champion and World Champion. Due to the success of the GB Paratriathlon team in the last year Jonathon Riall was able to secure a large amount of funding from the National Lottery along with new sponsors. The sport had gone up a notch with it being three years away from the Rio Paralympic Games.

Along with the excitement and the opportunity came the dedication, responsibility and pressure of not only performing but also the full commitment to the task ahead. Even with funding from the programme that was going into my bank account every month the one thing that I couldn't buy was time. My time was stretched and every waking second was dedicated preciously to some part of my life. But there was never enough and…I needed more.

My wife and I were still going to Relate counselling but we were struggling to agree on a solution. I knew she wanted to spend more time with me and her solution was to redirect time from triathlon training but that didn't work for me. What I now know is that we were asking the wrong questions. Rather than her asking "Will you give up triathlon?" we should have been asking "How can we spend more time together?" Whilst quitting triathlon would have given us more time, I then wouldn't have been happy and so that would not have worked either long term.

In February my wife and her dad took the kids away to Fuerteventura on holiday. I was gutted that they went without me but while they were away, apart from working, training and catching up with DIY jobs around the house I took some time out to do some thinking. My wife returned home to a warm and tidy house and my request that we sit down and talk. I had jotted down some notes that I thought would help us build bridges and move forward together. I related to the communication techniques suggested from our counselling sessions. I knew that there was a lot of water that had passed under the bridge and whilst I was committed it did feel like the hardest race ever. It was like paddling upstream with no sign of progress.

I had imagined she would come back happy and relaxed and that we could go through the things that I had thought about. Instead she didn't speak to me and said she had felt physically sick at the thought of coming home to me. I attempted to read the notes that I had made through a closed door of things that I had taken for granted and to express my feelings but I wasn't being heard. It certainly wasn't how I had envisioned her return.

My wife had also been doing some thinking of her own. I felt like I was trying everything possible to achieve our shared goal apart from the obvious which was quit training. My attempts for reconciliation were constantly sucked into a whirlpool of despair. I started to feel that it was useless even trying and it was becoming just a waste of time.

A couple of weeks later I had to attend a weekend performance training camp in Loughborough. The camps had improved even more and the variety of help, support and advice that was available was amazing. There were new staff and practitioners including doctors, physios and strength and conditioning experts. Coaches who were experts in their fields, nutritionists and bike mechanics as well as mind coaches. The purpose was to consider and monitor everything about the athlete to ensure they are enhanced to their elite capability in mind, body and soul. We were given personality tests, physiological assessments and also took part in a VO2 max exercise that monitors heart rate, blood lactate and oxygen uptake. I was very interested in the way the mind of an athlete works. On one such questionnaire I was asked if I ever talked to myself and I sheepishly answered that I did. I was so relieved to be told that this was in fact good practice and encouraged as long as there was a balance between positive and negative engagements. "I told you so!" I said to myself as I rolled my eyes. We participated in discussions and lessons on goal setting, working on our plans of what we were aiming to achieve for the season ahead as well as for the road to Rio. We looked at the hurdles and barriers that could prevent us from continuing on our journey and more importantly what proactive actions we could take. This reminded me of my successful instigation of injury prevention three years previously.

Another session that I immediately connected with was the introduction, explanation and breakdown of the book The Chimp Paradox by Dr Steve Peters. Recalling the mechanical issues that I experienced on the bike section out in Beijing helped me to identify with the messages from the book. I'd always been good at learning from my mistakes and consequently turning adversities into golden opportunities. The book explained how this takes place in the brain and how you can accept 'the inner chimp' inside you; how you can learn from it and go on to train your chimp. I grabbed the opportunity to have a one-to-one session with the life coach and we talked all things work, relationships and training. His philosophy for an athlete is 'Team You': what do you need as an environment, support and tools to make you the best that you can be? I made many notes and was keen to share them on my return home. Immediately after the camp we competed at the British Duathlon Championships where I won gold which was a perfect end to a fascinating couple of days.

Driving up the motorway I smiled to myself as it felt like I was heading towards my future, equipped with new tools that would help me mentally for the year ahead. I'd be able to perform to my best ability and become World Champion one last time before I retired from international competition. Part of the plan was to bring my wife on board with my mission and through expressing my feelings and desires I was confident about moving forward. One of the songs playing as I drove was 'Keep on Movin' by Five. Just like the lyrics I felt hyped about what was ahead of me, equipped with new knowledge and awareness. I just knew that better moments were coming my way, but I was wrong.

I sat down with my literature in front of me as I explained to my wife that it hadn't been a glorified holiday and that the things that I had learnt could also be used in all situations in life. (I was of course commenting on the classroom activities rather than the pool and track sessions.) I referred to my notes to aid me as I explained how I was aware of my vision and my goals for the year. What triathlon meant to me and how much pleasure and passion I got from representing my country. Pushing myself to achieve such sporting accolades by grabbing these opportunities that were there before me. I spoke with spirit and sentiment about the vision of achieving my goals in my sporting prowess. I explained how I didn't want to be on the journey alone and I needed help and support so that I could share and celebrate the successes and experiences. "Ok, I get what you're saying Steve, but that's your goal, that's not our goal!" was my wife's response. I frantically searched through my handouts from the camp to see if there was any comeback after comments like that, but there were none and we were finished.

CHAPTER 23

Suffering in Silence

Two months after my article was released in the triathlon magazine there was a response from a reader who felt compelled to send in a letter which was consequently printed in the magazine. He stated that he was clearly inspired by my recovery and achievements but also made comments regarding how an elite athlete representing his country, as in myself, struggled with time for training. Reading this made me feel justified in my frustration. I felt solidarity with the magazine and an alliance with this reader and fellow triathletes alike. Many of my friends and colleagues read the article and I was happy to share it with others. But not everybody accepted what had been written in the article and this was consequently made clear to me with repercussions that followed.

At my next appraisal meeting with my boss I was told that my position as Health and Safety Manager was being made redundant. There was no set date when it would take place but I was told that I could take as much time off as I wanted to search for jobs and go for interviews. I politely thanked them as I stood up in a daze and left the room.

Sat back at my desk I stared at my computer, trying to understand that on the one hand I was going to lose my job, my security and my income for my family but on the other hand we didn't know when this was going to happen. I didn't hate the job as such and I didn't want to leave. I also didn't really want to spend my time looking for another job as I had more than enough to deal with. "I'll deal with the situation…later," I said to myself. "Anyway, I've got months before anything needs to be done!" I was unaware that I was not just concealing my acceptance of the situation but I was also stifling my anxiety. I suppressed my thoughts, my questions and even my feelings. As instructed I carried on as normal, not talking to anyone about it…always smiling.

Once again I turned to music as my saviour and the song 'Hold On' by Skepta hit the right notes with words that consoled and reassured me, convincing me that when I was knocked down I had to get up and hold on. When I felt that there was no way out I had to have faith and hold on because I was indomitable.

On an early spring family trip to Holland to see the vista of blossoming tulips we were disappointed. The dark and exceptionally cold season had delayed the protrusion of any such brightness from the earth. Nothing was growing and nothing was blossoming. It rained on the desolate fields as we searched in hope to no avail.

My wife carried on with her cycling, achieving the amazing accomplishment of cycling from London all the way to Paris with a group of friends. I trained hard over the next couple of months, blanking out the dark thoughts of reality and instead focusing on the European Championships in June.

My training was taking a more natural and rural approach as I found myself running more through my local woods and with no watch on to time my progress. Instead I focused on a single tree on the horizon and tackled the uncompromising terrain to triumph. Battling through the undulating pathways I eventually reached it. Once there I would catch my breath and then breathe deeply. I'd perform my yoga and tai chi set while looking out on the beautiful view of the countryside. I was on my own, miles from anywhere and anybody and out here, I was at peace. I would push my body to the extreme on the way back until my lungs were raw and my legs were on fire so that I knew that I had been the best that I could be. In my head I had the words from the poem:

'The Song of the Ungirt Runners' by Charles Hamilton Sorley
The rain is on our lips, we do not run for prize.
But the storm the water whips and the wave howls to the skies.
The winds arise and strike it and scatter it like sand,
And we run because we like it through the broad bright land.

The bike was similar as I was spending less time on my road bike and more time on my mountain bike even though the chain was locked in the high setting. The gears were broken but instead of fixing them I just pedalled on, building up my resilience to push myself up the hills that faced me. Out of my seat and on my toes pushing and shaking as I focused, chin up towards my goal. I breathed in the distant surroundings in their green and undulated beauty. On the downhill I let rip, pushing it to the edge, out of my comfort zone with the speed technicality and overall risk on the crags and small pathways. The adrenaline pumped through my blood and caused me to shout and whoop out loud. It was a release and it was awesome and I was happy but afterwards it was back to reality. Back to the stresses of my life and the fatigue that followed.

The feeling of exhaustion was so tough and I was always tired after my training sessions. When I tried to get up in the morning my body said 'No'. I felt like a lead weight but with a stubborn mind I still managed to get up and swim. Knowing that I would find it difficult to drag myself out of the house in the early morning and off on my bike I took proactive measures.

My 'grab and go' system reached a new level as I actually wore my cycle gear to bed, minus the helmet and shoes. When my alarm went off and my consciousness kicked in I was fully aware of what the plan was and in automatic pilot mode I just got on with it. I was unhappy at work because I knew that they didn't want me there and in the evening I just wanted to go to bed because I was exhausted. Completing my goals made me so happy but I had to pay the price as I worked towards them. It got me thinking that surely the journey is a big part of achieving the goal. Although I accepted that it would be tough the fact that it made me unhappy maybe meant that the whole balance was wrong.

Training Notes May 2013: Sacrifice

> *Can I sacrifice so much for one goal? A year's worth of commitment, six days a week! The pain, tiredness and exhaustion. The stress, priorities and arguments. Is it too much to give? Or is it worth it to feed the need for this amazing opportunity?*

I kept my competitive edge up by entering local races like the Epworth Triathlon but even then I'd compare my results to that of able bodied athletes. Because I wasn't coming in the top ten I started being tough on myself and wanting to push even harder than I already was. I was trying to reach impossible and meaningless goals and in the process I'd beat myself up like a punchbag when I didn't achieve them.

Back at work, as instructed I carried on as normal and refrained from talking to anybody about my looming redundancy but it was cutting me up inside. I sunk into a dark place when there were discussions and meetings about future work and possibilities on the horizon. The hardest was delivering inductions for new starters into the company, building rapport and trust to relax them and make them feel at ease in their first week. This was killing me inside and I just wanted to scream out. After one such induction I had to take myself outside as I was shaking and my eyes were welling up.

I guess some people would have expected me to quit and move on, but not me. Call it stubbornness or the fact that I'm a fighter but whatever way you look at it, the point was that I stayed on. It wasn't affecting my work but it did start to affect my health. But still...I told no one and just carried on as normal.

Thoughts, Feelings and Reflections
May 2013: Low

I'm feeling low and I've lost my 'mojo'. I've lost my 'get up and go' and my enthusiasm.
I don't want to do anything. I hate work, can't be bothered to train and I'm feeling very nervous about the Europeans. I miss my wife while she's at her parents and I really miss the kids.
I had a great weekend and now I'm in the doldrums and I almost can't be bothered to pull myself out...but I must...and I will...just not quite yet.
I'll think of what I need to do to release some endorphins, task completion, music, exercise, organisation, communication. I know these things will work, I just need to do them. But not now... just not quite yet.

I was struggling, I was digging down deep on my positivity but I was scraping the bottom of a very empty barrel. I was falling and I needed help, I just needed someone to help me. The derogatory comments I received on a daily basis caused me to cry myself to sleep followed by a restless night. The morning filled me with dread and misery as I struggled to motivate myself for the day ahead. One morning, sat on the floor of my bedroom, my phone pinged with a new text message. I wiped my tears away and read it.

"Get your hair cut and pull yourself together."

These fabulous words of encouragement and motivation didn't have the effect that had been hoped for and by the time I arrived at work I was a mess. I didn't know how I had got there and I certainly didn't know what to do now as I sat there in the car park. I just stared forward like a zombie, not being able to move and my thoughts were just spinning round at a hundred miles an hour. I shook my head from left to right whispering "No...no...no". I didn't want to put up with any of this anymore. I just wanted it to stop. I was breaking apart, I just wanted it to end, I wanted everything to end! "No...no...no." I shook my head like I was going insane. I needed help and I picked my phone up with my shaking hand, wiping my eyes so that I could see the screen as I typed 'Samaritans' into the search engine. I wrote down the number on a scrap of cardboard packaging from an old sandwich box, cleared the screen and then dialled.

I don't know how long the call lasted but it was enough to get me through that day. I had talked and I had expressed myself and they had listened. There had been no answers or specific words of wisdom but just words of concern, care and understanding. I kept the number tucked away in my wallet, just in case. And having that gave me the strength to carry on. I knew that I could be strong when things went wrong but it was also good to have a 'plan B' in my back pocket.

CHAPTER 24

I'm Done and
I'm Finished

At last in mid-June came my first big event of the year, the European Championships. They were held at the beach and tourist resort of Alanya in Turkey. It was hot and humid and we were encouraged to arrive early to acclimatise. A huge entourage of athletes, coaches and practitioners accompanied the GB Paratriathlon squad and we were ready for action with our new kit and positive outlook. Every possible detail had been considered and addressed. Great Britain were leading from the front with regards to our elitism in all areas of this sport.

The same familiar faces were there at the start line including my racing archenemy Michele Ferrarin. There were again some new faces which was a growing occurrence the closer we got to Rio 2016. The swim was in the beautiful turquoise sea around two distant buoys and then back in to shore. I remember later seeing some underwater film footage taken of all of us para-athletes out in the sea. There were numerous arm amputees as well as some leg amputees and some with stubs from partially amputated limbs. As I watched the video with fellow para-athletes we joked that it looked like an excerpt from the movie Jaws.

Out of the water and I grabbed Taurus and was once again chasing down the Italian on the six lap circuit. The atmosphere was amazing and I could hear the cheering support from fellow GB triathletes "Go GB!!!" This also included my 'NouriSH me now' sponsor Lynwen who was also out there representing GB in the age categories. "Come on Steeeve!" they shouted as I pushed hard on the course and handled Taurus expertly round the tight corners. 'I've done five laps I'm now on my sixth, I've done five laps I'm now on my sixth, I finish at the end of this.' My mantra worked as I leapt off Taurus, through transition and out onto the run. It was hot! The wave of heat hit me as my legs adjusted to the new discipline.

One K down and I was flying now, through the streets of Alanya with the crowds cheering me on as I hunted down my prey. I high fived a few hands to bring in the element of fun, and a smile to my face. "Let's get those legs lifted Steve!" I said to myself. "Chin up, look forward, relax, smile…faster…faster now, keep going." I passed my friend Adrian from another category who was really struggling. Everyone presumed that he was suffering from heat stroke and they were passing him bottles of water or pouring them over him. In reality he had had a nasty fall on the bike and the flesh on the stub of his amputated leg was in a really bad way but he was carrying on, stifling the pain and focusing on the completion of the race in hand. He was not prepared to stop.

I had one K to go and was exerting all of my energy now as I powered my arms, forcing my legs to follow suit. Looking ahead there was no sight of Michele but I kept focused on my efforts and my race. I sprinted down the home straight and crossed the finish line looking like I'd run through a furnace…but still smiling…always smiling. I grabbed the silver medal that day with Michele a minute ahead of me. I'd been in this situation before. I couldn't have gone any faster on the day. I'd had a good race but I wasn't prepared to change my goal for the World Championships in London. My goal was the gold medal and I wasn't going to start leaning on excuses. Once again I was going to change my excuses into challenges. We shook hands and congratulated one another. His English was about as good as my Italian so our communication was mainly through body language and gestures but we understood each other well enough. I'd see him in three months' time, in London.

The first race of the season was over and we wrecked the 'all you can eat' buffet back at the hotel. We gorged out on the chips, burgers and desserts before some of us hit the town for a few beverages and later dived into the sea for a giggling midnight swim. It was a total release from everything. A release from the stresses of racing, from the purity of being an elite athlete and from life in general. Landing at Stansted Airport close to midnight, the queue for the taxis was ridiculous. I swiftly jumped on the bus into the centre of Bishop's Stortford where I planned to catch a taxi out to my mum's house where my car was parked. Twelve thirty on a Tuesday morning and there didn't seem to be any taxi ranks open. I started limping the one and a half miles and was so glad that on this occasion my bike was making its own way home due to an organised bike courier company. After half a mile of dragging my suitcase I was conscious of the constant whirring noise of the wheels echoing out through the residential area and attempted to carry my suitcase on my head for a bit, probably only for about five minutes. Finally I reached my car, quietly unlocked it and loaded up. I sent my mum a text message while she slept and set off up the M1 but not home…not yet.

As previously mentioned part of my job was carrying out site audits on our construction sites around the UK and where possible this included night shifts. I'd worked out that I would be passing the construction site as I drove past Melton Mowbray two hours into my trip. As I drove through the endless night I desperately broke out the holiday sweets that I had bought for work colleagues. I hoped that the sugar rush would keep my eyes open just a little bit longer for me to get to the site. I arrived and changed into my work clothes in the desolate car park. Hard hat, high vis, boots, glasses and gloves before grabbing the clipboard with pre-printed audit sheet that I had prepared whilst packing my GB tri suit. It was a surreal experience hobbling around the site with my silver medal in my pocket. Audit done, I completed the last hour and a half of my journey before getting home and grabbing a couple of hours' kip. The next day I went into work and typed up the results of my site audit with the exploits of my European achievements now a distant memory.

I called a meeting with my boss and a member from the HR team as I had done some thinking time while I was away and was now ready for action with a plan. I'd written out a script to make sure that I stayed on track about how I felt, what I wanted to express, questions I wanted to ask and answers that I needed. We sat down and they looked at me. I was tired and fatigued but I had control and composure and was ready for action. I read out word for word the narrative that was written on my sheet of paper.

> *"Over the last couple of months I've been struggling with the concept of redundancy."*

As I started opening up to the two of them my emotions started running ahead of myself. Flashbacks of my tears and 'episodes'. Already my throat was beginning to croak under the strain and my mouth began to quiver. *"I need to know what's going on…and…"*

My voice broke and the tears interrupted me. I tried again. *"I need to know what's going on…and…and so…"* I wanted to finish. I had a whole page of notes that I wanted to read out and get off my chest…but I couldn't. I felt that I had failed as the tears rolled down. The HR representative stepped in and ended the meeting. I was excused from work and it was suggested that I go and set up a session with a counsellor and book a doctor's appointment. I did both immediately and had my first session with the counsellor the very next day. I again wrote some notes in advance before my session.

I explained how I needed decisions and awareness of my future. I would have sleepless nights and wake up tired and feeling low. It felt like I couldn't do anything right and I would have a dizzy head, start hyperventilating, finding it hard to breathe, and I'd struggle to stop crying. I was stressed because I didn't know what the future held for me and also because of the amount of work I had to do even though I was leaving. I felt depressed about the inductions I had to do with new starters and lying to people. I just felt ever so lonely.

I don't know how helpful my sessions were but it was good to talk, to share and to offload and I guess that's what I really needed. I took the same notes to the doctor the next day and we had a good chat about them. I was signed off for a full two weeks on a diagnosis of 'work-related stress'. As she announced it my heart sank at the thought of the stigma attached. 'Signed off work with stress.' I thought I was stronger than this. After all that I had been through and suffered I thought I could handle myself. Why was this different...why?

I guess in the past it was expected that I would be struggling emotionally. I was going through trauma with life changing experiences and oodles of pain. Of course I was expected to be low, decumbent and to have hit 'rock bottom'. But here and now it was different. I had everything going for me, didn't I? I had a wife, kids, a career and I was a two times World Champion. The world thought I had it all. There was pressure to keep up the façade and pretence...always smiling! I had decided to not share how tough it was. I bottled it up. I didn't talk to anybody, I could have... of course I could have but I didn't. 'They've got their own worries, they don't need to hear mine. Anyway, I'll be ok. I've been through worse.' But every situation is different. The less I shared the more it built up and then...well, and then it just exploded like a volcano. Or like a gasket on an engine because mine had certainly stopped working. Or maybe it was like a dam bursting its banks with the water symbolising all my tears. Whatever the analogy, it had most certainly just happened to me. The one thing that was for sure now was that I was finally getting some help.

Signed off work for two weeks. Before I left I turned and asked, "What am I supposed to do in these two weeks? Is there a programme that I should follow or something or a report that I need to fill in?" She looked at me and smiled. "No Mr Judge, just do what makes you happy, and try and relax." I left the surgery feeling ten tons lighter and a two week openness in front of me and I smiled.

Training Notes June 2018: Plan or Ponder

Make a plan to do then you will do. Ponder about doing and you will keep pondering about doing.

My two weeks were spent on going out cycling with my wife and having some good quality family time with the kids as well as getting some training in. By the time I got back to work I was feeling a lot better. On my return I was asked to join my boss and HR in the conference room upstairs which happened to be the same room that I had been interviewed in nine years previously. I was presented with a redundancy package with a date and by the next week it was all completed. I collected my bucket, sponge, soap and towels. I removed my spare clothes that I had used when I'd cycled into work. I cleared my desk of all personal items and shut my computer down. There was no farewell speech, shaking of hands or drinks after work. After nine years there was no leaving card or goodbyes as I left the building. I sat in my car, put my shades on, window down and turned the music up as I drove away. Emotionally I was exhausted and spent, I was done and I was finished.

The very same afternoon I had a speaking gig arranged at Sheffield United Football Club. I absolutely loved sharing my story and helping the footballers to be inspired and motivated towards their goals...no pun intended. "Maybe a possible future career?" I thought to myself. Two days later I drove over to Liverpool which was the new location for the Paratriathlon British Championships. Things had certainly escalated since Rother Valley back in 2009 as I gave a pre-race interview with the TV station Channel 4. It was an interesting swim in the Docklands with clearly visible jellyfish below and consequently no camera operator filming us. Out of the swim and for the first time in the British Champs I was chasing in my category. There was a new athlete called Craig McNeil. He was like Aquaman as he streamed through the water to exit two minutes ahead of me with James Smith in my wake hunting me down. The bike was fast and flat and I was cruising with my toned and energised legs. Eyes on the prize, I needed eyes on the prize as I scanned the road ahead of me looking for Craig. Eventually I saw him, took him and swept into T2. I sprinted out of transition in first place and through the cheering crowds. "Come on Steeeve," they shouted and I felt strong. I ran with such speed and agility as the massive burden that I had been carrying for the last five months had been lifted off my shoulders. Now I was free, my white tiger uncaged galloped along, personified with its strong athletic beauty in full stride. I was liberated and happy and smiling again. I was on fire as I passed various other athletes from other categories and burst through the finish line a full five minutes ahead of James and thirteen minutes ahead of Craig. I was awarded British Champion for the fifth time and hugged my gold medal with just as much pride as I had done back in 2009. It meant so much to me and I knew that I would certainly miss these moments.

The pain I suffered the next day was extreme. I was limping like a pirate with a screwed-up face to compensate. As usual it was draining but inside I was euphoric with my performance and proud of my achievement, so no regrets. On the Monday morning I travelled to Leeds for a job interview with the Scout Association for a part-time role on the media team which I ended up securing. My wife had coincidentally been biting at the bit to go back to work full time and so me taking this job would give her the opportunity to fulfil this desire. Hence my new role would precipitate a new routine for the running of the house with new systems, efficient, slick and loads more fun time with the kids. I was excited and I was well up for it. The job would start in September and before I got fully stuck into it I just needed to complete the small goal of becoming World Champion for one last time. The summer was spent with my wife and kids on lovely idyllic British holidays in the Lake District and Cornwall. I was also able to secure plenty of cycling, running and lots of swimming in the open water.

As September started it was all change in the household as we both started new jobs and this new chapter of our journey. I got a buzz from my induction at Scout HQ, meeting the rest of the media team and staff. Sadly my wife's start to her job was not so good and by the end of the first week she was already looking for another one. My support for my wife could have been better but instead I submerged myself into my new job and my new role. With blinkers on I fought with ignorance against the raging turmoil that once again swirled around me. I wasn't going to be brought down again, not this time. My tunnel vision was locked on my ultimate goal as I dealt with the daunting nerve-racking prospect of representing my country for the very last time in the World Championships.

My kids were so excited as I gave them a big hug and they gave me a 'good luck' card which they had created. I packed it in my bag along with the ones from my mum, brother, sister and an A4 sheet of folded paper that was titled 'Steve Must'. On the handwritten list were five goals that had been chosen for me and number one on the list was:

"Give up International triathlon from September 13th" (My race day)

I folded the sheet of paper closed, placed it back in my bag next to my GB tri suit and left.

I joined up with the rest of the GB Paratriathlon team in Loughborough where we had a critical couple of days honing in on our training, coaching and any other arrangements. We travelled into the centre of London as a team with just two days to go until the final. I remember trying to assist with loading all the equipment and luggage but was asked to step back. "What do you mean?" I said. "Why not, why can't I help?" "You're an athlete," they said with a smile, "we'll carry your bags for you. Less chance of you straining yourself or anything." I smiled as I stepped back in compliance. Things had certainly come a long way in the last five years and Jonathon Riall and his BTF team were hellbent on continually moving things forward for Great Britain.

The triathlon festival opening ceremony was held in Trafalgar Square where I was involved in carrying one of the flags. There was such excitement and jubilation with representatives from all over the world. The next day in Hyde Park there was a frenzy of activity and a thrill of emotion as the course recce was completed by the athletes and race briefings were attended.

I was walking back to my hotel when I heard "Steve…Steve…over here." A fellow triathlete from Thailand introduced herself as Nini. "I've been reading about you in various triathlon magazines," she said, beaming with childish excitement. "I can't believe that I'm actually meeting you," she continued with a big grin on her face. After talking about her involvement in triathlon she asked me for a photo with her. I had a sudden flash back to San Francisco all those years ago when I had done the same to the National Triathlon Champion Mike Pigg and thought about where that subliminal message of inspiration from Mike had got me.

As well as a photo with Nini I also gave her a Go-en that I had in my wallet after explaining the story and meaning behind it. "Good karma will come to you if you are aware of your vision and seize opportunities," I said. Nini and I stayed in contact and four years later she sent me a message to thank me for my ongoing inspiration and the gift that she wore at all times. They had got her through some very tough times with regards injury and motivation struggles. She told me that she lived by my messages and using them had achieved her goal of becoming a doctor as well as the National Women's Thai Champion in triathlon.

Friday. Race day. The dark clouds above brought occasional light rain but there were definite gaps of blue sky ahead. My playlist blurted out 'The Phoenix' by Fall Out Boy, helping me to put on my race face with lyrical war paint, ready to release that which drags me down and instead rise from the flames. There was a huge crowd presence building around the park including my mum and brother who had managed to get there.

I did my normal preparation enabling me to feel relaxed, confident and able to go and be the best that I could be. For the final time I heard the tannoy announce: "Representing Great Britain…Steve Judge."

In the water, holding onto the pontoon and waiting for the horn to sound. "On your marks…HONNNK" and we were off, with the Italian like a fish. I pushed it as hard as I could with high elbow, reaching long and pulling strong. Out of the swim and through the long transition with Michele leading our category by a full three minutes. I was in second place and the other eighteen athletes in our category were chasing. Holding my tuck position as I gripped onto the horns of Taurus and together we were Minotaur hurtling around the closed roads of Hyde Park. With the water on the surface the officials were screaming at us to "Slow down, slow down". But at no point was this ever going to happen. All the hills and the miles of pain that I had put myself through meant that I was not going to "slow down". Then as the race unfolded I saw various athletes skid and fall. I witnessed wheels buckle and flesh torn. I quickly re-evaluated the situation and decided to slow down at certain points on the course.

The crowd were going wild as they shouted out "Go GB!! Come on Great Britain." Into T2 and I racked my bike and saw the Italian's bike already stationed. Helmet off, trainers on and I sprinted out and onto the two lap 5K run route. This was it, this was all I had left now. It was all or nothing. Pacing myself at a high tempo I looked forward, chin up, powered my arms and pumped my legs. I heard my mum cheering me on and I smiled to help myself lighten my step. It didn't last for long as I was focused on the path ahead. My brother cheered me on and shouted out to me as I passed: "He's two minutes ahead." Now, this was exactly what I wanted him to do, for him to tell me where my goal was but I also remember thinking, 'So what? What do you want me to do? Go faster?' I was flat out and couldn't possibly go any faster. The second lap and still there was no sight of the Italian. The crowd pushing me along all the way round. My tiger roaring with mouth open, grabbing as much oxygen as I could as my lungs screamed out for more. My legs were burning with the amount I was demanding from them and then up ahead I saw a glimmer. The athlete had just turned the corner but it was definitely the bright blue tri suit of Italy. I tried to notch it up a gear but there was nothing there. I pushed on at the same speed.

I estimated that I must have half a K left, about two minutes. James Smith was there encouraging me along at the side of the path. "Come on Steve, you can do it," he shouted. I was approaching the paraphernalia of the grandstand with the sound of the tannoy and the crowd and the finish line. But I couldn't see him. I couldn't see Michele through the twist and turns. I was running at full pelt as I entered the final corner and onto the home straight. The supporters were cheering and the flags waving as I sprinted with wings towards my goal. I thrust my arms into the air with clenched fists and yelled out loud with sheer delight. I'd done it, I'd finished and I had nothing left as I crossed the line with unsteady feet. I felt euphoria and exhilaration for the completion of the task and I was completely exhausted and utterly spent. I was done and I was finished.

Woohooo! Crossing the line with absolutely No Regrets because I was the best that I could have been. Hyde Park, London, World Championships 2013. Photo courtesy of British Triathlon Federation

On that day I learnt what true success really meant to me, with my dad's final words clear in my head. True success was about being the best that I could be and having no regrets. But it wasn't just about having no regrets on the day; it was about having no regrets on every day of my journey. The early mornings and the late nights. Pushing my body to its limit as well as listening to it. Being the best that I could be in everything. My diet, my nutrition, my equipment, my preparation. I had done everything to the best of my ability. And of course on the day, my swim, my bike, my run, my transition. Everything was perfect. I had been the best that I could be and because of that I had no regrets.

On that day I got beaten by just thirty seconds to grab the silver medal. I couldn't have done any more. And that's why when I crossed the line I was beaming with pride...always smiling. I had absolutely no regrets and that to me is what success is all about.

I found my brother in the crowd and thanked him once again for the strategic and powerful encouragement that he'd given me. I hugged my mum and squeezed her tight. Her endless and unconditional support, love, care, trust and encouragement was there in everything I did. This time she whispered in my ear, "You did it Steve...you did it!" and she squeezed me even tighter, not wanting to let go. My sister made it to the medal ceremony with her family and I gave her a huge hug for all of her extra loud and heartfelt support.

Very Important People. Hyde Park, London, World Championships 2013.

I congratulated Michele on his epic win as we stood there in Trafalgar Square on the podium accepting our medals. Who knew that the Italian national anthem was so long! I limped my way back to the hotel and collapsed on the bed. I had a couple of hours before I was to attend a celebratory meal for the GB team and their partners where my guest would be my mum. I lay there staring at the ceiling with many thoughts whizzing around in my head. Remembrance from the past days, weeks, months and years. I closed my eyes and breathed in...and breathed out. I was finally at peace and as I relaxed myself I stabilised my thoughts. My right hand reached over to my left hand where it clasped my wedding ring and tugged it off my finger. I placed it on the bedside table as I took in another deep breath...and then exhaled. I was exhausted and spent, I was done and I was finished.

Epilogue

Following that day I made certain decisions in my life and I consequently retired from international competition.

"Will you keep competing until the Paralympics games in 2016?" was a common question. The thought of continuing for a further three years sent shudders down my spine. The pain, exhaustion, sacrifices and consequences heavily outweighed the prospect and after all, that's all it was, just a prospect with no guarantee at the end of it. I no longer had that burning desire to compete at such a high intensity. With everything that I had been through over the last couple of years I was exhausted both mentally and physically. I felt as though I had been swimming against the tide and now it was time to stop. I looked at the medals, trophies and accolades that I had already achieved and would say "No thanks, I'm good." I now had other aspirations.

With the time that I acquired I've started giving back as I volunteer as a leader at the local Scout Group. I ensure that the programme that is delivered is full of fun, challenge and adventure. We work our way through the badges which they so love to achieve. Without them realising it they're receiving life skills and opportunities. Who knows where those badges will take them later on in their life.

6th Eckington Cub Scout pack with fellow leaders and helpers including Robert and Susannah. Eckington Woods, 2019.

I'm divorced now and live my new life in happiness with my two kids and have a loving and supportive partner. My song that now reflects my mood and outlook is very much 'It's A Beautiful Day' by Michael Bublé. The words are in sync with my perspective as I smile while the sun shines and the birds sing their song. And if the weather is cloudy I'll not be the one that's whining but instead see the blue sky beyond. I still keep fit and healthy and do at least one triathlon every year...just so that I can still call myself a triathlete. 'How do you know when there's a triathlete in the room? Don't worry, they'll tell you.'

You'll still find me running and cycling round Eckington, battling with 'those damn hills'. On Saturday mornings I often cycle to Rother Valley Country Park with my kids ready for the 5K parkrun. In the summer months you'll find us having an early morning swim in the lake with the amazing Sheffield Triathlon Club, before a quick run and then cycling back home for a bacon sandwich. I still see those benches dotted around the park which constantly reminds me of where I've come from and what I've achieved.

I worked for the Scout Association for three years until my contract came to an end. It was the best job that I had ever had. Helping people to promote Scouting through the positivity that it is. Sharing my knowledge and learning from others as well as witnessing the amazing work that goes on. Seizing opportunities to shout loud about Scouting which also included working closely with people like Bear Grylls and the Duchess of Cambridge. Over those three years I had increased my speaking appearances at schools and football clubs and organisations to pass on my messages of inspiration.

Just before I left people asked me: "So Steve, what are you going to do now?" Almost in a Superman pose with hands on hips and looking to the future I would turn to them and say, "I...am going to be...a motivational speaker." I'd learnt through my journey that I should follow my heart more and follow my gut. Find something that I really want to do, something that I'm passionate about and something that I need. I was given the amazing opportunity to go on a speaking tour of Mexico which not only gave me the experience of a lifetime but also gave me the confidence and the belief that I could make this work.

But people would ask me, "How are you going to do it, how are you going to make a living and run a business as an inspirational speaker?" And I would say to them (still with my hands on my hips), "I haven't got a clue... but I'll make it happen."

My goal was to be stood on stage as the bright lights beam down on me, sharing my story in front of thousands of people, to help, inspire and motivate them towards their own gold.

"GOLD!!!" Inspiring others to believe in themselves and work towards THEIR gold. T2 Talks, Hull, November 2018. Photo courtesy of Karl Andre on behalf of Trans2 Performance

I still reach up and touch the Go-en coin that hangs round my neck and heed the message that Taka gave me all those many years ago. "Be aware of your vision and seize opportunities" he said and that is something that I'm conscious of and continue to do every day. I've learnt that if you want something enough, if you are hungry for it and believe that you can do it, then you will make it happen. If you truly 'need' this thing then you will feed that need and work towards it. For me it was about going all out on something that I believed in and something that made me happy.

An analogy that I use is if you imagine me swimming in the sea. I'm a long way out and I'm a good swimmer but my goal, land, is far away. The only way that I'm going to get there is to keep swimming. I have to keep working hard because if I stop...I'll drown. Looking up and seeing my goal, that thing that drives me onwards is what motivates me. Now, I could hang onto a life raft to be safe a bit like having a part-time job to stay buoyant. But if I do that, if I hang onto this life raft then I'm never going to reach my goal. So I've pushed any such life raft away and I swim, indomitably, every day...towards my goal.

I still have my alarm set at 5.30 in the morning but instead of diving into a cold training pool I now walk into my study. I read a self-development book, I exercise and then I get into a yoga position where I visualise my goal. What I want to achieve. That thing that when I think about it I get excited, almost nervous in anticipation. I visualise it in such detail that when I open my eyes I'm smiling as I say to myself, "That was awesome…I want it". I give myself words of affirmation before picking up a pen and my notebook and writing down five things that will lead me to my goal… just five. This takes me to about seven o'clock and I go and wake the kids up, have breakfast and then get them ready for school. But when they're gone and I sit down at my desk I have those five things that I need to do that will take me towards my goal.

My overall goal or mission statement or my 'Why' is that I want people to experience the happiness, fulfilment and achievement of their true life goals. As the day progresses and the emails ping and the phone rings it's hard not to get distracted. Sometimes it's like fighting my way through a jungle but at least I know what direction I need to go in. The list of five things will take me towards my goal. That's what drives me, that's what I want and that's what I need.

Running my business as an international speaker I am always thinking about how I can improve:

What more can I do?
What more can I do?
What more can I do?

I'm constantly assessing my performance to ensure that I give my absolute best. Setting goals to continuously improve helped me to become Yorkshire Speaker of the Year 2017 and 2018 as voted by the Professional Speaking Association. You'll now find me speaking at schools, universities and business conferences. I spoke at Sheffield Hallam TEDx in 2015 and more recently alongside Sir Clive Woodward at the Action Coach Business Excellence Forum 2019. To receive standing ovations from over a thousand people clarifies and convinces me that I'm on the right path. I get great pleasure in passing on my new-found knowledge and experience as a speaker coach. I believe that everybody has a story that others can benefit from and if their desire is to share it then I can help them to do so in the most memorable and empowering way.

I have developed and run goal setting workshops. After an introduction into who I am and my journey I then help people to find out what their goals are. It's important to find out what their 'true' goals are. I then share the tools that I used to achieve. I know how to achieve; I've done it. From growing my leg back to walking again to becoming a World Champion to becoming a professional speaker. I just want to share my knowledge to help others. I know what it's like to achieve...it's awesome. People can go through their lives as mediocre and maybe content and that's fine, but are you truly happy? Doing something that you love and working towards and achieving your true life goal is one of the best feelings there is and I just want to help people experience this.

As I continue on my journey within my business and my life I continually set goals and work towards them using the messages that I have learnt through my rehabilitation and being an elite athlete. I know that there will be times when I'll struggle to achieve certain goals but it's important for me to stay focused and not change the goal but where necessary change the plan. I know that there'll be times when I feel that I've failed but it's critical for me to remember that there is no such thing as failure, only feedback. As I continue on my journey I understand that there will be barriers in front of me in one form or another. It's essential that I see these barriers as excuses and to turn those excuses into challenges. By doing that I can smash through those barricades and work towards my goal. But I think the most important thing that I've learnt on my journey comes from my dad's last words to me. To keep doing what I'm doing and in everything I do and everything I strive for I must always be the best that I can be, always! Because when I do that, then I have no regrets.

People always ask me what my goal is now. My continued goal is to be happy...always smiling, so it's more about what I'm doing to work towards that ongoing goal. At this moment in time my focus is about getting my messages and inspiration out there so writing this book has been a massive focus for me, but what next? What do you think? Maybe a film?

On my venture I'm always open to new opportunities. It's about seeing them, hearing them and smelling them and then grabbing hold of them with both hands and doing something about it. Taking action so that I can help people, inspire others and motivate many.

If you are interested in booking me as a keynote speaker, please get in touch via my website www.steve-judge.co.uk.

You can find details of my goal setting workshops and how to get in touch regarding coaching enquiries.

I'd love also to connect with you via social media in any of the following ways.

LinkedIn: Steve Judge
Facebook: Steven Judge
Twitter: @stevejudge
YouTube: Steve Judge
Instagram: @scoutjudge

Competing Results

ETU European Triathlon Championships PT3

2010 2nd Place ETU European Triathlon Championship, Athlone, Ireland

2011 1st Place ETU European Triathlon Championship, Pontevedra, Spain

2012 2nd Place ETU European Triathlon Championship, Eilat, Israel

2013 2nd Place ETU European Triathlon Championship, Turkey

ITU World Triathlon Championships PT3

2011 1st Place ITU World Triathlon Championship, Beijing, China

2012 1st Place ITU World Aquathlon Championship, Auckland, New Zealand

2012 1st Place ITU World Triathlon Championship, Auckland, New Zealand

2013 2nd Place ITU World Triathlon Championship, London, Great Britain

ITU World Triathlon International Events PT3

2010 1st Place ITU World Paratriathlon Event, London, Great Britain

2011 1st Place ITU World Paratriathlon Event, London, Great Britain

British Triathlon National Events Paratriathlon PT3

2009 1st Place British Paratriathlon Championships, Rother Valley
(T4 category)
2010 1st Place British Paratriathlon Championships, Holme Pierrepont
2011 1st Place British Paratriathlon Championships, Holme Pierrepont
2012 1st Place British Paratriathlon Championships, Holme Pierrepont
2013 1st Place British Paratriathlon Championships, Liverpool

British Triathlon National Events Paraduathlon PT3

2013 1st Place British Paraduathlon Championships
2014 1st Place British Paraduathlon Championships

Awards and Honours

Sport

2010 Male Paratriathlete of the Year, British Triathlon Federation
2011 Male Paratriathlete of the Year, British Triathlon Federation
2011 Outstanding Achievement Award, Sheffield Triathlon Club
2011 Outstanding Achievement Award, Sheffield Triathlon Club

Business

2017 Yorkshire Professional Speaking Association (PSA) Speaker of the Year
2018 Yorkshire Professional Speaking Association (PSA) Speaker of the Year

Hobbies

1983 Cub of the Year, Bawtry, South Yorkshire
1987 Scout of the Year, Bawtry, South Yorkshire
1990 Venture Scout of the Year, Bawtry, South Yorkshire
1991 Venture Scout of the Year, Bawtry, South Yorkshire

Link to Spirit, the YouTube video I made of cycling from Eckington
to Bawtry:
https://www.youtube.com/watch?v=cWrjlESNDWk

Acknowledgements

I would like to thank and acknowledge and thank those who have been a part of my journey. My life has been shaped by many experiences and people associated with those moments. People often ask me: "Bearing in mind all that you have achieved in your life, if you could turn back time and avoid the car accident, would you?"

My answer is that I absolutely would, because on that day in 2002 I nearly died. My life and the lives of those I loved were turned into turmoil. I suffered dreadfully through rehabilitation, both physically and emotionally. I now endure pain every day and can never forget what I've been through.

The fact of the matter is that I can't change things that have happened in the past. Things happen in life. How you cope with these situations impacts on how you deal with them. I'm lucky to have met many incredible people on my journey who have helped, supported and inspired me. These people have been mentioned in my book and so instead of doing a list of thank you's here, I'll let you go on a treasure hunt.

My journey brings me to the present as a professional speaker and now as an author as I complete my first book. As always, I've found it crucially important to have the right team around me to aid my progress towards my goal. I would like to acknowledge and thank the following people:

My book coaches Karen Williams and Sheryl Andrews, who have held my hand through this new experience and guided me practically and very much emotionally. My copy editor Louise Lubke Cuss, designer and typesetter Sam Pearce and also my proofreader Abi Truelove. Together you have helped this book become the professional publication that it deserves to be and that I am so proud of.

My mum, Dawn and Bruce, Theo, Andrew and Dave. Thank you for your time commitment and constructive feedback. Emma Sutton for your polite persuasion of enquiry of "how is the book going?" over the last couple of years.

My loving partner Jo who has been with me on every step of the 'book journey', helping me with support, feedback and encouragement. Thank you for listening to me as once again I talk about 'my book', but you do so because you understand how important it is to me which I appreciate and is one of many reasons why I love you.

My kids Robert and Susannah who I love so much and am so proud of. You both inspire me every day and let me know, in your own special way, that you love me too. Thank you for your enthusiasm in all my crazy endeavours.

I'd like to thank myself – Steve. Thank you for your dedication and commitment to the numerous goals throughout the journey, always. Most recently with the book as at times you yourself set the alarm clock for 4am to continue with your passion of getting this story out there and heard. Thank you for having the foresight to keep all the information, notes and poems in the loft so that they could now be used to share with others. Thank you for being open and authentic with your thoughts and feelings.

Lastly, I'd like to thank you, the reader, and I hope that I'll inspire you to not lean on your excuses and to live with no regrets.

Steve Judge

Lightning Source UK Ltd.
Milton Keynes UK
UKHW051129081219
354991UK00014B/501/P